Lasagna Gardening

A New Layering System for Bountiful Gardens: No Digging, No Tilling, No Weeding, No Kidding!

Patricia Lanza

RODALE

RODALE

WE **INSPIRE** AND **ENABLE** PEOPLE TO IMPROVE
THEIR LIVES AND THE WORLD AROUND THEM

Editor: *Nancy J. Ondra*
Project Editor: *Deborah L. Martin*
Book and Layout Designer: *Lisa J. F. Palmer*
Interior Illustrator: *Elayne Sears, Jane D. Ramsey*
Front Cover Designer: *Christopher Rhoads*
Back Cover and Jacket Designer: *Nancy Smola Biltcliff*
Cover Illustrator: *Douglas Schneider*
Senior Research Associate: *Heidi A. Stonehill*
Copy Editors: *Beth Bazar, Ann Snyder*
Manufacturing Coordinator: *Melinda Rizzo*
Indexer: *Lina Burton*
Editorial Assistance: *Jodi Guiducci, Lori Schaffer, Alison Ackerman*

RODALE ORGANIC GARDENING BOOKS
Managing Editor: *Fern Marshall Bradley*
Executive Creative Director: *Christin Gangi*
Art Director: *Patricia Field*
Production Manager: *Robert V. Anderson Jr.*
Studio Manager: *Leslie M. Keefe*
Associate Copy Manager: *Jennifer Hornsby*
Manufacturing Manager: *Mark Krahforst*

We're always happy to hear from you.
For questions or comments concerning the editorial content of this book, please write to:

Rodale Inc.
Book Readers' Service
33 East Minor Street
Emmaus, PA 18098

Look for other Rodale books wherever books are sold. Or call us at (800) 848-4735.
For more information about Rodale Organic Gardening magazine and books, visit us at:
www.organicgardening.com

Library of Congress Cataloging-in-Publication Data

Lanza, Patricia.
Lasagna gardening : a new layering system for bountiful gardens : no digging, no tilling, no weeding, no kidding! / Patricia Lanza.
p. cm.
Includes bibliographical references and index.
ISBN 0–87596–795–7 (hardcover)
ISBN 0–87596–962–3 (paperback)
1. Organic gardening. I. Title.
SB453.5 .L35 1998
635—ddc21   98-25315

Distributed to the book trade by St. Martin's Press

25 26 27 28 29 30   hardcover
23 24 25 26 27 28 29 30   paperback

To my family for being loving, understanding, and supportive,

and

In memory of Della Webb and Etta Neal, the grandmothers

Contents

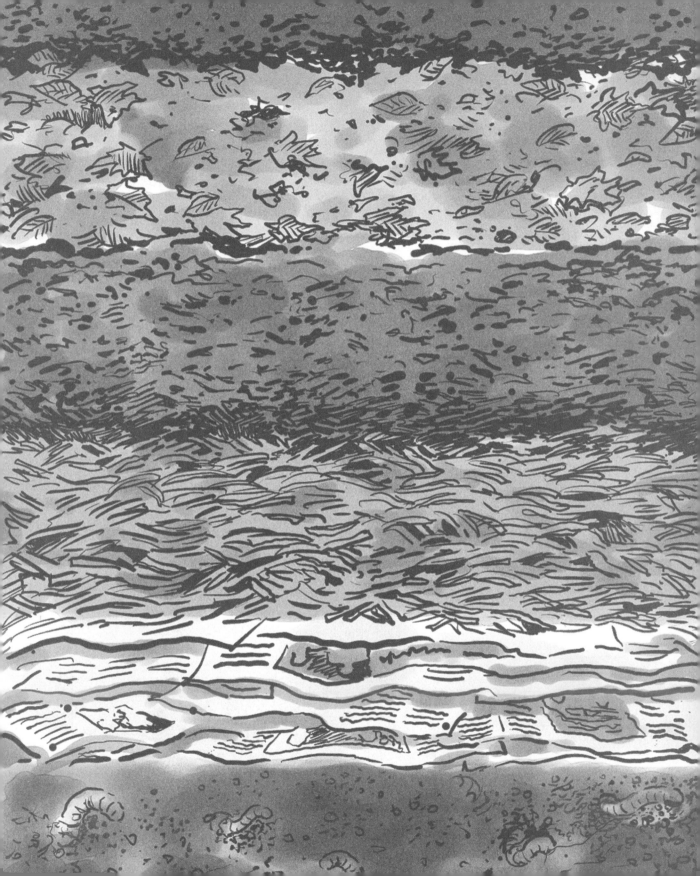

Introduction

 When I was a child, growing up in the Cumberland Mountains of eastern Tennessee, I would watch my widowed grandmother get ready to plant her garden. She would hitch the mule to an old plow and, throwing the reins over her shoulders, guide the plow up and down, making long straight rows. Grandmother was a small woman; the mule was big and the plow heavy. The soil was one part dirt to two parts rock. I can't imagine how hard it was to plow that garden, but watching her do it made a lasting impression on me. It was there the seed was sown that would grow into a gardener.

I tagged along beside Grandmother for most of the first years of my life. I learned to count by dropping seeds in furrows. As Grandmother prepared a hill for potatoes or squash, I came behind and carefully placed the seed potatoes or the right number of squash seeds. She would trust me to place a dipper of water into each hole where a tomato or cabbage plant was dropped. When planting was finished, she would bring out a Mason jar of dried flower seeds and, in 2 feet of space around the perimeter of the garden,

sprinkle them on top of the ground. She would use a lawn rake to mix up the soil a bit, then flatten the surface of the soil with the end of the rake. By the height of the season, my grandmother's garden was a beautiful sight. The rows of vegetables, in various stages of growth and ripening fruit, were surrounded by the border of brightly colored, mixed annuals. When friends or family came to visit, she would send them home with a wonderful country bouquet wrapped with a few sheets of wet newspaper covering the cut ends. The family saw the best of the blossoms in Mason jars on the kitchen table at supper time.

When the flowers were finished for the season, my grandmother would pull the bottom ends of her apron up in one hand, making it a carrying cloth, and walk along the outside edge of the garden. With her free hand, she pulled off the dried flower seeds and dropped them into her apron. She kept them in paper bags until she was sure they were dry; then she would store them in capped Mason jars for next season. Each year she would add new seeds to her flower mixture by gathering seeds from fellow gardeners.

During the summer Grandmother hoed weeds and carried water to keep her garden growing in the intense Tennessee heat. She would let me help pick bugs from potatoes and beetles from beans. I would drop seed corn into rows and hill up squash and melon mounds. I carried garden and kitchen waste to the compost pile long before I ever heard the word compost. As fall came around,

Grandmother stepped up her pace, for all she grew had to be canned, dried, or preserved. I still find it unbelievable that one little grandmother could have done so much.

When I look back at that time with my grandmother, I can't remember her talking very much, but each time she did I would pay attention. Watching and listening to my grandmother as she grew and preserved our food and medicines inspired me. Seeing a garden planted with a border of flowers each year gave me a longing for beauty. All of it seeped into my very being. She trained me to be a gardener and a hard worker without ever verbalizing her intent. Everything I learned from her makes me the gardener I am today.

I took all the knowledge I gleaned from this uneducated, but wonderfully intelligent, woman with me when I left the mountains. It came in handy when I married a man in the military and had to move every three years. I used that knowledge to help raise my family of seven children, run my home, and become a good gardener. I was always able to grow some of our food, find other food in the wild, and then preserve, can, and freeze that food. I kept my children near me in the garden where we planted, worked, and weeded our gardens together.

With each move we started a new garden and learned what grew best in each state.

With our last move to New York State, we became innkeepers with little time for gardening.

Our inn had only nine rooms, but 250 seats for food service. At first I had only an herb garden by the kitchen door where we could pick fresh chives, dill, basil, and parsley. Later I expanded the herb garden and grew enough herbs to dry, including oregano, tarragon, anise, and many others. My family and I learned the joys of picking and eating wild blueberries and growing rhubarb that we could harvest for the entire season. Gardening in the short, cool summers of the Catskill Mountains was a challenge for most vegetables, but the freezer was full of blueberries, raspberries, blackberries, currants, and chopped rhubarb.

As my children grew up and left home, gardening became a solitary pleasure. I soon found that traditional gardening—all that tilling, digging, hoeing, and weeding—was too much work. I began to search for easier ways to do all that was needed to have my vegetable, herb, and flower gardens. Memories of my grandmother returned. All I had learned so many years ago came back to me as I worked alone. But what I needed to do was adapt those lessons I'd learned to a new way of gardening: a way to have the best soil with the least effort. Lasagna gardening was my answer.

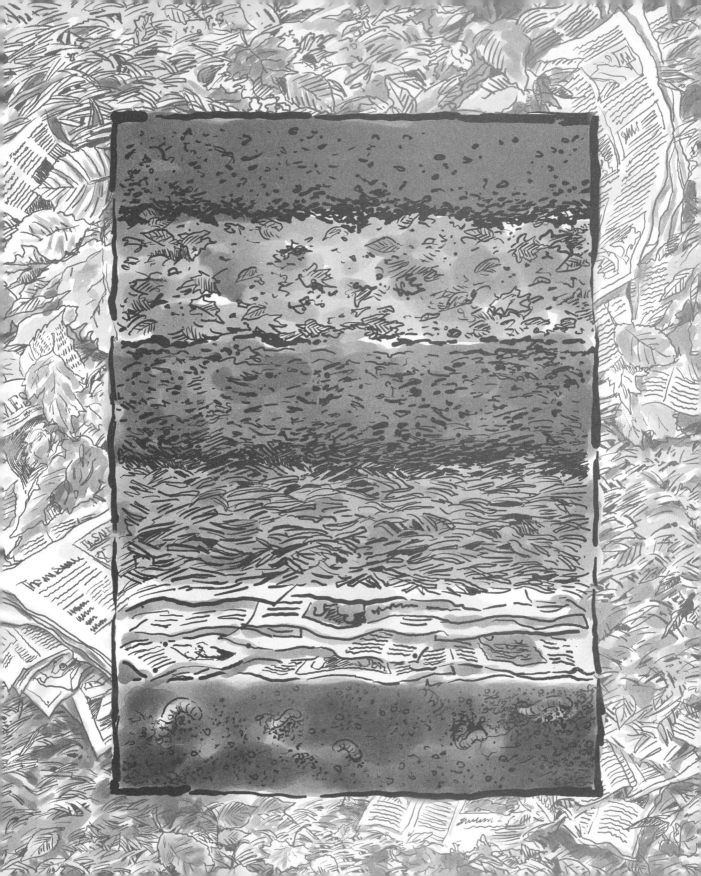

Chapter 1

Lasagna Gardening Basics

When I first started gardening, I thought I had to do it all. The gardeners I knew and the books and magazines I read said to remove the sod, then till, dig, and even double-dig the top 12 to 18 inches of soil before starting a garden. This message is intimidating. It's enough to make you want to throw in the trowel before you even get started!

I followed that approach in my own garden for many years. But when the children left home and I began to garden alone, I was hard-pressed to keep up with the demands of my job and keep the garden going. Then one year I was so busy that I didn't have the garden tilled at all. Instead, I piled it high with the contents of all the compost piles, several bales of peat moss, and lots of aged barn litter. I bought plants, plunked them in holes, and gave them a rough mulch of grass clippings each time I mowed. It was a mess to look at but a great garden for production. When I could find a plant among the weeds, I would harvest record numbers of fruits and vegetables. It was amazing!

Still, I felt guilty about the way the garden looked, so I tried to start and run the rotary tiller. It finally started, but I lost control when it hit a rock, and it went careening off on its own, like a chicken with its head cut off. The whole experience scared me to death, and I vowed never to try it again. During the rest of that summer, I thought about my neglected vegetable garden and its generous yield. Sure, anyone can have a great garden with deeply dug or tilled soil. But I liked the idea of doing less work and getting better results. The idea of lasagna gardening was born.

What Is Lasagna Gardening?

No, it doesn't mean growing your own lasagna! Lasagna gardening is a nontraditional, organic, layering method you can use to create better soil while keeping your gardens neat and attractive. (The name comes from the layers you'll be making to create your beds—they reminded me of making lasagna!) Based on a commonsense approach and readily available natural ingredients, lasagna gardening is an easy, time-saving way to install and maintain any kind of garden without removing the sod, digging, or tilling. Close planting and generous mulching greatly reduce the time needed for watering and weeding. And because of the healthy growing environment, lasagna gardens are plagued with fewer garden pests. Using no power tools, heavy equipment, or expensive additives, one person can easily create and enjoy a healthy, productive garden.

Why Lasagna Gardening?

The answer is simple: It saves work, energy, time, and money. After you make the beds, all you have to do each year is plant and

mulch—no tilling or heavy digging required. The ground stays cool and damp under the layers of mulch, so regular watering is a thing of the past. Setting the plants close together encourages them to fill in faster, so weeds don't stand a chance, and the few that do pop up are easy to pull from the loose mulch. Lasagna gardens give you a place to recycle nearly all of the wastes from your property, so you'll keep

Why Isn't Everyone Lasagna Gardening?

This method is amazingly simple and successful, so why isn't everyone doing it?

- *Some think they don't have time to garden. (If you want to do something, you'll find the time.)*

- *Some think gardening is too hard. (There's no such thing as a no-work garden, but a lasagna garden is pretty close.)*

- *Some think they are too old to garden. (You're only old if you think you're old.)*

- *Some have physical disabilities and have set limits on what they think they can do. (Never set limits.)*

- *Some want to, but just don't know where to start. (Keep reading, and you'll find out!)*

those garden trimmings and kitchen scraps out of landfills. Best of all, lasagna gardens are chemical-free, so you'll become a more earth-friendly gardener, providing healthy food for the table and a safe habitat for birds and butterflies. You'll surround yourself with beautiful and healthy growing spaces and enjoy the pleasure and stress-relief you only get from gardening.

Lasagna gardening is for busy people who have the urge to put their hands in the soil. It's for people who are power-tool challenged. It's for anyone who is not able to garden traditionally because of age or physical limitations. It's for the new gardener. It's for the environmentally conscious. It's for the legions of us who are stressed and overworked. It's the way to have it all without doing it all.

Getting Started

Creating any kind of garden, whether traditional or lasagna, starts with two basic questions: What do you want to grow and where will you put the garden? If you have a large property, you probably have your choice of sites. In this case, you can first decide what you'd like to grow, then choose a spot that fits the needs of those plants. If you want to raise vegetables, for instance, you'll look for a spot that's open and sunny, so you can grow the widest variety of crops.

Those of you with limited space are better off choosing a site first, then selecting plants that will thrive in the growing conditions that spot has to offer. Sure, most plants will grow in less-than-ideal conditions. But their yield or flowering will also be less than optimum, and they'll be more prone to pests and diseases. By matching the plants to the site, you'll be well on your way to creating a naturally healthy, top-producing, easy-care garden.

Tips and Time-Savers

Making Connections

One of the exciting things about gardening is that there's always something new to discover. Read everything you can. It's also fun to join a gardening club, where you can interact with other gardeners, from beginners to experts, and learn about something new at each meeting. The Cooperative Extension Service is another valuable but often-overlooked source of gardening information. Its offices offer a wealth of publications and guidance, including regional growing charts and plant lists. Take advantage of this service—your tax dollars support it! The Cooperative Extension Service is organized by county. Look for its listing in your telephone book, usually under "Government Services" or a similar heading.

Select a Site

If you have plenty of possible sites for a new garden, it can be difficult to decide on the perfect spot. I find it helpful to start with a plan of my property. This isn't anything formal: just an outline of the property drawn roughly to scale, with buildings, the driveway, and other permanent features (such as trees, large shrubs, play areas, patios, and walkways) sketched in. Make a few photocopies of this base plan, so you can make notes on one copy and pencil in different garden layouts on another copy without messing up the original.

(continued on page 6)

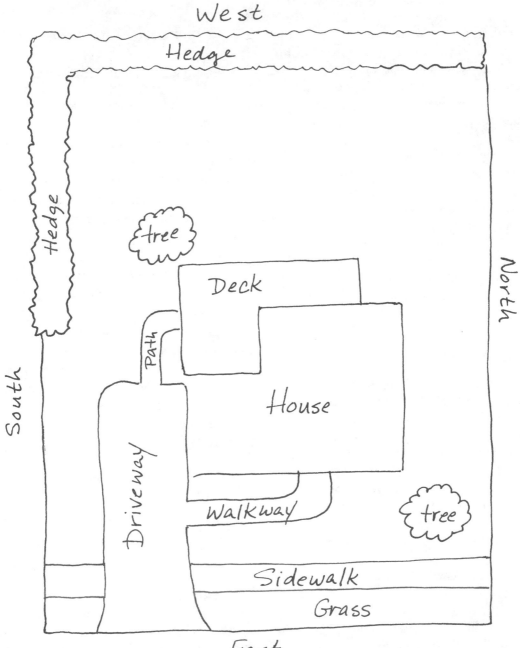

Start with a Base Map. Not sure where you want your new lasagna garden? To identify possible sites on your property, make a simple map of your yard, sketching in the existing features, such as buildings and trees.

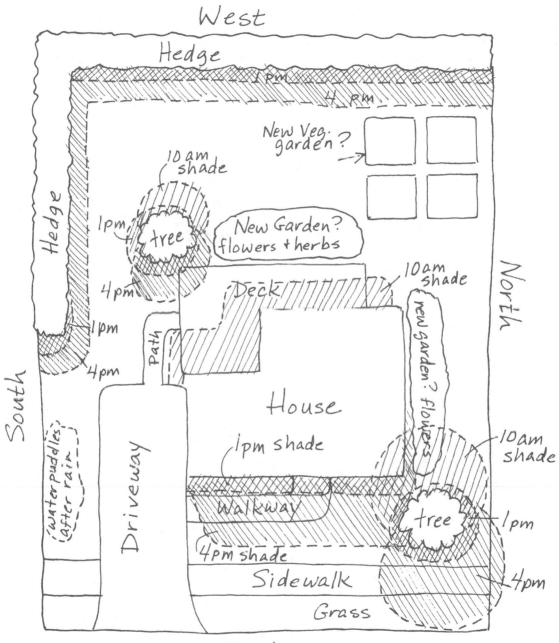

Now, Make Notes. Jot down comments about your soil conditions, shade patterns, and other observations right on a copy of your yard map. Besides helping you identify a good site right now, it will also be handy for planning future gardens.

Take a copy of your base plan and head out to your yard. Unless you're planning to replace an existing planting, you'll probably want to consider only areas that are currently in grass for your new garden. Now, take a good look around.

Sun and Shade. The easiest things to observe are the shade patterns cast by trees, buildings, and other features. On your plan, use a pencil or crayon to color in the areas that are in shade. Actually, it's smart to repeat this exercise in the morning, at midday, and again in the afternoon, so you can get an accurate assessment of how many hours of sunlight the different areas get during the day. If you're extremely organized, it's ideal to observe the shade patterns several times during the spring, summer, and fall before planting. An area that's in full sun at spring planting time can end up in full shade by midsummer, when nearby trees have fully expanded their leaves. When this much advance planning isn't practical, you'll just have to make an educated guess about the average amount of sun a particular site gets. If necessary, you can adjust some of your plant choices later on as you learn more about the spot you've chosen.

A site that's in full sun eight or more hours every day gets enough light to support a wide variety of vegetables, fruits, herbs, and flowers. Many of the same plants can get by on six to eight hours of sun, although they may not yield as much or flower as generously as when growing in full sun. Spots with less than six hours of sun a day can still support great gardens, but you'll need to choose your plants more carefully to find the ones that thrive in somewhat shady spots. To find out more about the light needs of specific plants, refer to their entries in the following chapters.

Water and Wind. Next, take a closer look at the ground. As you walk around, note any areas where water forms puddles after a heavy rain or spots that feel soggy underfoot, and mark them on your plan. These poorly drained spots are less than ideal for most garden plants, as soggy soil tends to rot roots, so it's better to choose a drier site for your lasagna garden.

Think about how the wind blows through your property, too. Some wind is good, since it circulates air around your plants and helps leaves and stems dry quickly after rain, discouraging diseases. An open site that's frequently exposed to strong gusts can be a problem, though, since the wind draws water out of plants quickly and may cause them to wilt. Wind can also knock down taller plants. If you live on top of a hill or another frequently windy location, choose a site where your lasagna garden will be sheltered by shrubs, trees, a fence, or a building.

Tips and Time-Savers

Anything Goes!

Unlike traditional gardens, lasagna gardens aren't limited by rocky or compacted soil. Since you'll be building the soil up, instead of digging down, you have a lot more flexibility when it comes to selecting a site. I've created great lasagna gardens on grassy sites packed down by years of car parking!

Decide What to Grow

You probably already have some idea of what you want to grow in your lasagna garden. This is a good time to write down a wish list of all of your ideas. If you enjoy cooking home-grown produce or eating it right from the plant, vegetables and fruits are likely at the top of your list. Cooks will get plenty of use from a garden of culinary herbs, too. If crafts are a favorite hobby, how about planting scented herbs for potpourri, or a cut-flower garden to provide a bounty of blooms for fresh arrangements or drying? Want to liven up your landscape with colorful plantings? Make a lasagna garden packed full of shrubs and perennials, or perhaps a mixture of dwarf conifers and rock-garden plants for close-up viewing.

Tips and Time-Savers

Planning Your Plantings

With careful planning, a single lasagna garden can serve several purposes. You might, for instance, combine vegetables, herbs, and flowers in one area. That way, you'll have your dinner veggies next to their seasonings, with a few flowers for a table bouquet! If you're just starting out, though, you'll probably find it easier to start small and concentrate on a single theme for your first lasagna garden. Once you see how easy it is, you can quickly create new gardens to fit all the things on your wish list!

Take a Soil Test

Once you've decided on a spot for your garden, and you have some idea of what you want to grow, it's time to take a closer look at your soil—specifically, its pH. pH is a measure of how acid or alkaline your soil is, which in turn affects how your plants will grow. It is measured on a scale from 1 to 14, with 7 being neutral. (A pH below 7 indicates acidity; above 7 is alkaline.) Most plants grow best when the soil pH falls somewhere between 6.5 and 7.2. So, how do you find out your soil's pH? Take a soil test!

Start by collecting a few spoonfuls of soil from five or six different spots in the area where you plan to put your lasagna garden. Mix them together to create a representative sample of the soil. Then, check the sample with a home test kit (available at garden centers), or send it to a soil-testing lab for a professional analysis. You can find a lab by asking the staff of your local nursery or garden center for their recommendations, calling your local Extension Service, or checking in your telephone directory under "Laboratories, Testing."

Lab tests cost more but give you a detailed report of your soil's nutrient content as well as its pH. Some also provide recommendations on what you need to add to counteract nutrient imbalances, based on the plants you want to grow. This full-scale testing might be a good idea if you are really curious about your soil, or if plants already growing on or near the site aren't as healthy or vigorous as you'd normally expect. To be honest, though, I've never had a professional soil test done on any of my gardens. I rely on a simple home test kit that allows me to check each garden's pH. I've found that the nutrient levels seem to take care of themselves, so I don't worry about them too much. Lasagna gardening gives you total control over what goes into your soil, so you can build soil that is pretty near perfect for growing most home crops.

Whichever testing approach you take, be sure to jot down whatever results you end up with. You'll refer back to these notes later, as you choose and apply your lasagna ingredients.

Gathering Lasagna Ingredients

The key ingredients in any lasagna garden are organic materials. These include peat moss, animal manures, shredded leaves, and other mulches; compost; and other materials recycled from garden and household wastes, such as grass clippings, coffee grounds, and vegetable peelings. Gather as much of these nutrient-rich materials as you can from your own property, and see if your neighbors are willing to share any organic materials they don't use for their own gardens. If you still need more materials, you can buy them from your local garden or home center.

Develop a Mulch Mentality

Understanding mulch—what it is, what it does, what organic materials make good mulch, and where to get them—is the first step in becoming a committed lasagna gardener.

So, what is mulch, and what does it do? Basically, a mulch is anything that covers and shields your soil from baking sun, drying wind, and pounding rain. This could include a layer of chopped leaves, a sheet of black plastic, or even closely spaced plants. But for the purposes of lasagna gardening, we're specifically interested in *organic* mulches. While these mulches cover and protect the soil, they also release materials that feed earthworms and other helpful soil organisms. In turn, these organisms release nutrients in a form that plant roots can absorb. Think of it

Earthworms: Living Garden Tillers

Have you ever left anything lying on the lawn that killed the grass underneath and left little tunnels? Well then, you've seen lasagna gardening at work. Those little tunnels are the work of earthworms, a gardener's best friend for soil building. The tunnels they make in their quest for food go several feet into the earth, even in compacted areas. I have felt my teeth jar when I tried to dig in soil that was hard clay and full of rocks, but earthworms can penetrate that. Their tunneling loosens the soil so air and water can enter. Plant roots can also use the tunnels as they grow outward in search of air, water, and nutrients.

Lasagna gardens are full of earthworms. Why? Because they provide the conditions worms thrive in: moderate temperatures, darkness, and moisture, with plenty of organic matter to feed on. Under the layer of newspaper or cardboard, earthworms are drawn to the cool darkness and ingest the paper and other organic material. As they digest leaves, grass, and other mulch material, they deposit earthworm castings, a humus-rich soil amendment. You build the right environment and provide food, and the earthworms do the rest!

this way: Organic mulches feed your soil, and the soil feeds your plants.

What are some good, easy-to-use organic mulches, and where do you get them? I've listed a sampling of the most popular ones in "Checklist: Mulch Materials," at right. Some of these you're probably familiar with; others, you may not have even considered before. One of the most useful mulches, for instance, is newspaper. Almost every home gets one or more papers a day, and they are a constant source of work: straightening, bundling, tying, and disposing. Newspapers are heavy when allowed to accumulate, and they are forever coming apart and lying about. Now, you can finally put them to good use. Dispose of all the colored and glossy pages and keep the regular part of the paper. What used to be a disposal problem becomes a great source of free mulch for your lasagna garden.

It's also worth looking into regionally available mulches. If you live in a rural area, for instance, you probably have easy access to hay and straw. Coastal gardeners can gather seaweed. If you live near a brewery or feed mill, you might be able to get spent hops, buckwheat hulls, or other by-products free for the hauling, or for just a few dollars. To find sources for these locally available materials, talk to other gardeners in your area, or check the classified ads in your local paper. When you develop a mulch mentality, you'll start finding mulch materials in the most unlikely places!

Checklist: Mulch Materials

Here's a list of ingredients that can be useful for building the layers of a lasagna garden. Some are widely available; others may be common only in certain regions. Use this list to get ideas, but don't be limited by it; many other great mulch materials are available if you look around for them.

- ✔ *animal manures*
- ✔ *compost*
- ✔ *corn cobs (chopped)*
- ✔ *grass clippings*
- ✔ *hay*
- ✔ *leaves (chopped)*
- ✔ *peat moss*
- ✔ *salt hay*
- ✔ *sawdust*
- ✔ *seaweed/kelp*
- ✔ *stalks (chopped)*
- ✔ *straw*
- ✔ *wood ashes*

Gather Household and Garden Wastes

Most of us spend a lifetime disposing of our waste products from home and garden as quickly as possible. You may have a garbage disposal where you push kitchen scraps out of sight. Yard waste is bagged and put out on the curb, all tidy and ready to be hauled away. But once you start lasagna gardening, you'll realize that you've been throwing away valuable organic matter—and paying for the privilege. Sure, it will take a bit of time to change old habits, but it's worth the effort.

The kitchen is a great place to start gathering organic materials. Place a covered plastic bucket under or next to your sink, to collect vegetable peelings, fruit skins and cores, used tea bags, coffee grounds, and other scraps. Keep bones, fat, and fish and meat scraps out, though, as they'll smell bad and attract critters if added to your garden. Every day or two, empty the bucket by scattering the ingredients directly onto a layer of a lasagna garden you're building, or add the contents to your compost pile (more on that in "Create Great Compost," below).

When you are out working in your garden, carry some kind of container with you to hold gathered leaves, spent flowers, and other soft trimmings. A 5-gallon bucket makes a convenient container for a small amount of material. If you're doing a serious garden cleanup, a tarp may be more practical for gathering and carrying your haul. Add the materials directly to a layer in a new lasagna garden, stockpile them in an out-of-the-way spot until you need them, or add them to your compost pile.

Create Great Compost

Some gardeners refer to compost as "black gold," and it's easy to see why. From humble origins—kitchen scraps, grass clippings, manure, leaves, bits and pieces of sod, and ashes from the fireplace, among other things—arises a dark, crumbly material that plants thrive in. When you add compost to a lasagna garden as one or more of the layers, you give back a gift of organic matter and nutrients that are vital to soil building.

Select a Site. Place your compost pile on level, well-drained soil in full sun. It could be close to, or in the middle of, your garden so you won't have far to haul your garden trim-

mings. It's also smart to consider access from your house so it's convenient for collecting kitchen scraps. Look for a site that's sheltered from wind and screened from your neighbors. *You* know how valuable compost is, but your neighbors may not have the same appreciation for the piles, so be considerate when choosing a composting spot.

Consider the Size and Shape. Plan on each completed pile being 3 to 4 feet on each side. You can make a freestanding pile or build an enclosure from anything that is handy— lumber, chicken or fence wire, hardware cloth, bricks, cinder blocks, hay bales, wood pallets, or railroad ties. Leave air space at the bottom by laying down a foot or so of heavy brush or a 6-inch layer of scrap wood in a grid pattern. If you build an enclosure, make sure air can also circulate through the sides, because bacteria and fungi need oxygen to do their work.

Feed Your Pile. Food for a compost pile includes just about anything that was once

Tips and Time-Savers

Collecting Compost Materials

Keep rubber gloves and premoistened towelettes in your car in case you spot bags of leaves or other compost ingredients when you're out running errands or on the way to an important meeting. You can stash the bags in your trunk and use the towelettes to clean up before the meeting.

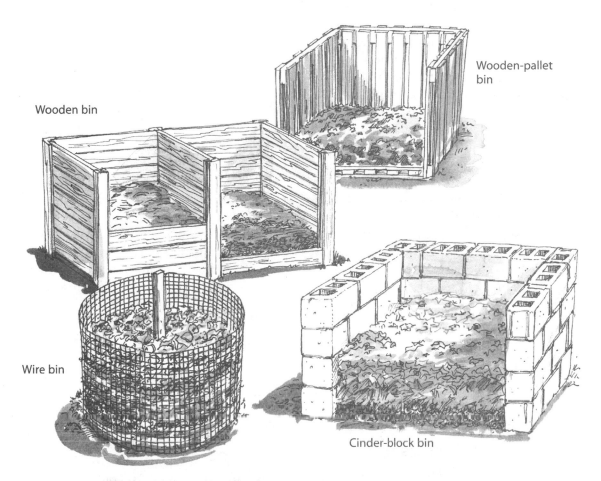

Wooden-pallet bin

Wooden bin

Wire bin

Cinder-block bin

Compost Options. Create a freestanding compost pile, or enclose it in a bin to keep it looking tidy. You can choose from a wide range of homemade and commercial compost bins. Just make sure the one you use can hold at least a cubic yard of material.

alive. The ingredients listed in "Checklist: Mulch Materials" on page 9 are as well suited for making compost as they are for mulching. Now, simply layer them to create your pile, alternating the layers of high-carbon and high-nitrogen ingredients. (When you add brown, dry material, such as leaves, straw, and hay, you are adding carbon. When you add moist—and often green—material, such as grass clippings, kitchen waste, and manure,

you are adding nitrogen.) I add 4 parts of high-carbon ingredients to 1 part high-nitrogen material, and this mixture is usually just right. High-carbon materials are generally abundant and easy to find. If you don't have enough high-nitrogen material, you can substitute a thin layer of bloodmeal (available from garden centers).

Small pieces break down most quickly, so chopping the ingredients speeds up the composting process. Chop kitchen scraps in a blender or food processor; crush eggshells with your hands. Run newspapers, leaves, stalks, twigs, and branches through a chipper/shredder. A lawn mower also works well for chopping up leaves. Dry material is easiest to shred, but you'll need to wet it a bit when you add it to the compost pile. Sprinkle the layer with a watering can or hose to get it as damp as a squeezed sponge—not soggy.

What doesn't belong in your compost pile? Avoid adding fats, meat, bones, and oils. These are slow to break down, they'll make your pile smell bad, and they'll attract animals to your pile. Also, don't add droppings from dogs or cats; these materials can carry diseases.

No Needles in the Compost, Please!

Needles and wood chips from pines and other coniferous trees work best just as they are, without composting. They make an excellent mulch for blueberries, azaleas, rhododendrons, and other acid-loving plants. If you do add them to your compost or use them as a layer in a lasagna garden, then you should apply lime to counteract the acid conditions produced by these materials as they decompose.

Use Your Compost. When the pile is finished (3 to 4 feet high), it's big enough to start heating up. The source of the heat is the millions of microorganisms that are feeding on and decomposing the pile's ingredients. After a few days, a well-built pile feels warm to the touch. When it cools off, let it sit for another week or two before using the still-somewhat-chunky end product. For a finer, more crumbly material, stir or fluff the pile thoroughly with a pitchfork, and let the material heat and cool again before using the finished compost.

Use layers of rough compost on unfinished lasagna gardens. Save finished compost for a decorative top-mulch and for container gardens, such as window boxes. Add a few handfuls to each planting hole, and mulch vegetables with it in summer to provide a nutrient boost. Sift finished compost to use as a fine seedbed on top of a lasagna garden.

Keep Making More! Once you've learned how to make compost, you'll never have enough. I always have at least two piles going—one being built while the other is cooking. Eventually, you'll run out of home-gathered ingredients and have to start looking elsewhere. Keep your eye out for compost ingredients your unenlightened neighbors aren't using. (I've created a community of ardent scavengers for organic compost material in my neighborhood, and now I have to go far afield to find extra materials!) In addition to your own kitchen scraps, ask your grocer or your favorite restaurant for lettuce and other vegetable trimmings. Local farms and horse stables are good sources of manure-laden barn litter, a super compost ingredient. If your community has a composting program, you may be able to tap into municipal compost piles; the material is often free for the hauling.

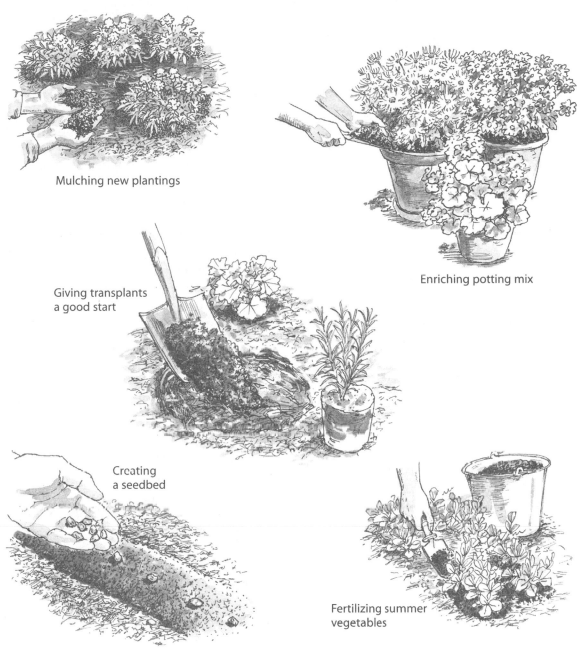

Mulching new plantings

Enriching potting mix

Giving transplants
a good start

Creating
a seedbed

Fertilizing summer
vegetables

Five Fast Uses for Compost. There's a reason gardeners refer to compost as "black gold"! It's a great addition to lasagna layers, but if your supply is limited, save it for special uses, such as sowing seeds outdoors, enriching potting soil for container plants, giving transplants a good start, or providing a handsome and nutrient-rich mulch for flowers, herbs, and vegetables.

Sheet Composting

If composting in a pile or container is not practical for you, because of space limitations or any other reason, don't give up—let your lasagna garden be your compost pile. Lasagna gardening is really just another name for sheet composting, a technique in which you arrange the same raw compost ingredients in low, broad layers, rather than in higher mounds or containers. The end result is the same: a crumbly, organic-rich soil amendment. I found this out by living in one of the coldest parts of the country, where the snow was so deep I couldn't get to the compost bin in winter. I began to make small compost piles where I wanted to build a new garden, piles that were nearer to the house and more accessible in the winter. Eventually I did most of my composting by sheets or layers.

Buy Additional Lasagna Ingredients

Unless you have an unlimited supply of homegrown mulch materials and compost, you'll probably need to buy some of your lasagna ingredients, especially when you're just getting started. Sphagnum peat moss is one of the most accessible and inexpensive materials

available to lasagna gardeners. Even after years of gathering mulch materials, I still rely on peat moss for building my lasagna gardens. In fact, I use peat moss after each layer of other mulches: newspaper, peat, compost, peat, grass clippings, peat, chopped leaves, peat—you get the idea.

Other purchased materials I use include bonemeal (which adds phosphorus, a necessary plant nutrient that promotes good root growth) and bloodmeal (a high-nitrogen material that can substitute for manures or grass clippings). Depending on the results of my soil test, I may buy and add lime (powdered limestone, which adds calcium and raises the pH of acid soil) or powdered sulfur (which lowers the pH of alkaline soil).

Assembling a Lasagna Garden

You've selected the perfect site and assembled all your ingredients, so let's get this lasagna garden started! First, mark the outline of the garden on the ground, with either stakes and string or a sprinkling of lime or flour. The actual size and shape of the garden are up to you. If this is your first garden, I suggest starting small. An area roughly 4 by 8 feet won't take a lot of ingredients but will give you room to grow several different crops. After you've tried the technique once, you can quickly create new lasagna gardens to expand your plantings.

For the first layer, you need something heavy to smother the existing grass and weeds. Most of the time, I use thick pads of wet newspaper. Lay them close together, so the edges overlap slightly to keep weeds from sneaking through. Another good option is flattened, overlapping cardboard boxes.

Super-Simple Garden Starting. Creating a lasagna garden is easy. Instead of digging up the sod, simply cover it with wet newspaper to smother the grass, then build your lasagna layers on top.

Next, add a 2- to 3-inch layer of peat moss to cover the paper or cardboard. (If you'll have paths through your lasagna garden, cover them with 4 inches of wood chips instead, and save the peat moss for the growing areas.) Now, spread a 4- to 8-inch layer of organic mulch material over the peat moss. Add another layer of peat moss, and another layer of mulch, and so on, until the beds are 18 to 24 inches high. I often top the layers with a scattering of bonemeal and wood ashes to provide extra phosphorus and potassium. That's it!

The exact materials you'll use for your lasagna depend on what you have readily available. Every time I build a lasagna garden, I use somewhat different layers, depending on the season, but the results are the same. Whatever you decide will be right: The important thing is to do it!

Tips and Time-Savers

Preparing the Paper Layer

When making a new garden on top of sod, use thick sections of paper. Newspaper works best if wet, so I soak it first in a large plastic bucket with thick rope handles. (The handles make the bucket easy to drag.) Surprisingly, newsprint is still readable even after being outside all winter. Sometimes I'm caught bending over in the garden and reading when I'm supposed to be working!

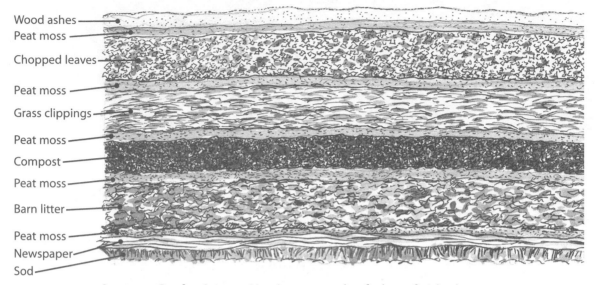

Wood ashes
Peat moss
Chopped leaves
Peat moss
Grass clippings
Peat moss
Compost
Peat moss
Barn litter
Peat moss
Newspaper
Sod

Lasagna Garden Layers. Here's an example of what a finished lasagna bed might look like in cross section, with alternating layers of peat moss and organic materials. The exact materials you use to create your own lasagna beds will probably be different, depending on what you have readily available.

Lasagna Gardening in Spring

With the months you've spent staring out of the windows all winter, you've had plenty of time to choose a spot for a new lasagna garden. As soon as the ground dries enough for you to start spring cleanup, you can mark the new spot, lay down newspaper, and begin the lasagna process.

There's quite a lot of material in the spring to get a lasagna garden going. If you didn't get around to cleaning up the previous fall (which is fine, as the stalks and seedheads provide food for birds), clean the gardens as soon as the ground thaws in spring and add this debris in layers to a new garden. This is also a good time to empty your compost bins. The material has had all winter to break down, so it should be nice and crumbly. I stockpile bags of leaves collected from the curb in the

fall for spring use. If my neighbor can spare some, I also use horse barn litter and spoiled hay. Once you've built the layers, you can plant right away or let it "cook" first (see "Planting a Lasagna Garden" and "Cooking Your Lasagna Garden" on the opposite page).

Lasagna Gardening in Fall

For the organic gardener, fall is the bountiful season. Leaves are the backbone of a new lasagna garden, as well as the compost pile. I use four times as many chopped leaves as I do any other organic matter. You've heard the expression "make hay while the sun shines"? In autumn, I "collect leaves till the snow falls."

Fall is the time of year when you can make real strides in soil building. Whether you are starting a new lasagna garden or rebuilding

Cooking Your Lasagna Garden

One great thing about lasagna gardening is the instant result: You can create a garden from scratch and plant it all in the same day. But sometimes you may want to "cook" your lasagna first, to reduce the height of the beds and get loose, crumbly soil quickly. It takes a little more thought to create the right balance of organic materials to encourage heating. Put about four times as much brown (high-carbon) material—such as peat moss, hay, straw, and chopped leaves, stalks, and twigs—as you do green (high-nitrogen) material: grass clippings, kitchen scraps, and fresh manure. Apply the material in 4- to 6-inch layers, adding a sprinkle of organic supplements, such as wood ashes, bonemeal, and lime or sulfur (if needed to adjust the soil's pH). If you have a ready supply of compost, by all means add layers of that also.

Once the bed is 18 to 24 inches deep, I cover it with black plastic and weigh down the edges with bricks. The plastic helps keep the materials moist and traps the sun's warmth for fast heating. I usually leave the plastic on for about six weeks. Most of the mulch will have broken down into a dark, crumbly material that's a joy to plant in.

an existing one, just lay on as many layers of organic material as you can find. Worms are your hardworking soil cultivators, and the lasagna layers provide a generous supply of worm food.

You can plant fall-built lasagna gardens right away, let them "cook" first (see "Cooking Your Lasagna Garden," at left), or just leave them to break down naturally over winter for spring planting. The first time I built a lasagna garden in late fall, I didn't finish until the first snow began to fall, and I never even thought about planting it. The next time I built a fall garden, the entire process took just an hour, and it was completely planted. Everything survived the winter, and from then on, I knew I could make a garden at any time of the year and plant it right away.

Planting a Lasagna Garden

A lasagna garden that's been "cooked" or left to decompose over winter will be dark and loose, much like deeply dug soil, so you can set out plants or sow seeds just as you would in a traditional garden.

The great thing about lasagna gardening, though, is that you don't *have* to wait to plant—you can build the garden and plant it all in the same day. To make a planting hole in a new bed, simply pull the layers apart with your hands. Set the plant in the hole, pull the mulch back around the roots, and water it thoroughly. To sow seeds in a newly built lasagna garden, spread fine compost or damp peat moss where the seeds are to go, then set the seeds on the surface. Sift more fine material to cover the seeds and press down. When the plants have two true leaves (the leaves that form after the first pair of "seed leaves"), pull some of the coarser mulch material around them to keep the soil moist and weed-free.

No-Dig Planting. Ready to plant your new lasagna garden? Don't bother digging—just pull back the layers with your hands, pop in a plant, and pull the mulch materials back around the roots.

Simple Lasagna Seedbeds. To create a good seedbed in a newly built lasagna garden, spread a row or patch of sifted, finished compost or damp peat moss where you want to plant. Sow the seed on top, cover it with more compost or peat moss, then press down to firm the bed.

Lasagna Gardening and Me

To get you as excited about lasagna gardening as I am, I want to tell you of the 30 gardens I installed and maintained over a six-year period. Why so many gardens? I began building a few to prove my theory: that this method was truly a good soil builder and could support all sorts of crops. Then, I needed a few display gardens for groups of people who were coming to hear my lectures. It was so easy, the few gardens grew to 30 before I knew it. I never planned to build that many gardens!

More than anything, I want you to be able to garden in a way you may not have thought of, and I want you to be successful in your efforts. You can learn something from my experience. Just because it is so easy, don't get carried away and get so many gardens going you can't maintain them. Besides the maintenance the established plants require (such as pruning and division), lasagna beds need new mulch layers each fall to provide fresh nutrients to the soil and to suppress weed growth. It's one thing to collect materials for a small home garden, but when the number of beds grows to double digits, it can become a full-time job!

My First Lasagna Garden

Later in the summer that I discovered the great yields from my mulched-but-not-tilled vegetable garden, I wanted to build a new garden. A grassy lot next to our inn offered a great location, with full sun and access to water. The ground was level, and we weren't using it for anything at the time. On the downside, the soil was compacted from years of use as a parking area. Overall, there were enough reasons in favor of the site and only that one against it, so I decided to give the garden a try. But this time, I was going to use my new approach.

With the aid of my surveyor son-in-law, I laid out a formal square herb garden, divided into four 3-foot-square beds with a circle in the middle. In the meantime, I had stockpiled materials to one side of the area: stacks of newspaper, a pile of wood chips for the paths, the contents of my largest composter, bales of peat moss, bags of chopped leaves, grass clippings, aged manure, some builder's sand, and last, but not least, bags of soil amendments bought on sale for a fraction of their spring price.

Right after Labor Day weekend, I began the new garden by laying down thick pads of wet newspaper on top of the sod. This was covered with a 2-inch layer of peat moss for the garden beds and 4 inches of wood chips for the paths. I had achieved the look of a garden instantly by covering the sod in this way. Each day, I added another layer to the beds: 4- to 6-inch layers of chopped leaves, grass clippings, compost, manure, other organic materials, and sand, alternated with 2-inch layers of peat moss. By the time Thanksgiving came, the garden lasagna was finished, and the beds were 18 to 24 inches high. We had been burning fires in the woodstove for several weeks, and I had saved the wood ashes. The last thing I did was sprinkle them on top of the gardens, as you would Parmesan cheese on a lasagna.

When spring came, I could hardly contain myself as I waited for the ground to thaw. The day I walked out to the garden, with my trowel in hand, I was in a high state of anticipation. Beds that had been 18 to 24 inches high had shrunk to about 6 inches, but everything looked good. Using the trowel, I dug down through the 6 inches of black, crumbly soil to the remnants of newspaper and on down another 3 to 4 inches. The underlying soil, which had been tightly compacted, was now loose. Altogether, I had about 8 inches of super soil to plant in. Earthworms had been hard at work and were still in evidence with each bit of soil turned. There were weeks to wait before it would be warm enough to plant, but I knew the experiment had worked far better than I had imagined.

Back at the weedy, neglected vegetable garden I had walked away from last fall, I began by pulling out dried stalks from last year's harvest. This left me with a weedy, grassy plot. I waded in and stomped down the weeds, then covered the whole thing with wet newspaper. Because it had been tilled for so many years, I simply poked holes in the paper, stuck in plants, and covered all the paper with mulch. I used spoiled hay around the plants and wood chips for paths. (Once paths are made, you no longer walk on the growing spaces.) As the plants grew, I mulched them with a manure-and-sawdust mix from my neighbor's barn. Last, I added a layer of peat moss to cover the manure/sawdust layer. The garden was neat and produced well. It was the second year the tiller had sat unused, so I sold it that fall. Lasagna gardening was here to stay.

The Experiment Continues

In back of my house, across the road from our inn, I installed four raised beds. After marking off four 12- by 14-foot spaces, I laid

Making the Transition. To turn an existing vegetable garden into a lasagna garden, tromp down the remaining topgrowth in fall or late winter, cover it with thick pads of wet newspaper or cardboard, and start building up the layers. (This can work with flower gardens too, but dig and set aside any perennials before building the layers, then replant them on top.)

down overlapping, flattened cardboard boxes on top of the sod and covered them with 6 inches of soil. Next, I covered the soil with 4 inches of peat moss. After wetting the area, I pulled the peat and soil back and set plants on the cardboard. After pulling the mix back around the plants, I mulched them with chopped leaves and wood chips. All the plants survived the winter. In spring, I moved the perennials to new homes and used the four beds for my vegetable and herb gardens.

Next, I began on the front of the house. There was no soil there, and the ground dropped off several feet from one side of the house to the other. I needed lots of fill. The road department was cleaning out ditches and looking for places to dump the contents. I received four dump-truck loads. All I had to do was spread it. Days of raking hardly made a dent, so one of my neighbors came and pushed it about with a small bulldozer. What would have taken me all summer was done in about an hour. Nothing takes the place of good neighbors!

A trip to the dump took care of my need for lots of newspaper for the first layer. Bales of peat moss covered the paper for the first 2 inches; bags of grass clippings and more peat moss added another 4 inches to the layers. The contents of two large compost bins provided another 3 inches, and fall was on its way with lots of leaves.

Before fall was over, the front garden was installed. A picket fence divided the space into two planting areas. Inside the fence, a gently curving fieldstone path led to the front door before going out a second gate at the other end. Near the house was a combination foundation planting and perennial garden. Low-growing thymes crawled between the stones, and near the fence assorted perennials formed a bank of color. At one corner of the house, I

planted a clump of Korean white birch *(Betula platyphylla)*, then a blue spruce *(Picea pungens* 'Glauca').

In late fall, outside the fence, I installed a bulb-and-perennial garden. In spring, the first blooms came in early March with a ground cover of yellow crocus. This was followed by early-blooming jonquils and hyacinths. Later, bright yellow daffodils and early red tulips came into bloom with a ground cover of blue forget-me-nots *(Myosotis* sp.). The ever-changing, flashy show of color lasted until it was time to plant annuals. This beautiful garden had gone together so quickly and, except for the bulldozer work, was relatively easy.

During the time I was building the four beds in back of the house and two gardens in front, I had also begun the first of the production gardens. There were to be eight raised beds on the south side of the house. The first four measured 8 by 12 feet; the next four measured 4 by 12 feet.

I marked off an area for one garden at a time. Next, I laid down thick pads of wet newspaper, then covered the paper with 2 inches of peat moss and 4- to 6-inch layers of organic material alternated with 2-inch layers of peat moss. By the time I had a garden installed, you could reach down through all the soil amendments and feel, first the warmth of decaying vegetation, then the cool earth near the paper. Underneath it all, considerable worm activity was already taking place.

Moving the First Garden

When the time came to sell the inn across the road from my house, the new owner wanted to return the area of my first lasagna garden to grass, and I wanted to move my plants and all that great soil. First I lifted all the plants and, using a very old wheelbarrow

Encourage the Worms

Earthworms are indicators of healthy garden soil. If earthworms are scarce in your soil, it could mean that your soil is compacted or low in organic matter, or that it has been treated with pesticides. If you do nothing more than lay down chopped leaves and grass clippings over your existing garden soil, you will see a difference in worm activity in a short time. (Of course, full-scale lasagna gardening will greatly help encourage earthworm populations.)

To increase your worm population even more quickly, buy worms from a mail-order supplier or at a bait-and-tackle store. Be sure they are common earthworms or night crawlers. Dump them in the garden, under the paper layer or between the mulch layers. They will begin eating, tunneling, and reproducing right away, and they'll quickly go to work on improving your soil.

wood chips that had covered the paths. The whole removal process pleased the new owner, and the plants and soil became a part of my new gardens.

It was necessary to get some gardens installed to house the new plants. I marked off a spot and laid down thick pads of wet newspaper for the first one. I covered the paper with 2 inches of peat moss, then with 6- to 8-inch layers of weeds, grass, hay, and horse manure. On top of each layer of mulch material, I added a 3-inch layer of peat moss and a sprinkle of bonemeal. Eventually, the bed was about 24 inches high. This time, I decided to try something different: I covered the bed with a piece of black plastic, held down with bricks around the edges. Every few days, I'd lift part of the plastic to feel the middle of the layers. It was hot, which meant it was really cooking. After about six weeks I removed the plastic and, after removing the heaviest stalks (which had not broken down), found the garden ready to plant. It gave me such pleasure to cook a garden lasagna, I did it often after that.

Lasagna Gardening: A Way of Life

The number of lasagna gardens grew at an alarming rate, and I gave impromptu talks as I worked. I was amazed at the number of people who stopped by to see what I was doing and stayed to watch. Some even offered to help. But with this method, creating new gardens was easy, even for a 50-year-old woman using no power tools and no help.

And so my life went for the next six years. Each year, I would finish building more gardens, all with different themes, and bring more and more people to walk the paths and listen to how it had all been done—to learn about a kind of gardening anyone could do with a

with an iron wheel, made the first of hundreds of trips across the road. Once the plants were removed, using a flat-bladed, straight-edged perennial spade, I took away all the soil that was above ground level. Last, I raked up the

little effort and just a few changes in attitude. I like to think I helped "would-be" gardeners get going with lasagna gardening.

I won't tell you here about each and every garden I installed over those six years, but before we are through with the telling and the reading, you will come to know them. We will connect in the spirit of gardening, and I hope you will make one or more easy garden lasagnas.

Changing Old Habits

As a youngster, you may have earned part of your allowance by raking up and bagging the grass clippings left after you or your parents mowed the lawn. In fact, bagging was a common method of getting rid of all kinds of yard waste. The very thought of compost conjured up scenes of untidy, odorous piles of refuse. Changing the habits of a lifetime is asking a lot. But is it?

If you are determined to make gardening a part of your life and you are looking for better, more efficient, and healthier ways to accomplish that, you may be open to suggestions for change. Where once we stuffed our kitchen wastes into disposals and all garbage into bags, then mindlessly carried them to the curb, we have now been forced to think about garbage. Towns mandated regulations to make us separate plastic, glass, and aluminum for recycling. Some people fought even that small change, though I like to think most were glad to be doing something to be more earth-friendly.

Municipalities took charge of recycling hard goods; now they are quietly forcing change in the way we dispose of yard waste. They started charging for bags to put leaves and grass in, then charging to have the bags taken away. We got hit in the pocketbook and that got our attention. Suddenly, it seemed worthwhile to mow or chip leaves, making them smaller and thus using fewer costly leaf bags. We could justify buying a new mulching mower, so the grass clippings could go right back onto the lawn. My point is, we have all made some changes already. And once you have made a commitment to change gardening methods, lasagna gardening is the next logical step!

Chapter 2

Vegetables in the Lasagna Garden

 Once you have an established lasagna garden bed, growing vegetables couldn't be easier. After planting, all you need is a little smart mulch management, and your chores are nearly finished. There's no such thing as a no-work garden, but this is close.

Getting Started

The process of making a lasagna garden to grow vegetables is the same as for any other lasagna garden. (For a review of the basic building steps, refer back to "Assembling a Lasagna Garden" on page 14.) When you lay down paper to kill the sod, you also create the perfect habitat for earthworms: darkness, dampness, and food. Then you cover the paper with layers of organic mulch, so it won't look like paper lying on the grass, and you make more food for your earthworms. They'll work even harder, tunneling through and loosening the soil while breaking down the organic matter into nutrients your vegetables need to produce generous yields.

25

Even in the vegetable garden, neatness counts! If you pile up organic matter helter-skelter, it looks like a mess. No one wants to see that. Most of us do not live in the wilds, without neighbors, but even if we did, we would rather see a neat garden than one that looks like a pile of garbage. Lasagna gardens are neat. They are organized layers of organic material that decompose without looking messy or smelling bad.

Design your lasagna garden beds so you can reach into every area without stepping on the soil. A comfortable width for most people is 3 to 4 feet across. The length of the beds is up to you. If you have room for more than one 3- to 4-foot-wide bed, lay paths between them to allow easy access for planting, mulching, and harvesting.

Interplanting: Making the Most of Your Space

When life leaves you scraps, make a quilt. When it seems you have no place to garden, look again. Take a walk around your yard, and you'll probably find a wealth of other spaces where vegetables could fit in.

Create a Beautiful and Bountiful Flower Garden

Even established perennial gardens can usually accommodate a few vegetable plants. The front of the border usually includes ground covers and low-growing flowers, but a variety of herbs can fit in well there too. You might even consider planting an edging of all

Keep Beds within Reach. Build individual beds no more than 4 feet across, so you can easily reach into the middle of the bed from each side. That way, you can plant, mulch, and harvest comfortably without stepping on the soil.

one vegetable or herb, such as bush beans or curly parsley. I like the look of a bush cucumber or squash plant in the middle "tier" of planting. If you use attractive supports for climbing plants like tomatoes, beans, and cucumbers, you could tuck them into the back of the border. Lay down stepping-stones so you can reach the middle and back of the garden for harvesting without walking directly on the soil.

Give Vegetables a Good Foundation

Interplanting vegetables with a foundation planting—that uninspired collection of evergreen shrubs lurking around the base of most homes—is an excellent use of space. With a little thought and some lasagna layers, you can convert an ordinary, straight-line foundation planting into a wider, curved bed housing a spectacular garden of flowers, herbs, and vegetables. You don't even have to remove

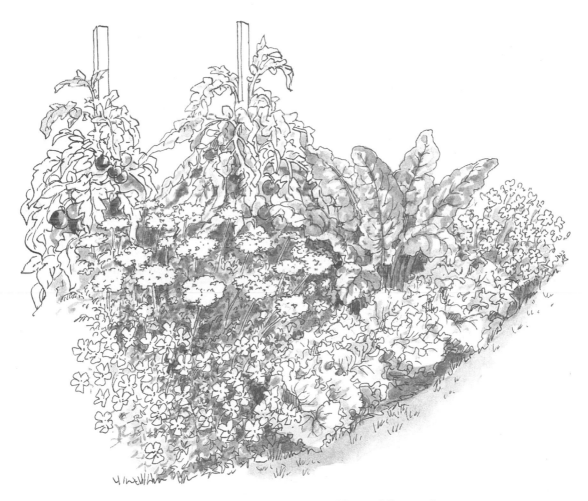

Mix It Up. There's no rule that says vegetables and flowers have to be in separate gardens! Make the most of your space by mixing up your plantings, and enjoy their beauty *and* their bounty.

the original trees and shrubs, though a bit of judicious pruning might be in order to shape them a bit and control their size. Remember, this area is the first thing visitors see when they look at your house, so an attractive appearance is important for creating a welcoming atmosphere.

Grow Up!

An arbor or trellis only takes a tiny bit of ground space, but it gives you a generous surface to support tall or climbing crops. Add one or more of these structures to an existing garden, or use them to dress up a blank wall or drab deck. Besides providing extra growing

Make the Most of Your Space. Foundation plantings can be more than just boring evergreens. Fill the space between shrubs with a few large vegetables, such as zucchini, then fill in with flowers and herbs.

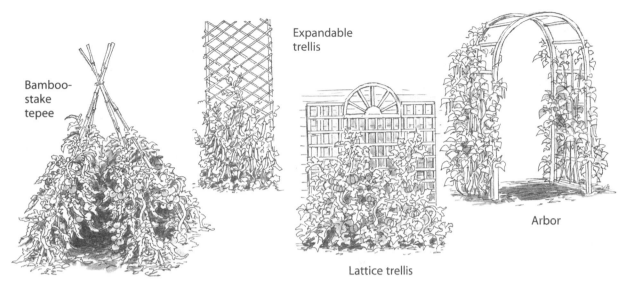

Bamboo-
stake
tepee

Expandable
trellis

Arbor

Lattice trellis

Support Your Crops. Growing vegetables on vertical structures, such as stakes, trellises, and arbors, gives you a clean, easy-to-pick harvest while taking up a minimum of garden space.

space, these supports make picking a snap! Tomatoes and cucumbers are two excellent choices for trellised crops. Scarlet runner beans are also great, with bright, edible flowers that attract hummingbirds, followed by long, green, edible pods filled with tender beans. Climbing nasturtiums can quickly fill an arbor with a cascade of edible leaves, stems, and flowers, followed by seeds that can be pickled and used as you would capers. In addition, the flowers are a beautiful bonus.

Luscious Vegetables for Lasagna Gardens

Lasagna gardening works great for just about any vegetable crop. Here I've highlighted some that I particularly enjoy growing. Many are traditional favorites; others, such as radicchio, you may be surprised to see. I've found that the lasagna system gives great results with these and several other crops that are just too much work with traditional methods. So read on, and see how you too can succeed with vegetables the lasagna gardening way!

Artichokes

Artichokes are easy to grow using the lasagna method, as long as you live in the right climate for them. I haven't grown them since moving to the Northeast, as the summers are too short and the winters too harsh, but they were always my favorite when I lived in warmer areas. Grown as a perennial in Zones 7 and 8, artichokes come back each year from offshoots of the parent plant. With their striking blooms and spiky, gray-green foliage, artichokes are fabulous in the flower garden.

Site and Soil. Full sun and well-drained, nutrient-rich soil are a must for great artichokes. A second-year lasagna garden will have the depth needed for sturdy plants. Other than regular mulching with rich compost, this easy Italian transplant requires little or no work to grow.

Planting. I have never seen artichoke plants for sale, but they are easy to start indoors. They need a very long time to mature, so get the seeds planted by the middle of February to give them an early start. Set out the plants when all chance of frost is over, spacing them 2 feet apart. Scatter 1 cup of a general organic fertilizer around each transplant, and scratch it into the soil with your fingers or a hand fork. Water well and mulch with 2 to 4 inches of compost.

Care. Add more compost every few weeks to keep the bed mulched all summer. In the fall, cut the stems and leaves back to about 8 inches and mulch with 2 feet of chopped leaves and grass clippings. In early spring,

Tips and Time-Savers

Artichokes

Plant lettuce, radishes, and other fast growers around the base of your artichoke plants in spring. By the time the artichoke leaves have filled in, you'll have harvested the quick-maturing crops.

remove the mulch, then scatter 1 cup of a general organic fertilizer around the base of the plant and work it into the soil.

Harvesting. First-year yields may be small, but the second-year harvest will be much heavier and the plant should produce well for at least four years. Cut off orange-size flower buds when they are firm and meaty but before they begin to open.

Eating. This is the best part. Trim off the tips of the harvested buds, then drop the trimmed artichokes into salted, boiling water into which you have added the juice of a whole lemon and then the remainder of the lemon. Place a crockery plate over the top of the chokes to keep them under the water. Cook for about 8 minutes, then remove the chokes with tongs and drop them into cold water for 1 minute. Serve on plates garnished with lemon and melted butter, or try spreading a little soft butter on the edge of the plate with some grated Romano cheese. Tear off each scale, drag the bottom through the butter and the cheese, then pull it through your teeth. When you get to the heart of the bud, tear away the hairy part and discard it, then eat the heart with a bit of the butter/cheese combination.

Bold Beauty. When you have eaten your fill, leave some of your artichoke buds unharvested and enjoy the fuzzy flowers in the garden or in arrangements.

Poppa Lanza would make a delicious stuffing for artichokes from Italian-seasoned bread crumbs, onion, garlic, and egg. To prepare the stuffing for two artichokes, moisten 1 cup of the bread crumbs with one egg. Sauté ¼ cup chopped onion with 2 cloves of crushed garlic in 2 tablespoons butter, then add to the bread crumbs. Steam the chokes, then set them in a lasagna pan. Pack stuffing between the scales, drizzle olive oil over each stuffed artichoke, and bake them at 375°F for 30 minutes. Serve with fresh lemon wedges.

Asparagus

Many gardeners needlessly deprive themselves of this tasty crop because they think it's too hard to grow. Traditional methods call for digging a deep trench, setting the crowns in the bottom, and then gradually filling in the trench with a soil-and-manure mixture. You had to continue this backfilling all summer, and you couldn't even look forward to eating any asparagus until 2 or 3 years had passed. That's not my kind of gardening, so I skipped growing asparagus for many years. But once I saw how well lasagna gardening worked, I tried everything, including asparagus, and got great results. You do have to be careful where you make an asparagus bed, because you don't want to move it. But in return, a well-prepared, properly planted asparagus bed can continue producing for 20 years or more.

Site and Soil. A heavy feeder, asparagus needs well-drained soil and at least six hours of sun. The fall before planting, build a lasagna garden on the site you've chosen for your asparagus, with a base of newspaper topped with 18 to 24 inches of layered organic material. By spring, the lasagna bed will have the ideal soil conditions for asparagus.

Asparagus from Seed

If you enjoy store-bought asparagus, imagine what it would taste like to eat some of your own growing. No amount of work would be too much, but you don't have to work hard, just work smarter.

The first year I lived in my house, the downstairs great room wasn't finished, so I used it as a seed-starting room. I set up sawhorses and plywood for tables and laid tarps on the floor. In early February, I filled my containers with seed-starting mix, planted the asparagus seed, watered, and waited. That room got so cold at times, I covered the trays with floating row cover and wished I had heating cables to keep the soil warm, as I knew asparagus seed was supposed to need warm temperatures to germinate. But even in my less-than-ideal conditions, the seed still sprouted and grew.

When the weather warmed outside, I carried the new seedlings to their bed and interplanted them with purchased one- to four-year-old crowns. I gave them a mulch of manure-enriched compost, and they grew well that first year. Next spring, I cut some of the first spears for about a week. I ate most of them in the garden but saved one cutting to be steamed and eaten with melted butter and lemon. What an incredible taste!

Planting. When installing a new bed, buy equal amounts of crowns (dormant buds with roots attached) that are of different ages—one, two, three, and four years old. Your first harvest will be better, and the bed will produce longer. The crowns look dry when you buy them. If you are not sure they have been disinfected by the seller, soak them for 15 minutes in a solution of 1 part household bleach to 3 parts water. If you can't plant right away, keep them covered with a damp cloth or damp sand.

In the spring, you'll know the time is right to plant when the soil in the bed has thawed and crumbles in your hand. Plant your asparagus in rows about 2 feet apart. Using a tool with a flat blade—I use a mattock—make two 3-inch-wide, shallow trenches about 3 inches apart in each row. This leaves a middle island with a slight rise between the two trenches. Place the asparagus crowns about 18 inches apart atop the rise, with their roots extending into the two trenches. Cover the crowns with 2 to 3 inches of a mixture of half soil and half compost. As the plants grow during the summer, continue covering with compost-enriched soil until the crowns are about 4 inches deep. Plan on 25 plants per person for fresh eating—even more if you plan to can or freeze.

Tips and Time-Savers

Asparagus

Keeping your asparagus healthy and productive for years to come starts at planting time. When buying the crowns, choose cultivars that are resistant to rust and fusarium, two fungal diseases that can attack susceptible cultivars. Keep the bed mulched heavily at all times, and if a weed gets in, remove it as soon as possible.

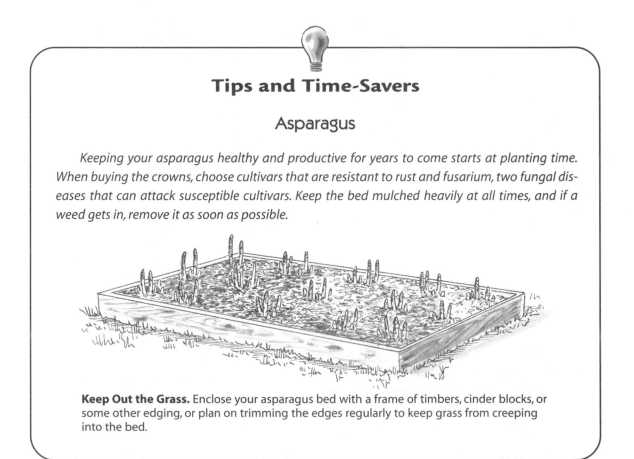

Keep Out the Grass. Enclose your asparagus bed with a frame of timbers, cinder blocks, or some other edging, or plan on trimming the edges regularly to keep grass from creeping into the bed.

Care. Don't begrudge a little extra work to a new asparagus bed, because it will repay you for years to come. When fall comes, give the entire bed a blanket of 8 to 10 inches of organic mulch, such as finely chopped leaves and grass clippings, spoiled hay, straw, seaweed, salt hay, rough compost, or barn litter. Each spring, feed the bed with a 4- to 6-inch cover of compost enriched with manure or barn litter. If you live in the colder regions, pull the mulch back on half your bed so the soil warms faster and growth starts earlier. Leave the mulch on the other half. It will take longer to start but you will have a longer harvesting season. Once the harvest season is over, the remaining shoots expand into ferny topgrowth. When the foliage turns bronze, cut it back to the ground.

Harvesting. Regardless of what you have heard about waiting several years to start picking, I've found that you can gather a small harvest the first spring after planting. Lay a 12-inch board between the rows so you can reach all the plants without stepping on and compacting the soil. Using a sharp knife, cut thumb-thick spears well below the soil level, twisting the spear as you cut. Limit the harvesting time to about two weeks, or until the spears are only pencil thick. In following years, lengthen the harvest by a week each year for the first six years. Once the bed is established, harvest every day during the season. An established bed produces a good harvest for six to eight weeks.

Eating. It's hard to resist eating the first tender spears raw, right from the garden. If some make it to the kitchen, steam until just barely tender and serve on a warm platter with melted butter and lemon, chopped hazelnuts browned in butter, or a dollop of hollandaise sauce. Or blanch the spears, marinate them in olive oil and vinegar, and serve cold.

Pat's Picks. 'Mary Washington' and 'Martha Washington' are old cultivars that produce female plants, so they channel much of their energy into seed production. On the other hand, new male hybrids such as 'Jersey Giant' channel most of their energy into the production of spears, making them much more productive. To get the highest possible yields from your patch, start with 'Jersey Giant', 'Jersey General', 'Jersey Knight', or another all-male 'Jersey' hybrid.

Beans

If you can decide what type of beans to grow, then you are a step ahead of me. Beans are such a fun crop to grow that most years I plant way more than I need!

Bush Beans

To get the best flavor and texture from bush beans, you have to grow them yourself and pick just before you are ready to cook. They are so easy and need so little care that you can grow all the beans you can eat all year in a small space. For the longest possible harvest, divide your batch of seeds into thirds, then plant every two weeks for six weeks. Here are some of my favorites:

- 'Blue Lake Venture' (55 days from seed to harvest): Extra early, germinates well in cool soil, and outproduces most green bush beans.

- 'Golden Rocky' (65 days): Tender pods with a beautiful golden color; long harvest.

- 'Jade' (60 days): Pencil-straight pods with a long-producing season.

❧ 'Royal Burgundy' (60 days): A good producer for cool-summer areas, with purple pods that turn green when cooked.

_____ *Dry Beans* _____

Dry beans come in dozens of cultivars, each with its own unique taste, shape, and size. They grow like bush beans but take a long time to mature. If you live in a warm climate, this isn't a problem. But if you live in a cool climate, like I do, you'll need to start the plants in peat pots several weeks before your last frost date to give your plants a head start on the season. Some of my favorites include

❧ 'Black Coco' (95 days from seed to maturity): Plump, black bean great for refried beans.

❧ 'Cannellini' (85 days): Rich and meaty, small kidneylike white bean.

❧ 'Cranberry' (75 days): Mild-tasting, oval bean the color of ripe cranberries.

❧ 'Dragon Tongue' (95 days): Eat as a snap bean when the pod is lime green, or let dry to yellow pods with bright purple stripes for shelling.

❧ 'Pinkeye Purple Hull' cowpea (50 days): Ivory peas with maroon eyes. Eat as a snap bean or let dry. Is it a bean or pea? I don't know, but it's a winner. Two crops a season in long warm summers.

_____ *French (Filet) Beans* _____

These are the gourmet "baby beans" meant to be picked while very slender. The 3-foot plants need support to keep off the ground. Filet beans are best steamed and served plain or tossed in olive oil and browned garlic. Try these:

❧ 'Astrel' (65 days from seed to harvest): Slim, stringless baby filet with unstoppable production and high yields.

❧ 'Fortex' (70 days): Imported seed from France. Early, productive, stringless, very long pods with rich, sweet flavor.

❧ 'Maxibel' (60 days): A full-size, dark green, stringless filet with great flavor.

_____ *Lima Beans* _____

Few gardeners are ambivalent about lima beans: It seems you either love them or hate them. If you're a lima-bean lover and want to grow your own, keep in mind that this cold-sensitive crop needs long, warm summers to mature fully. Some of the best cultivars include

❧ 'Fordhook 242' (75 days from seed to maturity): Heat-tolerant and highly productive, the granddaddy of bush limas.

❧ 'Henderson' (65 days): Light green, baby limas with the same buttery taste as their normal-size counterparts.

❧ 'Jackson Wonder' (65 days): Hardy, prolific, and tasty, whether fresh or dried; the traditional butter bean.

_____ *Pole Beans* _____

Pole beans produce long vines that need staking or trellising. They grow anywhere they can grab hold of something, and they tend to yield more than bush beans. A few favorites include

❧ 'Blue Lake' (70 days from seed to harvest): A classic with straight, stringless, dark green pods.

Grow Up! Growing beans is fun, but growing pole beans is the most fun of all. You can experiment with all kinds of supports: netting, strings, or even bamboo tepees.

* 'Kentucky Blue' (73 days): Offspring of 'Kentucky Wonder' and 'Blue Lake' with all their best qualities.

* 'Kentucky Wonder' (70 days): The original strain and the standard for pole beans; it's been around for generations.

* 'Violet Podded Stringless' (70 days): Germinates well in cool soil; very abundant harvest. The purple pods turn green when cooked.

Site and Soil. Beans grow best in well-drained soil that's high in organic matter, with a pH of 7.0 (give or take 0.5 in either direction). A new or established lasagna bed in full sun works fine for all types of low-growing and pole beans.

Planting. Buy good-quality bean seeds that are whole and clean. Beans like it hot, so wait until all chance of a frost is past and the soil is warm before planting. If you are planting pole beans, fix the poles into place before planting seed. The soil is loose and friable in a lasagna garden bed, so all you have to do is push the seed about 2 inches into the soil at 2-inch intervals. For bush beans used as a border, plant in a zigzag pattern to get full coverage and give a fuller look to the border. If you prefer straight rows, use a length of string pulled taut between two stakes to keep the rows straight. Cover the planted seeds and press down the soil over them to get good contact between the seed and soil.

Care. Keep the soil evenly moist until germination. Once the true leaves (the leaves that form after the first pair of "seed" leaves) emerge, add a layer of a clean mulch (such as straw, dry grass clippings, or buckwheat hulls) to keep the soil moist and the foliage clean.

Tips and Time-Savers

Beans

Beans combine well with many other crops, so you can get a generous harvest from even a small space. Try planting bush beans along the perimeter of a lasagna bed: They will grow up and over the edge, taking up hardly any room at all. Beans are also great for providing shade for smaller crops. Radicchio, for instance, thrives in the space under bean plants and is ready to pick about the time you harvest the last bean. If you're growing pole beans, take advantage of their shade by planting lettuce or other small greens once the bean vines are well up their supports.

The mulch also keeps weeds from invading your bean patch. In northern regions, protect young bean seedlings by covering with a floating row cover until the seedlings are up and have one or two pairs of leaves.

Don't work around your beans when the foliage is wet. The film of water allows disease-causing organisms to spread quickly from plant to plant. Bean beetles are the only pest I have to deal with, and they are easy to pick off and drop into a can filled with soapy water. In the fall, take away all surface bean debris but leave the nitrogen-rich roots in the ground. Don't plant beans or peas in the same place two years in a row to avoid a buildup of soil-dwelling pests and diseases.

Harvesting. Once bush, filet, and pole beans start producing, you need to pick them every two or three days; regular picking extends your harvest and increases the yield. Start picking when the pods are slender; let bush and pole bean pods fill out a bit more for the main harvest. Let dry beans mature on the vines until all the beans and vines are dry and brittle. Cut the vines close to the roots, hang in a dry place, then pick and shell the beans as you can find time. Lima beans are ready when you feel the beans fill the entire pod.

Eating. In the South, it is a custom to fry bacon or "fatback," add fresh green beans snapped into 2-inch pieces, cover with water, and cook until they are brown and unrecognizable. Delicious! I was in my thirties before I could eat a steamed green bean; to me it tasted raw and had no flavor. Once I was introduced to crisp, flavorful green beans, and had cultivated a taste for them, I began to try ways to improve on the taste. My family's favorite is to steam the beans until just crisp, drain, and set aside. In a sauté pan, add olive oil and chopped fresh garlic (other yummy additions include thinly sliced onions and sliced mushrooms).

Lure Beetles from Your Beans

One of my favorite gardeners, Douglas Bury (owner of the Antrim Lodge in Roscoe, New York, for 40 years, and an avid gardener), has a very easy way to keep Japanese beetles out of the garden. He has a wild grapevine growing on a fence that acts as a divider separating the front yard from the back of his property. The vine fills the fence with a solid cover of green growth and acts as a natural beetle trap. Leaves are riddled with holes from beetle feasts. At any time over the summer you can pick coffee cans full of beetles, but they are nowhere else in the garden.

Beetle Buffet. If you can't beat the beetles, give them their own spot to eat! Japanese beetles flock to grapevines, leaving your beans beetle-free.

Cook until the garlic starts to brown, add the cooked beans, and toss until they are hot and covered with oil.

Weekend Gardeners. When you can garden only on weekends, pick every bean on the day you arrive in the country and again just before going back to the city. Water well (don't get the leaves wet), and use extra mulch to keep soil cool and moist. Outline the patch with stakes and string with glittery Mylar strips hanging from it to keep animals at bay.

Beets

Beets may be an acquired taste, but once you develop an appreciation for them, you'll want to grow a generous supply. Fortunately, they don't take much fussing, and they are ready to pick in just a few weeks. Beets are a great choice for a child's garden, as they are fast growing and fun to pull.

Site and Soil. Beets prefer full sun and well-drained soil with a pH of 7.0. A new or

Beet Basics. Beets come in a range of shapes and sizes. Grow the small, round-rooted types for pickling or canning whole; cylindrical types are great for slicing.

Care. Beets need to be kept evenly moist, so give them plenty of mulch. Don't let them dry out or they become stringy. Other than that, beets need little care.

Harvesting. Beet greens are a wonderful vegetable by themselves. You can eat all the thinnings and pick side leaves from plants while you are waiting for the beets to mature. Harvest the roots when they are about 2 inches wide. Young, tender beets are the most flavorful.

Eating. Cook beets with just the foliage cut off; when tender, the skin slips off easily. Add raw onion to pickled beets when serving. Cut beets into cubes and serve with sour cream flavored with fresh chives. Use beet juice to color eggs at Easter; the red is a soft-washed color. All beets have green tops that can be harvested separately for cooking alone or with other greens.

Pat's Picks. Dutch import 'Kleine Bol' ('Little Ball') produces tiny baby beets developed for the gourmet market trade (50 days from seed to harvest). 'Monopoly' (55 days), another Dutch import, is a good choice if you don't like thinning seedlings; just place each seed where you want the plant to grow. Italian heirloom 'Chioggia Striped' (50 days) is a

established lasagna bed works fine. Beets grow best if you used bonemeal when preparing the bed; otherwise, sprinkle it on as you plant. Hold back on the manure as beets are light feeders.

Planting. As soon as the soil is thawed and crumbly in spring, sow beet seed 2 inches apart in shallow trenches 6 inches apart. (I use a weeding tool with a blade like a large screwdriver to make the trenches.) Cover by brushing soil over each trench with the side of your hand. Press the soil firmly over the seed so it makes contact. To extend your harvest, plant short rows every two weeks. Each beet seed produces a cluster of seedlings, so thinning is necessary. Thin when the seedlings have two true leaves (the leaves that form after the first "seed" leaves) to leave 4 inches between plants.

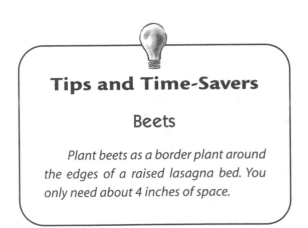

Tips and Time-Savers

Beets

Plant beets as a border plant around the edges of a raised lasagna bed. You only need about 4 inches of space.

dependable, sweet-flavored red beet that has red and white stripes on the inside. 'Golden' beet (50 days) is a beautiful yellow-orange color with tender flesh; try it grated onto a green salad. Harvest 'Sangria' early for baby beets or wait until the roots are mature (55 days); they won't get tough skinned.

Weekend Gardeners. Beets are so easy, they're a great addition to a weekend garden. Plant them near beans as they need the same amount of water and mulch.

Tips and Time-Savers

Broccoli

Broccoli grows best when covered with a generous layer of organic mulch, but if you're really pressed for growing space, try growing your leaf lettuce around your broccoli plants to act as a living (and harvestable) mulch.

Broccoli

I'm not going to try to sell you on the merits of broccoli, but it is a truly wonderful vegetable to grow and eat. Because it tends to be a heavy feeder and thrives in rich soil, broccoli grows best in lasagna gardens.

Site and Soil. Grow broccoli in full sun, in a lasagna bed rich with compost and frequent additions of manure. Prepare the bed in fall for spring planting.

Planting. Start your own plants from seed in late winter, or buy transplants. You want them to be about four weeks old when you set them out, as soon as you can work in the garden. Broccoli plants can withstand a lot of cold if you've hardened them off properly (see "Handling Hardening Off" on page 185 for details). Before planting, give the transplants liquid kelp to get your broccoli crop off to a good start.

Set plants out 18 to 24 inches apart in a zigzag pattern to make the most of your growing space. Make a 2-inch-deep trench along the rows, add a sprinkling of bonemeal to the trench, and cover with soil. Add a 2-inch layer of mulch, and lay a sheet of floating row cover over the plants to protect them from the cabbage looper moth.

Double the Yield. To increase your harvest of sideshoots, cut off the main broccoli head when it is tight and still small.

Cabbage, Carrots, and Cauliflower—Oh, My!

Cabbage, carrots, and cauliflower are three crops I usually don't give space to, because they are so labor-intensive and take a long time to mature. In addition, they are plentiful and cheap at the market. However, there are exceptions. One year, for instance, I ordered broccoli plants and got cabbage by mistake. I planted them in the front perennial bed. They got a generous helping of mulch and, except for a glance now and then, nothing else. I grew big solid cabbages that year.

I grew regular carrots once. They were labor-intensive, what with all the thinning and such, and the leaf mulch to carry them through the winter was 3 feet high. Yes, they were the sweetest root vegetables I've ever tasted, but this book isn't about how hard you can work,

but how easy. My exceptions are short-rooted, fast-maturing carrots that I can harvest during the normal growing season. 'Baby Spikes' (55 days) and 'Little Finger' (65 days) are sweet and dependable. Both of these short-rooted carrots can grow fine in a new lasagna bed.

My family won't eat cauliflower, so I don't bother with it. But if your family feels differently, the growing guidelines for broccoli should work equally well for this relative. The one difference is that cauliflower needs to be "blanched" to produce those white heads. When the heads are about 2 inches across, pull the leaves up over them and gather the leaves with a string or rubber band. The heads will be ready to pick four to seven days after tying.

Don't Crowd Carrots. Scatter carrot seed as evenly as possible when you sow. When the seedlings emerge, thin them to the spacing suggested on the seed packet to give the remaining roots room to grow.

Blanching Cauliflower. To get bright white heads on your cauliflower, pull the outer leaves up and fasten them over the center to block out the sunlight.

Care. Applying a layer of mulch when you plant and adding to it at weekly intervals keep the soil cool and moist and prevent weeds from sprouting.

Harvesting. Broccoli plants produce one large center head and lots of small sideshoots. Cut the main head with about 5 inches of stem with a clean sharp knife.

Eating. One of my favorite ways to prepare broccoli is simply to steam it and serve with fresh lemon wedges. Another favorite is to sauté 2 cups of trimmed broccoli florets and stems with 6 cloves of crushed garlic and $1/4$ cup extra-virgin olive oil in a covered sauté pan. In another pot, prepare angel-hair pasta. Cook the broccoli and garlic exactly as long as you cook the pasta. Drain the pasta, then mix in the broccoli, garlic, and oil.

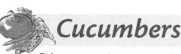

Cucumbers

I love growing cucumbers and each year try to think of a new way to support them so they will produce even more fruit. This heat-loving crop is a favorite for fresh eating or pickling.

Site and Soil. Cucumbers need the good drainage and rich soil of a new or established lasagna bed enriched with liberal doses of manure. They are heavy feeders. Most cucurbit crops (including melons, squash, and pumpkins as well as cucumbers) should not be planted in the same place for at least three years to avoid the buildup of disease and pest problems.

Planting. Cucumbers like it hot! The lightest freeze means the death of them, so wait until all chance of frost is gone before planting. In northern climes, start plants indoors in peat pots about three weeks before you plan to set them out. When the soil is

---

Tips and Time-Savers

Cucumbers

If your garden space is limited, install a trellis or netting to grow your cukes upward. Or try one of the bush cultivars; these compact plants will even grow well in containers if you keep the soil surface mulched and water daily.

---

warm, set out the plants, pot and all, into a lasagna bed, and cover them with floating row cover until the weather is dependably warm. In more moderate climes, plant directly outdoors in rows or hills. Set seeds 1 inch deep and 2 inches apart. Thin to 2 inches apart and provide supports for vines to climb on.

Care. No cultivating is needed around cucumbers when you plant in a lasagna bed. You mulch instead of cultivate. By applying more mulch you get the same results as if you had hilled up the plants. Cucumbers are shallow rooted so it's important to protect them with a generous layer of mulch. Six inches of mulch at all times helps to keep the soil moist, but cucumbers still need 1 inch of water a week, either from rainfall or irrigation.

Harvesting. Pick cucumbers when they are still young and firm for the best flavor. Once plants start producing, the fruits grow quickly, so check the vines daily and keep the fruits picked to encourage further production. Try to hold the vine at the point where the fruit is connected so it won't tear when you pick the fruit.

String Cradles for Super Cukes

One year, my friend Doug Bury had put in an early cucumber patch and was just going to let the vines run, so I asked him to do an experiment for me. Doug had planted four short rows in a small raised bed in front of a 6-foot stockade fence. He had enriched the bed with lots of manure and covered the soil under the plants with newspaper. The paper was then covered with buckwheat hulls. I asked him to tie string cradles from the top of the fence to posts in the front of the bed. Once the string cradles were installed, he tied strings hanging down into the bed. My theory was that the cucumbers would send out runners that would climb the strings, then they would climb the cradles and finally run across.

I went two or three times a week and helped the plants get a hold on the hanging strings. Soon they were on their own, climbing the strings, up the cradles and finally to the top of the fence. We had cucumbers in every stage of growth all summer. All too soon we lost control of the picking. We handed the fruits over the fence to neighbors, made dill and sweet-and-sour pickles, ate them at every meal, and took them to every gathering. The best part, other than the incredible harvest, was the clean paths. We didn't have to walk on plants to get to the fruit. Another bonus was that the trellises allowed good air circulation around the vines, so the leaves dried quickly after rain and were less prone to disease problems. This string trellis system was a great experiment and succeeded far better than I had envisioned.

Cradle Your Cucumbers. For the best harvest, train your cukes to grow up, rather than letting them sprawl. With a little help, they readily climb strings, and the fruits will be at the right level for easy picking!

Eating. Cukes are a natural for fresh eating, alone or in salads. If some of your fruit gets too big and seedy, try this oriental recipe: Peel and quarter 2 cucumbers and cut out all the seeds. Slice thin and combine with 2 tablespoons rice wine vinegar, 1 teaspoon sugar, 1 large clove of garlic (minced), 2 teaspoons soy sauce, and 2 chopped scallions (including the green tops). Add hot sauce to taste. Let stand for an hour in the refrigerator before eating.

Pat's Picks. 'Lemon' cucumbers (61 days from transplanting to harvest) are a 100-year-old American classic, producing large loads of lemon yellow cucumbers just a little bigger than a real lemon. Pick the fruits when young and eat them raw or pickle them. 'Marketmore' (56 days) is a dark green cucumber that's great for slicing; it has a crisp crunch. This cultivar produces shorter vines that are well suited for small spaces.

Eggplant

For warm-climate gardeners, eggplant is a delight in the garden as well as on the palate. North of Zone 6, I wouldn't bother growing eggplant. You might get a few fruits if the weather is warmer than usual, or if you use a few tricks to extend your growing season, but to my mind, it isn't worth the trouble. Remember, gardening is supposed to be easy!

Site and Soil. Eggplant needs full sun and well-drained soil. This crop is a heavy feeder, but don't add soil amendments with too much nitrogen (such as manures). Instead, prepare your lasagna bed with extra compost, plus a sprinkling of dolomitic lime.

Planting. Start eggplant seed indoors in late winter, or buy started seedlings. Wait until all chance of frost is past before setting them out in an established lasagna bed. Placing

Ornamental Edibles. Eggplant fruits come in a variety of shapes and colors. You'll enjoy their beauty in your garden as well as on your table.

plants in various warm parts of your garden, rather than all in one spot, can help to fool all the pests that love to feed on eggplant.

Care. Protect plants with floating row cover until the weather is dependably warm. When plants are bushy and starting to branch out, watch for blossoms. As soon as plants start to blossom, feed with a mulch of fresh compost. If you see signs of pests—such as tiny

Tips and Time-Savers

Eggplant

Eggplant is a beautiful plant, even pretty enough for the perennial garden. I love to have a few, but never more than four plants. Even then I may have too much fruit.

holes (caused by flea beetles) or yellowish specking (due to spider mites)—on the leaves, spray the affected plants with a strong blast of water from the hose. Check plants again every few days, and spray again if pests return.

Harvesting. Pick eggplants when they are still small and the skin is tight and glossy. Use a sharp paring knife to cut the fruit from the stem.

Eating. Slice a freshly picked eggplant in long, $^1\!/_2$-inch-wide pieces. Dip in a garlic- or rosemary-flavored olive oil and grill over charcoal for 3 minutes on each side. Or dredge the slices in flour, dip in egg wash (egg mixed with water), dip into seasoned bread crumbs, and sauté in olive oil; drain on paper towels. Layer the drained slices in baking pans with tomato sauce, top with grated cheese, and bake for 30 minutes in a 375°F oven. Serve with pasta. Yum!

Pat's Picks. 'Little Fingers' (60 days from transplanting to harvest) is a great little finger-type eggplant. The fruits develop early and can be harvested in quantity as babies. Italian heirloom 'Rosa Bianca' (75 days) is beautiful—the plant, the fruit, and the taste.

Endive

Salad gardens are not complete without endive. One of the easiest leafy green crops to grow, it becomes even easier when you grow it in the humus-rich soil of a lasagna bed.

Site and Soil. This undemanding plant grows in sun to partial shade. An established lasagna bed topped with lots of mulch is ideal. An application of dolomitic limestone will supply extra calcium.

Planting. Low-growing endive makes an excellent border for taller crops. Start seed indoors in spring and set out plants after the

Tips and Time-Savers

Endive

Most home gardeners grow too much endive at one time, so they end up with an overabundance all at once and then none the rest of the season. I suggest growing only four to six heads at a time. If you want lots of endive all summer and right into fall, make small plantings every two weeks.

last frost date, or sow directly in the garden after the last frost date. Space plants or thin seedlings to stand 8 to 10 inches apart.

Care. Endive is not demanding but likes constant moisture. Drip irrigation is ideal, but if you don't have an irrigation setup, just mulch heavily and water once a week if you have a drought.

Harvesting. Harvest the outer leaves as soon as they are a few inches long. Continue harvesting in this manner until you are ready to take a full head. Blanching gives endive a milder taste and more tender texture. Three or four days before harvest, cover the center of the head with a shield that blocks most of the light but leaves spaces for airflow. A small woven basket will do the trick.

Eating. Endive adds a tasty touch to green salads or soups. This pretty green makes a great garnish too!

Weekend Gardeners. Endive is a wonderful green for the weekend garden, as it doesn't require much care, and just a few plants can supply tender greens over a long season.

Blanching for Better Flavor. Endive can have a rather strong taste. If you prefer a milder flavor, blanch the plant by covering it with a basket to exclude sunlight for a few days before harvest.

Garlic

If you've never tried growing garlic, you've missed a terrific experience. You can't have too much of this herb, for it's a must-have for cooking, and it makes great gifts. I devote one entire 4-by-12-foot bed to garlic production each year. It's fun to watch and, with the addition of extra composted manure in a lasagna bed, undemanding. Here in upstate New York I plant the cold-hardy cloves in the fall and wait for spring to add another layer of mulch to suppress weeds.

Site and Soil. Good drainage is a must for garlic or it rots before it gets a chance to grow. Established lasagna garden beds in full sun provide perfect growing conditions. For the best crops, feed heavily with finished compost and a layer of aged manure. Move your garlic to a different spot each year, so each bed gets to rest three or four years before holding garlic again.

Planting. Buy "seed" garlic with big firm cloves from a reputable source. (Don't use the garlic from the supermarket as it has been treated to retard green growth.) Also, make sure the garlic you buy is suited to your climate; California garlic does not grow well in the Northeast. I like hardneck garlic from New York State or an area colder than mine, such as Maine, Canada, or Russia. (See "Growing Great Garlic" on page 171 for details.)

Late summer to early fall is the ideal planting time for garlic. Gently break the bulbs into individual cloves. Plant in rows, pushing each clove, root end down, about 2 inches into the soft soil. Brush the row back and forth with the side of your hand to cover the cloves. Mulch lightly.

Care. Top the bed with a winter mulch of straw or hay. In the spring, a long center stem grows up and forms a bud. The end forms an attractive curl and you will be tempted to leave

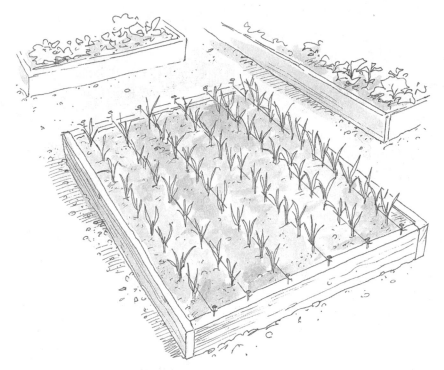

Keep Your Garlic Straight with Strings. I plant garlic in a lasagna bed that is framed with 2-by-6-inch boards. On the short sides, I make marks at 4-inch intervals on the top edge of each board, then hammer in a 3- or 4-inch finishing nail partway at each mark. Then I tie string lengthwise from end to end to mark the rows for planting.

Tips and Time-Savers

Garlic

When you haven't the room for an entire bed of garlic, plant it in groups throughout the garden. (I like to plant in clumps of odd numbers: usually three, five, or seven.) By planting in groups, rather than one clove here and one there, you will remember where the garlic is.

it. Don't! If allowed to stay, it will take energy from the head as it makes seed, and you will get smaller heads of garlic. Continue mulching through spring and summer to prevent weed growth.

Harvesting. Once the stems have started to turn brown, it's time to harvest. Using a garden fork, I loosen the rows of garlic and then lift the heads out without breaking the stems. (Even in the loose soil of a lasagna bed, I always end up breaking a few stems if I try to pull the bulbs without loosening the soil first.) Gather into bunches with a few heads in each; fasten together with a rubber band and hang them in an airy place to dry.

Prevent Plants from Blooming. When you see your garlic plants sending up flower stems, it's time to get out your clippers. Cut the curly stem end with the bud and use it the same way you would a clove of garlic.

Eating. Most of my recipes start with "First you take a clove of garlic. . . ." Besides drying the heads, you can preserve garlic by adding cloves to vinegar or by freezing in small containers. Once you begin growing garlic, pesto is only a bunch of basil, a little grated cheese, some olive oil, and a few pine nuts away. For easy pesto preparation, blend peeled garlic cloves and the other ingredients in your food processor, then package in individual amounts and freeze for later use. If you have a really good crop of large heads, try roasting some. Using a sharp knife, cut off the top of each head and drizzle olive oil over it. Set on a cookie sheet and roast in a 350°F oven until tender.

Weekend Gardeners. Fall-planted garlic gives you a great crop in very little space with little maintenance; just remember to trim off the flower stems in spring for the best harvest.

Kale

Kale is one of my favorites, and it's easy to grow in a lasagna garden. It's one of the best greens crops for the Northeast, and you need only a few plants to keep you in healthy nourishing greens.

Site and Soil. Making a lasagna bed in the fall ensures that you have the perfect loose medium with good drainage to grow kale in the spring. Once I've made the layers needed for a lasagna bed, I sprinkle wood ashes on top. If you don't burn wood, use dolomitic lime. Kale needs full sun and a pH of 7.0 to produce well.

Planting. Set plants out or direct-sow seeds in early spring, as soon as the ground has thawed. Kale planted under floating row cover can even take some freezing nights. Space plants 12 to 18 inches apart. There's no need to plant another late crop, as kale overwinters and you can pick new growth from old plants in the spring.

Care. Mulch plants to keep the soil cool, moist, and weed-free. Floating row cover keeps cabbage moths away from plants, preventing pest damage.

Harvesting. Starting in early spring, harvest outer leaves regularly and add to soups and salads. Once summer heat arrives, forget the outer leaves and pick from the center rosette.

Eating. I make a soup with strips of kale, diced potatoes, and onions. Combine the ingredients, cover with water, and cook until the vegetables are tender; flavor with olive oil or bacon. Or chop kale into fine strips and add to stir-fry. The very first outer leaves are sweet and tender and good in salads but are too strong later.

Pat's Picks. Try 'Red Russian' kale, with gorgeous, finely toothed, gray-purple, red-veined leaves, for a beautiful growing experience.

Extend the Harvest. Leave kale plants in the garden in fall, and they'll produce new growth next spring. When summer comes and the plants send up flowerstalks, harvest those stalks too.

Tips and Time-Savers

Kale

For fun, try "Wild Garden Kale Mix" (60 days from planting to harvest) from Shepherd's Garden Seeds. Broadcast the seeds of this heirloom mix and enjoy the variety of leaf shapes and sizes.

Lettuce

Everyone can grow lettuce. The only problem is most folks grow too much. Restrain yourself and make several smaller plantings instead of using the whole pack of lettuce seeds at one time.

When shopping for lettuce seed or transplants, you may notice some terms describing the growth habits or uses of the plants. *Butterhead* lettuces, such as 'Buttercrunch' or 'Bibb', produce loose heads with buttery-tasting leaves. *Loose-leaf* lettuces grow as spreading, loose-bunching leaves that grow back when cut; 'Oakleaf' and 'Ruby Red' are two favorites. *Romaine* lettuces, such as 'Apollo', produce upright heads or long, narrow leaves. They grow slowly, but you can harvest a few of the outer leaves while you're waiting. "Mesclun" refers to a mix of lettuces and other sweet or tangy greens grown and harvested together for exciting salads.

Site and Soil. Lettuce likes it cool, with a bit of afternoon shade. (Planting taller crops next to your lettuce can provide the right amount of shade.) Prepare a new lasagna bed to create a loose, well-drained site, and add high-nitrogen amendments (such as fresh grass clippings) to the top 2 inches. For even earlier planting, prepare the bed in fall.

Planting. Plant lettuce seeds $1/4$ inch deep outdoors in a prepared seedbed in early spring; sow in rows or broadcast leaf-lettuce seed over a wider band. Get a head start on heading lettuces by sowing seed indoors in peat pots. Set out transplants as soon as the soil is thawed and crumbly, and cover them with floating row cover to protect them from cold nights. For the earliest possible crop, you can even plant seed in the fall.

Care. Head-forming lettuces need some room for growth and good air circulation to keep fungal disease from developing; thin to 10 to 12 inches between plants. Mulch with compost and then a light top-mulch to keep the soil cool and moist.

Harvesting. For best flavor and crispness, pick lettuce in the morning or late in the day, just before dinnertime. You can start harvesting leaf lettuce while plants are still small; simply use scissors to snip off the outer leaves as needed. (The thinnings are also great in salads.) Harvest head-forming lettuces when the heads are firm. Lettuce plants bolt (send

> ## Tips and Time-Savers
>
> ### Lettuce
>
> *In summer, replace the plastic hoop covers you used in the spring with shade cloth to keep lettuce sweet. To prevent head-forming lettuces from bolting, wound the stem slightly below the soil level with a sharp trowel just as the head starts to feel firm.*

up flowerstalks) when the weather gets too warm, and the leaves become too bitter to eat. Leave the stalks in the garden, and new leaves will emerge in a few weeks.

Eating. There's more to lettuce than salads. I make a great but simple soup by heating chicken broth, then adding finely chopped lettuce during the last minute of cooking; add a dash of soy sauce before serving. This is a fine way to use an overabundance of lettuce.

Special Care for a Long Lettuce Season. Give transplants extra cold protection by covering them with plastic supported by wire hoops. Remove the plastic after a few weeks, then cover the hoops with shade cloth to extend your harvest.

Pat's Picks. I especially enjoy the beauty of red lettuces. Some of my favorites include 'Italian Red Perella' (52 days from seed to harvest), 'Juliet' (61 days), 'Merveille des Quatre Saisons' (60 days), 'Red Oakleaf' (50 days), 'Rouge D'Hiver' (60 days), and 'Rubens Romaine' (56 days).

Onions

Sure, you can always buy onions at the grocery store, but it's more fun to grow them at home.

Site and Soil. Onions thrive in well-drained, humus-rich soil in an area that gets six to eight hours of sun. They need constant moisture, which means that the soil is damp to the touch (like a well-squeezed sponge), not soggy wet. This is easy to achieve in a lasagna bed with lots of mulch added. A new bed works fine for small onions, but if you want to grow the big-bulbed kinds, an established bed produces better results.

Planting. Growing onions from seed gives you the widest choice of cultivars, but it takes a long time, and lasagna gardening is all about saving time. Starting with sets (small bulbs grown commercially the previous year and sold through catalogs or garden centers) is a real time-saver. Simply push each small onion 1 inch deep, and space them 4 to 6 inches apart. I don't cover the sets with soil, as onions like to have their tops out of ground.

Care. Mulching is the key to successful onions. Pile it on as soon as the stems form and continue mulching to keep weeds out of the bed. If you see little black bugs (onion thrips), spray the plants with a strong blast of water; repeat as needed if pests return. Cut off the flowerstalks to force energy to the bulbs rather than seeds.

Tips and Time-Savers

Onions

The best mulch I've ever used on onions was shredded office paper. It looked great and allowed the soil to stay moist but let the top part of the onion get air. (Only the roots need to be in the soil; it's fine if the bulb part is exposed.)

Harvesting. Once leaves begin to turn yellow, bend them down to the ground toward one side of the bed. When tops are fully yellow, loosen the soil with a garden fork to lift the bulbs toward the surface. If there's no rain in the forecast, leave the bulbs in place on top of the soil for a few days so they can "cure." If the weather is cloudy and damp, place the onions on a screen in a dry place for a few days. Clean dirt off by rubbing the bulb gently with your hands while wearing gloves with an abrasive surface. Don't wash them—you want them to be dry for storage in a cool, dry place.

Eating. I can't cook without onions! Add them to soups, salads, omelettes, meats—basically anything but desserts.

Pat's Picks. I like to grow bunching onions for the green tops and how they look in the garden. Perennial Welsh onions are dependable and prolific, a constant source of flavorful green tops and small sweet bulbs. Egyptian onions produce a similar harvest but are self-seeders instead of true perennials. Their tiny bulblets form on the top of a central stem, sometimes sending out green shoots before they fall and root themselves.

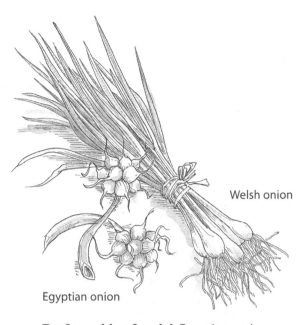

Welsh onion

Egyptian onion

Try Something Special. Egyptian and Welsh onions are attractive enough to grow as ornamentals, but they also provide a good harvest. I like to cut the young green stems for early soups and salads.

Peas

Growing peas is one of my favorite things, and I love sharing them with everyone who visits my garden. It's so easy to grow peas anyone can do it in less time than it takes to shop for them. The trick is to stay away from the old-fashioned kinds that have to be shelled. Save yourself the hassle by growing snow peas or snap peas; both have edible pods. Snow-pea pods are picked while still flat and eaten raw or stir-fried. Snap peas are a cross between snow and regular garden peas. If you grow so many you can't eat, freeze, or give them away fast enough while the pods are tender, you can shell your snap peas and eat them like regular peas.

Site and Soil. You can't go wrong if you pick a cool, well-drained area of the garden. You don't need much space: even a 1-foot-

wide lasagna bed, with a support fence down the middle, will work fine. Prepare the site in fall so it's ready for planting very early in the spring; use lots of organic material with added bonemeal and wood ashes.

Planting. Unlike most vegetables, peas can go in before the last frost. In fact, I have planted so early that snow covered the garden after planting and nothing happened to my crop. Make sure you order your seeds early, so you have them on hand when the weather is right for planting.

To support the vines, I use steel fence posts that have angled pieces at the bottom to

Tips and Time-Savers

Peas

Peas grow and produce best in cool temperatures, so the length of your harvest season depends greatly on where you live. For instance, I garden in three areas in upstate New York. One of my gardens is on top of a mountain, and the peas up there grow and produce all summer. In my new home in the valley, I can get them to produce most of the summer if I keep the plants cool with some shade cloth. Forty-five minutes east, at my place of business, The Potager, in the Wurtsboro Valley, I can grow peas for only two months, even if I shade them with tall plants on the south side of the pea fence. Providing shade takes a little extra thought, but it's worth it if you want the best possible harvest for your area.

Pretty Pea Fencing. I like to make my pea-climbing fence out of green garden twine. I weave it back and forth from post to post, each year using a different design.

keep them upright. My beds are enclosed with boards, so I just measure 6 inches in from a board and pound the stake in. (My beds are 12 feet long, so I use four posts, spaced 3 feet apart.) In the spring, when you get an early warm spell, tie one strand of string to the posts, about 5 inches above the bed surface, to keep a straight planting line. Next, push the pea seeds into the ground, on both sides of the string, with your fingers. Rake the sides of the row back and forth with the side of your hand. That's it! All you have to do now is wait until the plants grow to the top of the string.

Care. Once your pea vines get growing, you'll need to add more strings between the posts to support the climbing stems. Other than this, peas are pretty care-free, and if you keep the roots mulched, even weeds aren't a problem. Mulch also keeps the soil cool and moist so watering isn't needed except in drought. A compost mulch meets your plants' nutrient needs, so you don't need to fertilize.

Harvesting. Once the peas start coming in, you need to pick them every day or two. By keeping them picked, you are sending a signal to the plant to keep producing more flowers and pods. I grow only what I think I can eat, but every year I still have plenty to give away.

Eating. Edible-pod peas are great raw right from the vine, in salads, or as a dipping vegetable. Or stir-fry in a bit of olive oil just to heat. Serve as the vegetable course or add to other crisp vegetables.

Pat's Picks. For snow peas, try 'Oregon Sugar Pod 11' (60 days from seed to harvest; freezes well), 'Mammoth Melting Sugar' (68 days; wilt resistant), or 'Dwarf Gray Sugar' (57 days; a space-saver that doesn't need staking—great for containers or small gardens).

For snap peas, try 'Sugar Snap' (70 days from seed to harvest; big, meaty pods on 6-foot vines), 'Sugar Daddy' (62 days; pods are slender and thick fleshed; the best for freezing), or 'Sugar Ann' (60 days; early, productive dwarf).

Peppers

Whether you like mild, green bell peppers, sweet frying peppers, or colorful and zesty hot peppers, there's a perfect pepper for every taste. Starting from seed gives you the widest choice of cultivars, but it takes time and some effort. To keep it simple, start with purchased transplants.

Grow the Best Peppers Ever. For the biggest and longest harvest, feed peppers weekly by adding fish emulsion (diluted according to package directions) to the buried water jug. (Placing a stick in the opening of the buried jug will help you find the opening later on, when the plants have filled out.)

Site and Soil. Peppers like it hot! Locate your pepper patch in the warmest place in the garden, one that is protected from wind. If you live in a cold, windy area with short summers, find a place close to the house where heat radiates off the house walls onto the plants. A well-drained lasagna bed built the previous fall is the perfect place for peppers. As you prepare a lasagna bed where you plan to grow peppers, add bonemeal and dolomitic limestone.

Planting. Wait to set out plants until the soil is thoroughly warmed and night temperatures stay above the fifties. By this point, the plants should have 8 to 10 leaves and be starting to branch. Set them out as deep as they are growing in their pots. Space plants 1 to 2 feet apart, depending on their mature size. Protect transplants with floating row cover during cool nights.

Water well at planting time, and then mulch. In cool-summer areas, a combination of black paper (available at garden centers or through garden-supply catalogs) and aluminum foil gets peppers off to a great start. I cover the whole bed with the black paper and set out plants through slits I've cut in the paper. Then I add a circle of aluminum foil over the mulch around the base of each plant. The black paper absorbs heat and warms the soil, while the foil reflects extra light onto the leaves. The foil also confuses pests, protecting your plants from insect damage. In windy areas, support plants with stakes.

Care. Peppers are light feeders, but they do need a steady supply of water. If you have a drip irrigation system, you can easily provide the needed water; if not, try the "gallon bottle feeder system." Poke a pinhole in the bottom of a 1-gallon plastic bottle, then bury the bottom two-thirds of the bottle next to a pepper plant. Leave the cap off and place a stick in the opening. (Spray-paint the top of the stick a bright color to help you find the opening of the jug when the plants bush out.) Fill with water weekly, using a funnel. To water several plants at once, poke two or three holes in one jug, and fill it more often.

Harvesting. Begin harvesting green peppers when the first ones are big enough to use. For red peppers, leave them on the stem until they change color. Use a sharp knife to cut peppers from the main stem instead of pulling them off.

Eating. Enjoy crunchy fresh peppers raw in salads, or try them fried, roasted, or stuffed and baked. Bell peppers can be cut into different shapes and sizes and frozen for later use. They can also be roasted, cured in oil, and then canned. I like to grow yellow, orange, and purple bell peppers and use them to hold dips, for color in salads, and as additions to vegetable mixes. Hot peppers are wonderful for livening up homemade vinegars and making your spicy foods even spicier.

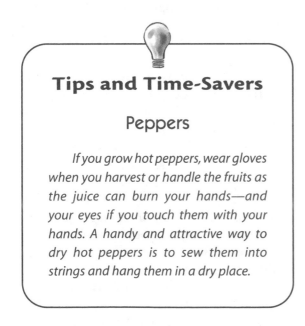

Tips and Time-Savers

Peppers

If you grow hot peppers, wear gloves when you harvest or handle the fruits as the juice can burn your hands—and your eyes if you touch them with your hands. A handy and attractive way to dry hot peppers is to sew them into strings and hang them in a dry place.

Potatoes

I have lived in potato country most of my life. What is potato country? Rocky, sandy, poor soil, found mostly in the mountains. Potatoes like good drainage and can tolerate acid soil. In fact, if you add too much lime or nitrogen-rich amendments, you'll get scabby tubers. Right there, potatoes save you time, as you don't have to fuss with special soil preparation. Growing potatoes is lots of fun, and they will grow just about anywhere as long as you keep the tubers from getting any light.

Before I discovered lasagna gardening, I planted my potatoes in furrows and then kept them hilled up all summer. It was a lot of work. Then one year, I covered a fairly new bed with several sheets of newspaper and placed the seed potatoes right on top of the paper. I covered the seed potatoes with about 10 inches of hay right away, then added more hay through the summer as the vines grew. By the end of the season, the plants were literally propped up with hay. The ease of this system made growing potatoes a pleasure, but the neatest part was how clean the tubers were. You don't dig them from the soil; you just lift the hay and they are lying there, ready to be picked up. Sure, the tubers were a bit smaller than soil-grown potatoes, but the easy harvest was a fair trade-off.

One of the things that potatoes do for a lasagna gardener is help to break up the soil. It makes for a better garden in years to come if you grow potatoes first.

Site and Soil. Place your potato bed in full sun. Potatoes like good drainage and can tolerate acid soil. In fact, if you add too much lime, you'll get scabby tubers. My newspaper-and-hay method practically eliminates soil preparation, but the moist soil of an established lasagna bed enriched with bonemeal or rock

Tips and Time-Savers

Potatoes

If you are short on space, buy one or two 30-gallon garbage cans and cut them in half crossways. Cut large holes in the bottom piece for drainage, or simply remove the whole base. Place the top half next to the bottom half on top of the soil. Plant seed potatoes in the bottom of each can half, and fill with mulch as the plants grow.

Contain Your Crop. Planting potatoes in garbage can halves gives you extra growing space. Once the plants have matured and turned yellow, dump the cans over and pick up your harvest.

Super-Simple Potato Planting. It's easy to plant potatoes the lasagna way—just scatter them over the newspaper, then cover them with layers of hay through the summer.

phosphate (rather than nitrogen-rich compost) produces an even better harvest of large tubers. Avoid planting potatoes where you have grown them or their relatives (including eggplant, peppers, and tomatoes) in the past three years.

Planting. For the best results, buy certified virus-free seed potatoes from a reputable source. (Seed potatoes are not seeds, but potatoes with lots of eyes.) I'm not going to tell you not to plant the old potatoes that started growing when you left them in the kitchen cabinet for a few weeks. I've done it lots of times. I even grew my biggest potato in the compost pile. But I do know that this route doesn't always produce the best harvests.

Plant your seed potatoes in early to midspring. If you want to save money, cut the seed potatoes into pieces with two or three eyes to produce the largest number of plants. If you plant them whole, however, they will give you bigger potatoes, and they will be less likely to rot. Spread several sheets of newspaper over the planting area, then set your seed potatoes 1 foot apart over the paper. Cover them with 10 inches of mulch.

Care. Add more mulch as soon as the plants emerge and keep it up until the plants are starting to die back. You'll use a lot of mulch by the end of the season, so keep a few bales of hay or straw on hand. Grass clippings also make great mulch, so if you have a large property, you can grow your own mulch, as I did. I had an acre of grass to mow right next to my potato bed, so I let it grow up and enjoyed the summer wildflowers that appeared. When the weather forecast called for a few dependably sunny days, I cut the tall grass with my mower raised as high as it would go. I mowed the plot all in one direction so that the cut hay formed windrows. (If you mow back and forth, the clippings will scatter all over the plot, and you'll spend more time and effort raking them up into rows. Let your mower do the work!) Once the windrows were dry on top, I flipped them over with a pitchfork to give the hay on the bottom a chance to dry. It was easy to keep my bed of potatoes mulched with readily available material.

Harvesting. For early potatoes, slip your hand under the mulch once the plants begin to

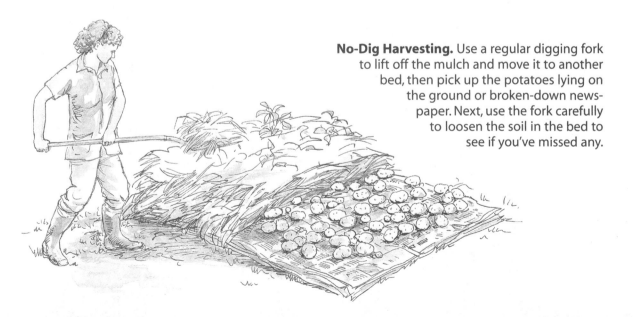

No-Dig Harvesting. Use a regular digging fork to lift off the mulch and move it to another bed, then pick up the potatoes lying on the ground or broken-down newspaper. Next, use the fork carefully to loosen the soil in the bed to see if you've missed any.

blossom and harvest a few tubers that are the size you need. The main potato crop is ready when the topgrowth starts to turn yellow. Let the tubers lie out in the sun for a day to dry and toughen the skin, then store them in a cool dry place.

Eating. New potatoes usually come about the same time I am picking the first beans. I like to cook the beans and potatoes in one pot, southern-style. I add some fresh chopped scallions and crumbled bacon if I'm feeling very southern; otherwise I just add salt, pepper, and butter and serve with skillet cornbread. If you have sliced tomatoes to go with this dish, it just doesn't get any better!

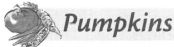

Pumpkins

I don't grow many pumpkins myself anymore, but I watch this fellow Ed Korth and he is the best pumpkin grower I know. He has a system that is so good I have to tell you about it. (The guidelines below also work well for growing winter squash.) There are all kinds of pumpkins, but Ed grows the kind that get big enough to win prizes at the fair. He has as much fun growing them as kids do picking them and making jack-o'-lanterns.

Site and Soil. Pumpkins, whether large or small, are heavy feeders and need lots of water. Give them a site with full sun and rich, evenly moist but well-drained soil. They can grow in either a new or established lasagna bed.

Planting. Ed starts the seeds indoors, then sets them out in hills of finished compost, planting three plants in each hill. A generous layer of mulch covers the soil until the vines fill in.

Care. During the summer, Ed removes the weaker-looking vines to leave only the best plant in each hill. Once the fruits start to form, he chooses the four or five biggest ones and

Tips and Time-Savers

Pumpkins

For fun and a child's delight, grow 'Jack-Be-Little', a true miniature pumpkin that takes 100 days to mature. These bright little pumpkins can be started indoors in peat pots, set out along a fence, and trained to grow up, taking space that usually goes to waste.

Pretty Minis. The small, bright fruits of 'Jack-Be-Little' pumpkin add a fun touch to a children's garden. Growing them on a fence or trellis takes up a minimum of space.

covers them with netting to keep birds and animals from pecking at them. He picks off the other, smaller fruits, as well as any blossoms. Keeping the flowers off encourages the plants to put their energy into ripening the chosen fruits.

Harvesting. You'll know a pumpkin is ripe when it is fully colored and you can break the fruit's stem from the main vine with one hand without much effort.

Eating. Just once in your life you should make a pie from a pumpkin you've grown. Wash the skin and cut the fruit in half. Take out the seeds and the pith around them. Place the two halves upside down in a pan with 2 inches of water in the bottom in a 350°F oven, until it feels tender when pierced with a fork (about an hour if you use 'Small Sugar'). Scoop out the meat and put through a strainer to remove the stringy part. Use your favorite recipe for pumpkin pie.

Pat's Picks. If you are short on space or have a short growing season, grow one of the bush cultivars, such as 'Hybrid Bush Spirit' (90 days from transplanting to harvest). This cultivar ripens two to three weeks before others.

If you have a bit more space, try 'Small Sugar' (95 days from transplanting to harvest). It has sweet, smooth-textured flesh and weighs only 6 to 8 pounds, which means you can train the vines to grow up a fence and support the fruit with mesh bags or old panty hose tied to the fence.

Pumpkins for Small Gardens. If you have limited space, try a small-fruited pumpkin such as 'Small Sugar'. Train the vines to grow up a fence, and support the fruit with mesh bags or old panty hose tied to the fence.

Radicchio

Thanks to all the chic restaurants, glossy food magazines, and trendy food shows on TV, the secret about radicchio is out. Beautiful but pricey, this tasty crop offers a distinctive nutty, and slightly bitter, flavor. Radicchio takes a long time to mature but it is worth the wait.

By the way, when you're flipping through seed catalogs for radicchio, don't give up if you don't find it under "R." Each catalog seems to list it differently: Check under "Chicory," "Greens," "Italian Vegetables," or "Salads."

Site and Soil. The only thing that radicchio, one of the most forgiving plants, doesn't like is standing water. It grows in either a new or established lasagna bed. Cool weather and a little shade help extend your harvest.

Planting. To sow seed in a lasagna garden, sprinkle seeds on top of the bed in early spring and rake them in, first one way, then another. Using the flat head of the rake, tamp the soil down where seeds are sown. When plants have about eight true leaves (the leaves that form after the first two "seed" leaves), thin seedlings to stand about 8 inches apart. When plants have grown for another two weeks, thin again so their leaves don't touch, which can cause rotting. For a head start, you can instead sow seed indoors in late winter to early spring. The seedlings will be ready to plant out in the garden in four to six weeks; set them about 10 inches apart.

Care. Give plants a layer of light dry mulch, such as dry grass clippings or buckwheat hulls, to keep the soil moist and discourage weeds. Other than that, there's not much to do.

Harvesting. Begin harvesting the outside leaves as soon as the head has formed. You can harvest some or all of the heart using a sharp knife and cutting into the center growth. The best-tasting leaves are the ones you harvest after the weather has turned cool. If you leave some of the plants in the ground through the winter, you can extend your harvest. When the blue flowers form, harvest them for salads; they also taste like radicchio.

Eating. Raw radicchio leaves chopped into a mixed green salad are sensational. All a salad like this needs is a light vinaigrette dressing. Chopping mature radicchio leaves into a mixed stir-fry of other crisp greens, like bok choy, imparts a stronger flavor to an other-

wise bland mix. To create an interesting first course, fill the inside and most tender leaves with your favorite flavored cream cheese.

> ## Tips and Time-Savers
>
> ### Radicchio
>
> *Most radicchio plants come in dark green with a deep red blush. I've found, however, that plants that have grown in some shade and matured after the first frost are more likely to produce bright red leaves with white streaks toward the center. You can also help ensure that bright color by choosing cultivars carefully. Some of the best-colored ones include 'Castelfranco', 'Firebird', and 'Rossana'. Some cultivars require cutting back in late summer to form well-developed heads. That's fine if you're willing to do the extra work; otherwise, choose those that don't need cutting.*

Gourmet Gardening. Radicchio has become a familiar ingredient of mesclun, a zesty mix of baby lettuces and other greens. This crop's inner bright red, white-veined leaves add a lovely touch of color to salads.

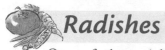

Radishes

One of the quickest crops to grow, radishes should be in every garden. They are easy to plant, easy to care for, and easy to harvest. Problem is, we usually sow them too thick and too many at one time. To have a steady supply of well-shaped radishes at the peak of flavor, make several smaller sowings through spring, and steel yourself to thin them properly.

Site and Soil. Radishes demand soil that's evenly moist but not soggy; other than that, they can adapt to just about any growing condition. A fall-built lasagna bed will have more than enough loose soil for most radishes by spring planting time.

Planting. Radishes thrive in cool weather, so get them in and get them out before it gets too hot. Plant a short row every two weeks as soon as all danger of frost is over and until daytime temperatures are consistently above 75°F. The seeds are tiny, so work slowly to space them about 1 inch apart and $1/2$ inch deep. Mark each row with the planting date so you can easily see when you planted your last crop.

Care. Thin to 2 inches apart when the plants have two to four leaves, then apply several inches of a fine-textured mulch, such as grass clippings, chopped leaves, or sifted compost, to keep the roots moist. Other than that, radishes don't need special care.

Harvesting. Pull spring radishes when they're up to 1 inch in diameter. Look for the ground swelling slightly around the base of the leaves as a clue that the radish is ready to pick.

Eating. Who can resist pulling the first radish, rubbing off the dirt, and eating the crunchy root in the garden? Not me! In the kitchen, radishes help make the first greens of summer more interesting and add needed color

Enjoy the Diversity. Radishes come in a range of shapes and colors. If you have grown more than you can eat, they keep well in the vegetable compartment of the refrigerator in vegetable bags.

Tips and Time-Savers

Radishes

Plant radish seeds around the edges of raised beds; they will be long gone by the time slower-maturing crops need the space. Or, for a handier harvest, plant some radishes in a container right outside your kitchen door; you can also grow a respectable crop in window boxes and planters.

to salads. Well-scrubbed fresh radishes served with a little dish of salt make a different first course. If you harvest more than you can eat, store them in vegetable bags in the crisper compartment of your refrigerator.

Pat's Picks. I can't resist showing off when I have beautiful vegetables coming into season. I pick or dig several kinds of show-off vegetables and, leaving the stems and leaves on, arrange them in a basket and use them as a centerpiece. Radishes are among my favorites for this sort of arrangement, as their bright red roots are certainly eye-catching. For extra interest, try growing a seed blend such as 'Easter Egg', which will produce roots that are white or shades of red, pink, and purple. While it's great fun to harvest them for centerpieces, don't forget to save some for your salads—they taste good too!

Rhubarb

There's more to rhubarb than pie! Since moving to the Northeast, I have grown champion rhubarb. I use it in many ways and never seem to have enough so I bought a freezer just for storing rhubarb. On the cold mountaintop where my country inn was located, I harvested rhubarb for the entire season. The kitchen staff never finished cutting and packaging stems until the season was truly over. In the beginning I used it as an ingredient in jam. I loved the chunky texture it gave strawberries and blueberries. I made it into pies, sauces, quick breads, and muffins, and included it in cobblers, tarts, and fruit glazes for poultry and ham. What more could you ask for?

Site and Soil. Full sun is the best location for rhubarb, although I've even seen it growing in the shade of several large hemlock trees. Give the plants a new or established lasagna bed in a well-drained spot outside your regular vegetable garden, as they take up a lot of room. Also keep in mind that these plants are long-lived perennials, so they'll grow in the same place for many years.

Planting. Dig a depression in your lasagna bed and set in the roots. Fill in around the roots with compost to cover them. Give them lots of water, and mulch heavily.

Care. You get bigger stems for a longer time if you mulch the plants with aged manure or compost in spring and fall. Picking the largest stems regularly lengthens your harvest-time and allows for good air circulation around the remaining stems. Keep an eye out for emerging flower stems: larger, rounder stalks usually growing up from the middle of the clump. Pull these off at the base of the plant to keep the clump producing.

Harvesting. Start pulling red or green stems from the outside of the clump as soon as they are $1/2$ inch in diameter. Never take more than one-third of the stems at one time. To

Plan Ahead. Make sure you know where you want your rhubarb to grow before planting, because it will stay there for a very long time!

Tips and Time-Savers

Rhubarb

When you head to your lasagna garden for harvesting, carry a basket with you so you can gather several crops at once. Pick rhubarb stems first, as they take up a lot of room. Take only as many as you can process right away, since they dry out fast. Cut the stalks into pieces and freeze quickly for later use. (You will have more time in the winter to cook and make jam than you do in the summer.)

Shallots

Shallots are expensive to buy but easy and inexpensive to grow. They have a mild, smooth onion flavor, sweeter than garlic; even those who are onion-shy will enjoy using them. As a bonus, the entire plant is edible: both the tops and the bulbs.

Site and Soil. Shallots will grow anywhere that drainage is good. The best shallots I have ever grown were in a sunny new lasagna bed. There were only 3 to 4 inches of layered soil amendments on top of paper in a garden I had put together in the early spring. I simply pushed the individual cloves into the ground and brushed a little "soil" around them with the side of my hand.

Planting. Shallots are not hurt by late frosts, so get them out as soon as you can push

harvest, take hold of a stem down close to the soil line and pull up and twist at the same time. Break the leaf off near the top of each stem, then gather the stems in your harvesting basket. (The leaves themselves are poisonous if eaten, but you can make use of them as mulch by laying them around the bottom of the plant.)

Eating. Some people swear by cooked rhubarb used as a warm sauce, much as you would serve applesauce. For others, the season isn't complete without a strawberry/rhubarb pie. You can put pieces of rhubarb into anything you would put apples or other fruit in. I've found that rhubarb takes on the flavor of any fruit you put with it. In my blueberry/rhubarb jam, for instance, I use only half the quantity of blueberries I need for plain blueberry jam. The end product is still predominantly blueberry flavored, but with a great chunky texture.

Edible Landscaping. Shallots are a snap to grow—just plant them and forget about them until it's time to harvest. They need very little space, so it's easy to tuck them into various parts of your garden.

Tips and Time-Savers

Shallots

Short on space? Plant a few shallots in groups among other crops in the vegetable garden or in a perennial bed. Mark where you planted them so you don't forget to dig them!

them into the soil. (I order my shallots early so I can take advantage of warm days and warming soil temperatures.) Plant the sets 1 inch deep and 4 to 6 inches apart. If you have the time, it's smart to mark the row before you plant, with a line of string tied between two stakes. This will help you keep the row straight. If you plant in a crooked line, you'll see the evidence as the new shoots emerge. (Of course, the plants don't care if their row is crooked, but a straight line looks nicer.)

Care. It takes one to two weeks for shallots to sprout. Don't mulch or cultivate them, as the bulbs form on top of the soil, and fussing around them may injure the plants. That's it! They are very easy.

Harvesting. When harvesting the tops, take only a few leaves from each plant. Wait to harvest the bulbs until the tops have begun to droop and turn yellowish tan. Separate the bunches into cloves and hang them in net bags to dry. Save some shallot bulbs for planting next year.

Eating. The fresh green tops are great in soups and salads. Substitute shallots for onions or garlic in any recipe. Cook whole bulbs in stews.

Spinach

One of the easiest greens to grow, spinach adapts well to life in a lasagna garden. This cool-weather crop doesn't take up much space—try it as a border for other crops. I like to have a long harvest, so I make several spinach plantings two weeks apart through spring. You need a lot of plants per person (roughly 30 or so) if you plan to cook it; a large bowl of spinach quickly wilts into a small amount of cooked greens.

Site and Soil. Spinach grows just about anywhere but thrives in nitrogen-rich, well-drained soils that have lots of organic material added. It can adapt to either a new or established lasagna bed.

Planting. Spinach likes it cool! You can plant as soon as you can get the seed into, or on top of, the soil. If you prepared the bed the previous fall, you can even scatter the seed on

Make the Most of Mulch. A loose top-mulch helps to keep the soil cool and your spinach leaves clean. I like to use shredded office paper, when I can get it—it looks great!

top of the snow. Plant seed $\frac{1}{2}$ inch deep and 2 inches apart, or scatter the seed evenly in a wider band, sprinkle fine compost over it, and press down the area with your hand or the back of a rake.

Care. Thin plants to stand 4 inches apart. Mulch with a nitrogen-rich material, such as manure-enriched compost or grass clippings, and cover that with a loose top-mulch. Water if you have a dry season.

Harvesting. You can begin picking the outer leaves of spinach as soon as they are big enough for your needs. Leave the center of plants growing until you just start to see a flowerstalk elongating in the middle of the

plant; then harvest all the topgrowth by cutting at ground level.

Eating. Good washing is essential for spinach: No one likes gritty greens. A raw spinach salad with chopped boiled egg and sliced mushrooms with a warm, sweet-sour dressing is heavenly. To make the dressing, cook some bacon (set it aside to cool), and brown flour in the drippings. Add water, vinegar, salt, pepper, and sugar to taste. The dressing should be thin. Drizzle it onto the raw spinach, add the eggs and mushrooms, and top with crumbled bacon.

Tips and Time-Savers

Spinach

For an extra-early harvest, sow a crop of spinach in late summer and leave the plants in the ground under a cover of mulch. They will begin to grow again in spring as soon as the soil warms. To extend your spinach harvest well into summer, sow a new row every few weeks through spring. Sowing two or three different cultivars is another way to increase your harvest, since they'll mature at different rates. Some cultivars, such as 'Italian Summer' and 'Nordic IV', have been selected for their good heat resistance.

Summer Squash

The only difficult thing about growing summer squash is limiting yourself to just a few plants. All kinds of summer squash are prolific, forming new flowers each day. I like a combination of tiny yellow squash and teeny, tiny zucchini. Two hills of each kind will be more than enough for a whole family.

Site and Soil. Build a lasagna bed in full sun, with layers of the richest ingredients you have, such as composted manure, fresh grass clippings, or compost enriched with organic fertilizer (a few handfuls of fertilizer per wheelbarrow of compost). A new or established bed 3 feet wide by 12 feet long can hold four plants, giving you all the summer squash you need. Short on space? Build a hill in a flower garden or foundation planting where you have a 3-foot-square space, and use all the same ingredients. One or two plants in a hill provide an ample supply of squash!

Planting. In cool regions, start plants inside in peat pots. Plant two seeds per pot, and cut away the weaker seedling. In milder

climates, sow seed directly in the garden a week or two after the last frost date. Plant in hills spaced about 3 feet apart, with two seedlings per hill. Mulch young plants with lots of rich compost covered with a layer of straw or grass clippings. Use floating row cover or hotcaps to protect plants from cool nights until the weather is dependably warm.

Care. Except for mulching and watering, if the summer is very dry, summer squash need minimal care. Proper spacing, healthy soil, and liquid seaweed (diluted and applied according to package instructions) encourage strong growth that resists pests and diseases. Several bugs and beetles may feed on the leaves; pick them off and drop them in a can of soapy water. If you notice leaves wilting, try injecting BT solution (an organic insecticide available at most garden centers) into the plant's stems to control squash borer larvae.

Tips and Time-Savers

Summer Squash

Picking squash when they're young will keep the plant producing and get the best produce to your table. No one wants overgrown summer squash. Overripe yellow squash turns hard, and zucchini can become baseball bats if you aren't on top of the picking. I don't even make bread out of overgrown squash; I just toss it in the compost pile.

Barriers Keep Pests at Bay. To keep slugs and snails away from squash seedlings, surround the plants with a ring of wood ashes.

Harvesting. Most important, check plants, especially under the leaves, every day for squash ready for harvest. Gather yellow or green squash when they're 4 to 5 inches long and the skin is so tender your nail pierces it.

Eating. Slice an equal number of tiny yellow and green summer squash, add a sliced onion, and sauté in a small amount of olive oil until just tender. Add salt and pepper to taste.

Pat's Picks. I always grow 'Early Prolific Straightneck' (50 days from transplanting to harvest). I love the pale yellow skin and delicate flavor. Compact 'Hybrid Jackpot' zucchini (44 days) has a pale green skin with flecks of yellow and is a space saver. A bush-type yellow squash for those with limited space is 'Hybrid Crescent' (53 days).

Weekend Gardeners. Keep squash picked each week or get a caretaker for your plants. If you miss a week coming to your country place, you could have a great harvest of baseball bats.

Swiss Chard

Swiss chard is so delicious you can never have too much. It's also one of the most beautiful plants in the garden, especially 'Ruby Red' or 'Rhubarb' chard, with its glowing red stems and leaf veins.

Site and Soil. If you garden in a mild-winter climate, Swiss chard will come back for several years, so pick an out-of-the-way spot so it can grow undisturbed. In cooler areas, this crop is an annual, so you can plant it in a different place each year. Swiss chard is not a heavy feeder, but it will produce larger stems if you enrich the soil with compost and other organic material. I suggest planting chard in a lasagna bed that has been established for at least a year. Choose a site where plants will get at least six hours of sun a day.

Planting. First, I soak the seed overnight to hasten sprouting. I then place them $1/2$ inch deep in double rows, zigzagging the seeds so the plants will be about 10 inches apart. I usually don't thin chard but start to harvest the outer leaves to give the plants air space.

Care. Start mulching as soon as top-growth appears, and keep mulching through the summer. Other than that, no care is needed.

Harvesting. Cut outer leaves as soon as they are 4 to 5 inches long, and continue cutting all season. To extend your harvest, mulch with a light material, such as hay, after the weather turns cool.

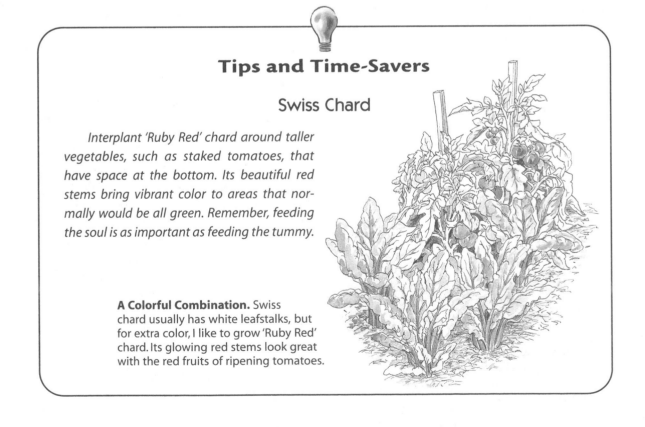

Tips and Time-Savers

Swiss Chard

Interplant 'Ruby Red' chard around taller vegetables, such as staked tomatoes, that have space at the bottom. Its beautiful red stems bring vibrant color to areas that normally would be all green. Remember, feeding the soul is as important as feeding the tummy.

A Colorful Combination. Swiss chard usually has white leafstalks, but for extra color, I like to grow 'Ruby Red' chard. Its glowing red stems look great with the red fruits of ripening tomatoes.

Eating. My father-in-law was the best cook. He was also a great gardener and loved to eat. He would cook Swiss chard in salted water with a little olive oil in it. He cooked pasta al dente in another pot and combined them with a little juice from the chard pot. He served it in large pasta bowls with a heavy sprinkle of grated Romano cheese. With a piece of hot crusty bread, it was a great meal.

Tomatoes

If given a choice of one crop to grow, most gardeners would pick tomatoes. There are so many wonderful kinds of tomatoes, you could start now and grow different ones every year for many, many years. Tomatoes are so easy to grow you almost always plant too many; fortunately, it's fun to share!

Site and Soil. Tomatoes need full sun and protection from wind. I get the best yields when I plant in a lasagna bed that is one or two years old, but I have also planted right on top of paper in a brand new bed and been satisfied with the results.

Planting. You really need to start with plants since tomatoes take a long time to mature. Buying transplants is an easy way to go, but if you want the widest selection of cultivars, grow your own plants from seed. It takes about six to eight weeks to have plants ready for the garden.

Set plants out once the weather is warm and all danger of frost is past. If your seedlings have sturdy stems, set the plants upright. Pull the soil up around each plant and make a little well around the stem. If your seedlings have long, leggy stems, lay them horizontally in a trench several inches deep, then cover with compost or other mulch, leaving just a few inches of the stem tip exposed. Water planted seedlings thoroughly and mulch with several inches of organic material. This is also a good time to install some sort of support system—a sturdy stake or trellis or a wire cage. Don't let your tomato plants sprawl on the ground. Besides making harvesting much easier, a support keeps the vines off the soil (so fruits stay clean) and minimizes disease problems.

Care. As the plants grow, continue to add more mulch. If you're using a stake or trellis for support, keep tying the stems to the support with twine.

Tomatoes need a constant source of water and food. To meet their needs, poke a pinhole in the bottom of a gallon jug or a large soda bottle, and bury the container up to its "shoulder" next to the plant. Fill with water, and insert a stick to make it easier to find the jug once plants fill in. Add more water about once a week, along with fish emulsion diluted according to package instructions. Don't be tempted to add more fertilizer than the directions recommend; excess nitrogen can leave you with bushy plants that produce more leaves than fruits.

Harvesting. Depending on the cultivar you grow, you can look forward to your first harvest roughly 55 to 100 days after you set the plants in the garden. (The cherry types tend to ripen quickest, while the large slicing types usually take the longest.) There are so many different colors of tomatoes now that you can't just say they are ready when they turn red. Check the seed packet or plant tag to find out what color your chosen crop should be when ripe, and harvest accordingly.

Eating. There are as many ways to cook and eat tomatoes as there are gardeners to enjoy them. I love them warm from the garden, when you bite into them and the juice

Tips and Time-Savers

Tomatoes

Wire tomato cages are good for more than just supporting your crop. For instance, you could place an extra cage in the middle of your tomato patch and use it to start a mini compost pile to feed the plants. Another great use is to place it around a plant and cover it with a sleeve made from a large, clear plastic bag with the bottom opened. Push the plastic down on warm days; pull it up and tie the top to protect the plant during cool nights.

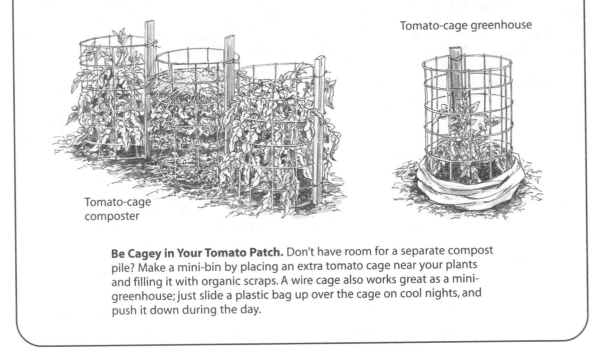

Tomato-cage greenhouse

Tomato-cage composter

Be Cagey in Your Tomato Patch. Don't have room for a separate compost pile? Make a mini-bin by placing an extra tomato cage near your plants and filling it with organic scraps. A wire cage also works great as a mini-greenhouse; just slide a plastic bag up over the cage on cool nights, and push it down during the day.

runs down your chin to your elbow. I also enjoy eating fresh tomatoes cold and sliced, quartered, or diced. My absolute favorite of all time is sliced tomatoes with fresh mozzarella cheese, fresh basil, olive oil, and balsamic vinegar. Add a piece of crusty bread to dip in the mingled juices, and you have a feast! Of course, you can also enjoy them baked, sautéed, broiled, or fried, alone or mixed with

other vegetables. Did I forget sliced, dipped in flour, then in egg wash (egg mixed with water), and last in seasoned bread crumbs? Fry them slowly in olive oil until they are brown and crispy on the outside and tender in the middle.

Pat's Picks. A tomato for all seasons? Absolutely! For cool climates with a short growing season, try 'Sub-Arctic Plenty' (45 days

Remove the Sideshoots. It's worth taking a few minutes to pinch or snip off tomato suckers—the shoots that grow out from the junction of a leaf and the main stem. Otherwise, the plant will put its energy into this leafy growth instead of producing more fruits.

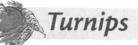

Turnips

Being southern born I have a real love for greens of all kinds, so it would be unthinkable to leave out one of my favorite foods and one of the easiest vegetables to grow!

Site and Soil. You can grow turnips anywhere. A new lasagna bed with 4 to 6 inches of loose organic material sitting on paper will do very well.

Planting. Plant very early in the spring. Mix the turnip seed with sand to give it bulk and make it easier to scatter evenly. Lay down a row of peat moss on top of a lasagna bed and sprinkle the seed/sand mix on top. Cover the seed with more peat or fine compost and press down with your hand or the back of a rake. Water with a fine mist.

Care. Thin so plants are about 3 inches apart and add mulch. As plants grow, add more mulch to keep soil cool and moist. Water if the weather turns dry.

from transplanting to harvest), 'Oregon Spring' (58 days), or 'Prairie Fire', 'Cold Set', or 'Stupice' (60 to 65 days). Midseason ripeners include 'Carmello' (70 days), 'Porter Improved' (75 days), 'Delicious' (77 days), 'Long-Keeper' (78 days), 'Big Beef Beefsteak' (78 days), or yellow-fruited 'Taxi' (65 to 70 days). For later harvests, try 'Old Flame' (80 days) or 'Oregon Star' (85 days). In addition, there are plum, pear-shaped, cherry, green, orange, and yellow tomatoes. I could go on with improved cultivars that started like 'Sweet 100', got improved to 'Sweet 1,000', and yes, now there's a 'Sweet 1,000,000'. There is, indeed, a tomato for all seasons and purposes.

Plenty to Pick. If you are looking for a prolific food crop, you've found it. You can get one to three crops of turnips and lots of greens if you plant successive crops every two to three weeks.

Harvesting. You can begin taking greens from the outside growth when the leaves are 4 inches high. If you want to harvest the turnip roots, do it when they are young and tender—3 to 4 inches in diameter.

Eating. For a tasty way to prepare turnips, cut off the greens and place them in a sink of cold water, then peel and dice the roots. Wash the greens in several sinks of water until they come out clean. Cut away the rib on each leaf, fold several leaves together, and cut them into strips. Cook the sliced greens and diced roots until tender in a pot with enough salted water to cover. Strain and serve with olive oil and hot vinegar.

For a real southern treat, cook a pound of bacon, then set it out to cool and drain. Pour the bacon grease into the pot of salted water with turnips and greens. Cook until the whole mess is unrecognizable. The liquid is called "pot liquor," and you need a pan of "iron skillet" corn bread to sop it up. Serve the greens in bowls with crumbled bacon on top.

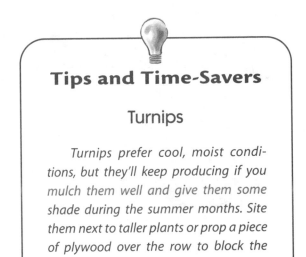

Tips and Time-Savers

Turnips

Turnips prefer cool, moist conditions, but they'll keep producing if you mulch them well and give them some shade during the summer months. Site them next to taller plants or prop a piece of plywood over the row to block the hottest sun.

Watermelon

You need 80 to 120 days of frost-free weather to grow watermelon. To get a head start, you can start plants in your house in peat pots. Watermelons need lots of space or a sturdy support to climb. If you do decide to let them climb, you have to help them up and tie them to a trellis. When the fruits come, you have to support them in bags that stretch and tie onto the trellis. 'Sugar Babies' is a great compact choice for trellis growing.

Site and Soil. Watermelons are heavy feeders and need loose, rich, well-drained soil. I planted my last crop of melons in a two-year-old lasagna bed that was loose down about a foot, and that seemed to be enough. I added several inches of manure-enriched compost to the bed before planting. Watermelons need full sun and some kind of structure to grow on. I put up a 6-foot frame of stakes and fence wire.

Planting. Start a few plants indoors in midspring or buy transplants. If they aren't in peat pots, wait until a cloudy day to set them out, as the sun can damage their roots. Make a depression that holds the rootball up to the top of the pot it was growing in. Pull the soil up around the plant, making a well around the base of the plant to hold water. Fill this well until the soil is soaked. Mulch with a heavy layer of compost, keeping a well around the base of each plant.

Care. Watermelon plants need lots of water and continuous feeding. Poke a pinhole in the bottom of a large plastic soda bottle or gallon jug, and sink it to two-thirds of its depth, near the base of each plant. (Placing a stick in the opening will help you find the bottle or jug when the plants have filled out.) Use a funnel to fill the bottle with water. Add more water,

Tips and Time-Savers

Watermelon

For a fun crop in a limited space, try growing 'Sugar Babies' watermelons in a container. Set one half-barrel on top of another half-barrel turned upside down, and plant two plants in the top one. (Make sure the containers have drainage holes before you fill them.) Keep the soil moist with a daily watering, and feed once a week. It's a neat thing to watch as the vines spill out of the barrel, and it makes an interesting conversation piece. Celebrate with a watermelon tasting at the end of summer.

A Barrel of Watermelons. You don't need a large garden to grow watermelons! Just plant a compact cultivar in a large container, such as a wooden half-barrel. Supporting the container on top of another barrel lets the vines cascade down, while the developing fruits rest on the ground.

along with liquid seaweed (diluted according to package instructions), about once a week. You must help the vines get started up their trellis and tie them on with pieces of stretchy material. Old panty hose work well for tying and holding the fruit.

Harvesting. Harvesting watermelon at the right time takes some practice and knowledge of what size your chosen cultivar should be when ripe. If you planted 'Sugar Babies', your melons should all be about 10-inch rounds with dark green rinds. They should be ready in 80 to 90 days after setting out, but if you have a cool summer it could take longer. Take one out of its bag to test and see if it is ripe; then you can judge the others.

Eating. My grandmother and I used to sit on the back porch eating watermelon with a saltshaker close at hand. (We didn't worry about blood pressure in those days!) She would lay out newspaper to catch the seeds and rinds and we would dig in.

Chapter 3

Growing Herbs the Lasagna Way

 The gardener and the herb patch—one of the most easy-going and rewarding relationships you will ever have. Herbs make few demands: average soil, a little mulch, and some sun. In return, perennial herbs give you years of harvest and enjoyment. Other than planting each year, annual herbs need little more. Tender perennials even come inside with you for the winter, asking only for a place away from direct heat, some indirect light, and a little water.

An herb garden is a source of pleasure during all four seasons. During spring and summer, herbs respond to stroking by releasing lovely fragrances. Some add flavor to foods; others repel insects. Some herbs can protect bulbs and vegetables by keeping animals away from your garden. Some blooms are edible; all are beautiful. In late summer into fall, when everything else is slowing down, you get the pleasure of harvesting and preserving your herbs, and in winter, you get to play with them. Having an herb garden is like having your own craft store: You'll have an ample supply of fragrant leaves and colorful flowers for fresh or dried arrangements,

73

wreaths, potpourris, and so much more. Once bitten by the herb-and-craft bug, you can't help finding different ways of using what you grow. But it's not necessary to make something from your herbs: You could just grow them and enjoy their beauty and scents right in the garden. Regardless of what, or why, you plant, an herb garden will weave a magic spell around you, enriching your life.

Getting Hooked on Herbs

Herbs have been a part of my life since I was a child, living in my grandmother's home in eastern Tennessee. She and I did just about everything together: milked the cow, gathered eggs, planted the garden, cooked meals, cleaned house, and washed and ironed clothes. We took walks in the woods and fields surrounding the farm, where Grandmother collected leaves, roots, and bark. When I stepped on a rusty nail, Grandmother washed my foot with homemade lye soap, prepared an herb poultice, placed it on the wound, and wrapped it in a clean rag. When I had a cold, she rubbed my chest with homemade herb salve. This was my introduction to herbs. When I had a family of my own, I began to use kitchen herbs. For the next 23 years, as we traveled from one United States Navy base to another, I planted backdoor herb gardens at each new home. It wasn't until we retired from the navy and permanently settled in upstate New York that I practiced herb gardening on a large scale.

The first garden to be installed at our new home and business was an herb garden between the kitchen and the taproom doors. A former owner had paved right up to the foundation of the building. In order to create a garden, we first had to remove the blacktop. Once the blacktop was removed, we found that the soil underneath was sour. It was rock, clay, and red shale with no drainage. There was nothing to do but haul in topsoil, spread it over the bad soil, and build retaining walls to hold it in place. That garden did go in, by sheer force of will. We took what neighbors and visitors shared, made holes in the topsoil, and planted everything they brought. It was a wonderful herb garden, and much admired by all who saw it. Eventually, though, I began looking for a way to create new gardens without so much work. This eventually led me to lasagna gardening.

The site for my new herb garden was where an old dance hall had stood for 90 years. We had used it as a grassy parking lot for several years after we dismantled the building. For my first foray into planned herb gardening, I designed a series of raised beds, built on the lasagna principle, with easy access paths. The hard part of building formal gardens is getting the lines straight, so it helps to have a surveyor in the family! After my son-in-law Bill had surveyed the garden and placed markers, my daughter Melissa and I strung cord to large nails and marked the boundaries of the beds and paths. The ground was so hard we had trouble driving the nails in. Bill and Melissa both wondered at the wisdom of making a garden on such unfriendly ground.

Nevertheless, I went ahead with the installation of my first garden lasagna for growing herbs. I laid whole sections of wet newspaper directly on top of the sod for the paths, then covered the paper with 4 inches of bark mulch. It looked neat and tidy, just the way paths are supposed to look.

Next I covered the garden beds with wet newspaper—again without removing the sod—and began the layering process. I covered the newspaper with 2 inches of peat moss, 4 inches of grass clippings, 2 more inches of peat moss, 4 inches of chopped leaves, 2 inches of peat moss, 4 inches of compost, another 2 inches of peat moss, 4 inches of barn litter (a mixture of horse manure and sawdust), 2 inches of peat moss, and a dusting of wood ashes. The finished garden lasagna was about 2 feet high and neat as a pin.

In the spring, the lasagna beds thawed quickly and I was able to see how well it had all worked. I ended up with 6 to 8 inches of loose soil for planting. The first year, I just pulled aside the soil and set prestarted plants in place. It was almost instant gardening. The only care I had to give that garden all summer was placing more mulch around the plants. No digging, no tilling, no watering, no weeding, no kidding!

The Basics of Herbs in Lasagna Gardens

You may have heard or read that herbs grow just fine in poor soil. Well, that's true for a few herbs, such as rue *(Ruta graveolens)* and yarrows *(Achillea* spp.). But believe me, most herbs will grow much, much better if you give them a spot in a lasagna bed. They'll thrive in the nutrient-rich soil, so you'll get even better harvests. Plus, the raised surface of a lasagna bed drains quickly, so you'll avoid those soggy spots that quickly rot and kill many herbs, especially during the winter.

To me, the greatest benefit is that lasagna gardens are kind to self-sowing herbs, so you can enjoy the plants for many years after just one planting. In regular gardens, you're always digging, tilling, or cultivating the bare soil, so the herb seeds get buried too deep or get destroyed as they sprout in spring. In a lasagna garden, they just fall in the mulch and pop up later on. I don't know why the mulch is so good for keeping weeds from sprouting while still allowing herb seeds to come up. Maybe it's because there are just so many herb seeds, some have to sprout! (I do give the self-sowing herbs a helping hand by dropping the seedheads back on the bed when I trim my herb plants.)

There's no special trick to creating a lasagna garden for herbs; just build it the same way you would any lasagna bed, using whatever organic materials you have available. You can build the garden in fall and wait until spring to plant, or create it and plant it right away any time the ground isn't frozen. Either way, you'll have a tidy, beautiful garden to look at right away. If you set out purchased plants, rather than grow all your herbs from seed, you can enjoy your new herb garden instantly, and you'll have herbs to harvest more quickly.

Keep Them Clipped.
Most herbs thrive with frequent trimming. If you don't need the clippings for cooking or crafts, just let them drop around the plant to add to the mulch.

Sun Vinegar

Once you have established herb gardens, you can harvest and use what you've grown. One of my favorite ways to use fresh herbs is to make sun vinegar. I make it in gallon-size glass bottles, then rebottle it in smaller, decorative bottles for table use. Many herbs are great for making flavorful vinegars, but chive blossoms are particularly beautiful and tasty.

When your chive plants are in full blossom (lots of blooms and buds), pick the flower heads. Wash and shake the blooms to remove any insects. Fill clean bottles half full of blooms, then pour white, distilled vinegar to the top of the bottle. Cap and place in the sun for one to two weeks. When the vinegar is pink and the blossoms are white, your chive-flower vinegar is ready. Strain the vinegar and discard old blossoms. Rebottle and add new blossoms and a few chive stems. Store the finished vinegar out of sunlight to retain the delicate pink color. The mild onion taste is perfect for garden salads and steamed greens.

Once you've seen how easy it is to make chive-blossom vinegar, you'll enjoy experimenting with other herbs, either singly or in various combinations. Some other good herbs to try include burnet, rosemary, and tarragon.

Herbal Garden Art. I like to use my herb-vinegars-in-progress as garden ornaments while they are steeping. Set a few bricks or an upside-down basket in the garden to make a pedestal, then set the jug on top.

After planting, herbs need only a minimum of care. Mulch soon after planting, and keep adding more through the season as the organic matter breaks down. That's it! Just remember to take time to walk through your garden frequently to enjoy the beauty and scents of your herbs. If you choose to harvest some for cooking or crafts, pick them around midday, when all the dew has dried off. Fresh herbs are a delight, but if you have a generous harvest, you might want to dry some for winter use. I like to toss the trimmings in paper bags, then hang the bags in a warm, airy place. The bags draw the moisture out of the herbs, speeding drying, and keep the herbs from getting dusty. Freezing is another fast and easy way to preserve many herbs.

Herbs for Lasagna Gardens

Here's a sampler of my favorite herbs for lasagna gardening. Some you'll recognize right away; others are a bit more unusual but fun to try. While most herbs have multiple uses, some are just ornamental and not meant for cooking. Before eating any herb from your garden, make sure you know what you are picking. It's smart to get your culinary herbs from a reputable grower, so they'll be labeled properly. And if you're trying an herb for the first time, use it sparingly, until you become familiar with the taste; some are surprisingly strong.

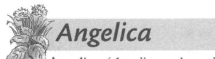

Angelica

Angelica *(Angelica archangelica)* is a truly spectacular-looking plant. This imposing biennial or perennial herb grows anywhere between 3 and 7 feet tall, with celerylike leaves

A Fabulous Focal Point. Angelica looks beautiful in the flower garden as well as in the herb garden. Its tall stalks and huge flower heads create an eye-catching accent in the back or center of any bed or border.

on long stalks. After the first year, the plant produces a center stalk topped with giant, greenish white flower clusters. It's a beauty!

Site and Soil. Angelica thrives in cool, moist soil and partial shade, but this adaptable herb also grows well in less-than-perfect conditions. Zones 4 to 9.

Planting and Care. Start with purchased plants, or sow seed outdoors in spring or early fall. Thin seedlings to leave about 3 feet between plants; mulch well. Once your plants bloom, clip off most of the clusters after the

Tips and Time-Savers

Angelica

Angelica seeds germinate best when they are less than a year old. If possible, try to get some seeds that have just ripened on a friend's plant, and sow them right away, where you want the plants to grow. Once your plants flower, you will have plenty of seed (and seedlings) to share with others!

kind, produces bushy, 18-inch-tall plants with wrinkled, bright green leaves. This annual herb also comes in a variety of other sizes, shapes, colors, and flavors. It's fun to experiment with these other cultivars, such as mound-forming 'Spicy Globe' and purple-leaved 'Purple Ruffles'.

Site and Soil. Basil plants need a warm, sunny spot with rich, well-drained soil.

Planting and Care. Start basil seed indoors about six weeks before your last frost date. Transplant to the garden after all danger of frost is past; space plants about 1 foot apart. Protect with row cover on chilly nights.

flowers fade, leaving a few to set seed. The seeds that drop will produce new plants to keep your crop going.

Harvesting and Uses. Cut a few of the new shoots in spring; candy them and use as cake decorations (see "Tips and Time-Savers: Borage" on page 80 for details). In France, angelica is grown as a major crop and, in addition to cake decorations, used to make jams and jellies. A tea made from the leaves is said to give even the most trying person a more angelic demeanor. Angelica seed is used commercially in making liqueurs, as flavoring for wines, and in perfumes.

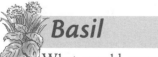

Basil

What would summer be without the warm, spicy scent and flavor of basil? Sweet basil *(Ocimum basilicum),* the most common

For Bushier Basil. Pinch off the shoot tips of your basil every week or two, and your plants will respond by producing bushier growth and more leaves. Save the shoot tips for the kitchen!

Tips and Time-Savers

Basil

If you have an extra-good basil harvest, chop the leaves in a food processor and add enough olive oil to make a loose paste. Pour the mix into ice-cube trays and freeze for winter use in pesto, soups, or sauces.

Harvesting and Uses. Pick off the leaves and shoot tips as you need them. Regular harvesting encourages plants to produce more leaves. Fresh basil and just-picked tomatoes are a perfect combination. Try topping sliced tomatoes with some extra-virgin olive oil, balsamic vinegar, and fresh mozzarella, and serve it with crusty bread to sop up the juice—it's the best lunch you'll ever have!

A Border Beauty. Borage's starry blue flowers add a welcome touch of color to both herb and flower gardens. Let the plants reach their full size to fill a large space, or cut them back for bushier growth.

Borage

Borage *(Borago officinalis)* grows to 3 feet tall, with broad, hairy leaves and heavenly blue star-shaped flowers. Besides adding beauty to herb and vegetable gardens, this bushy annual herb makes a pretty filler for bare spots in perennial gardens. Even if you never harvest your borage, you'll enjoy looking at it!

Site and Soil. Borage needs a sunny location with evenly moist but well-drained soil.

Planting and Care. Sow seeds outdoors in fall for spring growth. Thin seedlings to stand about 18 inches apart. Borage plants can get large, so if your space is limited, cut the plants back by about half after the first flush of blooms fade; the plants will get bushier and produce another set of flowers.

Harvesting and Uses. Pick borage's cucumber-flavored leaves for salads when they are young. Add the flowers to punch or salads, or candy them for dessert decorations.

Tips and Time-Savers

Borage

Candied borage flowers look beautiful on desserts. To candy flowers, use a soft, clean paintbrush to coat them with beaten egg white, then sprinkle them with granulated sugar (superfine is best). Let dry for a day or two, then store between layers of waxed paper in a sealed glass jar.

Site and Soil. Burnet needs sun and well-drained, alkaline soil. Zones 4 to 9.

Planting and Care. Sow seed outside in fall for spring harvest. Thin seedlings to stand 12 to 18 inches apart. When the flowerstalks appear, you have two options: either pinch them off or leave them. Removing the flowerstalks will encourage your plants to produce more of those wonderful ferny leaves. If you leave the flowers on, they will drop seed, and new plants will pop up throughout your garden.

Burnet

Burnet *(Poterium sanguisorba)* is a hardy perennial herb with mounds of tender, green leaves that smell and taste like cucumber. In summer, tight clusters of pinkish flowers bloom atop wandlike stems to 2 feet tall. You'll love the look of this herb in your garden.

A Change from Parsley. Burnet's ferny, blue-green leaves are tasty in their own right, with a mild cucumber flavor, but they also make a beautiful and unique garnish.

Tips and Time-Savers

Burnet

When you thin your burnet patch in spring, don't discard the seedlings you remove. Those tender, young leaves are ideal for adding cucumber flavor to salads and sandwiches.

Harvesting and Uses. Pick the fresh leaves as needed; they are good for early salads. The leaves are also tasty added to vinegar or cool drinks, or chopped and mixed with cream cheese. Blend the leaves with butter for fish and chicken. They also make a lovely garnish.

Caraway

Caraway *(Carum carvi)* grows in clumps of feathery green leaves, with 2- to 3-foot stems topped with white flowers the following year. The seeds of this biennial herb give rye bread its distinctive flavor.

Site and Soil. Give caraway a sunny site with well-drained soil. Zones 3 to 9.

Planting and Care. Caraway doesn't transplant well, so start with seed sown directly in the garden. Make the first sowing just after the last frost, and keep sowing every two weeks through summer to get a steady supply of leaves. Sowing caraway seed in fall will give you an even earlier harvest.

Harvesting and Uses. This herb earned a place for a short time in my white flower garden, but its prolific self-seeding got it tossed out of there and put back in the cook's garden. I don't bother collecting the seeds, as I find they need careful drying to prevent mildewing. I do like to pick the fresh leaves and use them as a component of a bouquet garni (a little bundle of aromatic herbs tied with string, so you can remove them from a soup or stew before serving).

Save Thinnings for Salads. Once your caraway seedlings have a few leaves, they are ready to use. Every few days, pull out some of the seedlings to leave space for others; use these thinnings as part of your harvest.

Tips and Time-Savers

Caraway

If you let the flowers mature on your caraway plants, you will have plenty of self-sown seedlings—you'll never have to plant caraway again!

Catnip

Catnip *(Nepeta cataria)* is not just for cats, although they love it. This vigorous perennial herb grows to 3 feet tall, in bushy clumps of fuzzy green leaves and dense spikes of small white to pinkish flowers in summer.

Site and Soil. Grow catnip just about anywhere. A lasagna bed in sun or light shade will suit it just fine. Zones 3 to 8.

Planting and Care. Start with purchased plants for instant impact. Restrain catnip's spread by planting it in a large plastic pot, then sinking the pot (almost to the rim) in the ground. Space plants about 18 inches apart. Frequent trimming will encourage bushier growth.

Hedges for Edges. Looking for something different to edge a flowerbed? Try a catnip hedge! Its gray-green leaves look great with more colorful blooms, and the plants adapt well to regular trimming.

Tips and Time-Savers

Catnip

If you know someone who's already growing catnip, chances are they'd be glad to share some with you, so you won't have to buy it. Figure on growing at least one clump per cat; that will give you plenty of trimmings for kitty toys.

Harvesting and Uses. Pick leaves as needed for fresh use, or cut whole stems in summer. Enjoy the fresh or dried leaves in tea. Catnip responds beautifully to shearing, so I like to use it as a low hedge. Use the dried trimmings as stuffing for cat toys.

Chives

Oniony-flavored chives *(Allium schoenoprasum)* produce 1-foot-tall clumps of slender green leaves accented with lavender-pink pom-poms of flowers in spring. This perennial herb is an attractive addition to any lasagna garden.

Site and Soil. Give chives a spot in full sun with well-drained soil. Zones 3 to 9.

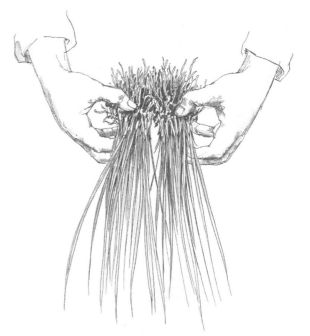

Multiply by Division. Divide chive clumps every three to four years to keep them vigorous. Simply dig them up in early spring and break them with your hands into two or more sections.

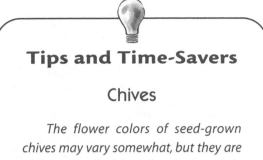

Tips and Time-Savers

Chives

The flower colors of seed-grown chives may vary somewhat, but they are all beautiful. Besides using the flowers in cooking or as a garnish, try picking and drying them for arrangements and other dried flower crafts. Gathering the blooms will also help reduce self-sowing.

Planting and Care. Start plants from seed sown indoors, or divide an existing clump. Space clumps about 10 inches apart. Chives readily self-sow if you let some of the flowers ripen on the plants.

Harvesting and Uses. Clip off leaves as needed. Harvest the flowers just as they are coming out of bud. Both leaves and flowers add a mild onion flavor to salads, stir-fries, vinegars, and salad dressings. (See "Sun Vinegar" on page 76 for details on making chive-blossom vinegar.)

Choose the Right Site. Comfrey is an attractive herb, but it gets big and spreads quickly by seed and creeping roots. Give it a space near your compost pile, where it will be handy for picking.

Comfrey

Comfrey *(Symphytum officinale)* is a perennial herb best suited for large gardens. A single plant grows to 3 feet tall, with broad, fuzzy leaves and nodding pinkish blue flowers.

Site and Soil. Comfrey thrives in rich, moist soil and adapts to sun or partial shade. Zones 3 to 9.

Planting and Care. It's easiest to start comfrey from an existing plant, so buy one or—better yet—find a friend who already has a patch, and ask for a division in early spring. Cut off the spent flowers to prevent self-sowing.

Harvesting and Uses. More than just a pretty plant, comfrey is also wonderful for speeding up the composting process. Cut the fresh leaves and spread them in layers as you

Extending Your Harvest. Coriander leaves, often known as cilantro, taste best when they are young and tender. Sowing small amounts every two weeks will give you a steady supply through the season.

build your pile, then add water, and poke some holes in the pile to get the right balance of air and moisture for the "cooking" process. I find that compost is ready twice as fast when I use comfrey this way. Plants regrow quickly, so you'll always have plenty of leaves to use.

Harvesting and Uses. Pick young, tender leaves as you need them for fresh use. Cilantro used to be saved for Mexican cooking, but now you'll find it called for in a wide range of recipes.

Coriander

Also called cilantro or Chinese parsley, coriander *(Coriandrum sativum)* is an easy-to-grow annual herb. Its 2-foot stems bear bright green leaves and are topped with clusters of tiny white flowers. You either love or hate the flavor of this strongly scented herb.

Site and Soil. Plant coriander in full sun, in an area of well-drained soil.

Planting and Care. In Zones 6 and north, get an early start by starting seed indoors; set out after the last frost date. Elsewhere, sow directly outdoors after the last frost. Sow again every two weeks through summer. I like to sow thickly and use the thinnings as part of my harvest.

Dill

The ferny, green, aromatic leaves of dill *(Anethum graveolens)* are attractive as well as tasty. In summer, the 30-inch stems of this annual herb are topped with flat clusters of tiny yellow flowers.

Site and Soil. Dill thrives in full sun and rich, well-drained soil.

Planting and Care. Sow seed outdoors in early to midspring, after danger of frost. Thin seedlings to stand 8 to 10 inches apart, then mulch. Other than that, dill needs little care.

Make the Most of It. Sure, dill leaves are flavorful, but don't forget to use the stems and flower heads as well—they are tasty too! You can even use the seedheads; pick and chop before the seeds turn brown.

Tips and Time-Savers

Dill

In my opinion, dill has the best flavor when its seeds are starting to form. I like to harvest the seedheads just as the seeds are forming (while they are still green) and chop them up along with the leaves and stems for cooking. Don't forget to leave a few seedheads to mature on the plant, though, so you can get self-sown seedlings.

Harvesting and Uses. Clip off the leaves, stems, and flower heads as needed for fresh use. Dill, cucumbers, and sour cream are a natural combination. Or make refrigerator pickles by mixing vinegar, water, garlic, and sugar in a large jar, along with whole small or sliced cucumbers and several dill seedheads. As you remove the pickles, keep adding more cukes and dill through the summer.

Fennel

Fennel *(Foeniculum vulgare)* is a big herb, growing to over 5 feet with finely cut leaves and clusters of tiny yellow flowers. I like to grow Florence fennel *(F. vulgare* var. *azoricum),* which has a tasty, bulblike base as well as flavorful foliage.

Site and Soil. Plant fennel in a well-drained lasagna bed in full sun. Zones 6 to 9.

Planting and Care. Sow seed outdoors after all danger of frost has passed, or buy plants. Try not to disturb the roots when transplanting. Thin seedlings or space transplants to stand 6 to 12 inches apart. Cut off most of the spent flower heads, unless you plan to collect the seeds; otherwise, you'll have fennel plants popping up everywhere!

Gathering Your Fennel. Harvest Florence fennel bulbs when the leaf bases begin to thicken, cutting just below the swollen part of the stem. You can also snip the leaves as needed for cooking or garnishes.

Harvesting and Uses. Snip fresh leaves as needed. Harvest Florence fennel bulbs by cutting just below the swollen base. Slice the base and serve raw as an appetizer, or roast it along with root vegetables. Fennel seeds add a distinctive flavor to Italian sausage. They are also widely used in baking for their licorice flavor.

Tips and Time-Savers

Fennel

Fennel needs lots of room, but it looks great in the back of a perennial border or foundation garden. Whether you grow the common green fennel or the brown-leaved bronze fennel (Foeniculum vulgare 'Purpureum'), it is definitely an attention getter!

Feverfew

Feverfew *(Tanacetum parthenium)* offers dainty, daisylike flowers atop 3-foot stems from summer into fall. While common feverfew has lobed, light green leaves, there is a more compact cultivar, known as golden feverfew (*T. parthenium* 'Aureum'), with wonderful yellow leaves.

Site and Soil. This adaptable herb can grow in sun or partial shade. It thrives in the well-drained soil of a lasagna bed. Feverfew is usually hardy in Zones 4 to 9, but it may not be fully hardy in colder areas.

Planting and Care. Start with purchased plants, and set them about 1 foot apart. Mulch after planting, and again through the growing season. Other than that, feverfew needs virtually no care.

Harvesting and Uses. Feverfew's tiny white flowers make it very valuable in the white flower garden. It also fills large gaps in a perennial garden over a long blooming period if you keep the spent flowers cut back.

Removing Finished Flowers.
Feverfew is pretty, but it can end up everywhere in your garden if you allow all the flowers to set seed. It's best to cut off most of them as they fade, leaving just a few to self-sow.

Tips and Time-Savers

Feverfew

Feverfew plants can be short-lived in some gardens, but they set seed so generously that you never have to be without this pretty herb. Simply dig up the self-sown seedlings in spring and transplant them to where you want them to grow.

Horehound

The early growth of horehound *(Marrubium vulgare)* resembles green rosettes, later expanding into interesting wrinkled, gray-green leaves on stubby branches. Mature plants can grow to 2 feet tall. I loved this plant in my white flower garden but lost it after a particularly hard winter; it is perennial in moderate climates but not reliably winter-hardy north of Zone 6.

Site and Soil. Horehound needs full sun and thrives in dry, sandy soil, but it will adapt to the well-drained soil of a lasagna bed. Zones 6 to 9.

Planting and Care. Since horehound plants are not easy to find, you'll probably have to start seed indoors or directly in the garden in spring. Allow about 18 inches between plants.

Please Touch the Herbs. Horehound is a handsome addition to any garden. Its felty leaves just beg to be petted, and its gray-green color makes a wonderful backdrop for white or brightly hued blooms.

A Hyssop Hedge. Hyssop makes an attractive, unusual hedge. Clip plants often with hedge shears for a formal shape, or just trim them lightly for a softer look.

Harvesting and Uses. Pick fresh leaves when you need them. For drying, cut whole stems a few inches above the ground in early to midsummer. You can use fresh or dried leaves to brew a tea or flavor a sweetened cough syrup to use for colds. Horehound has been used medicinally since early Roman times, and you can still buy horehound candy today.

Harvesting and Uses. Hyssop is grown primarily for its good looks. Enjoy its shrubby habit and colorful blooms in a flower garden, or use it as a miniature hedge for edging beds, borders, and walkways.

Hyssop

A hardy perennial herb, hyssop *(Hyssopus officinalis)* produces a short, tough hedge of narrow, dark green, aromatic leaves. The bushy, 2-foot plants are topped with beautiful blue, pink, or white flowers in summer.

Site and Soil. Hyssop appreciates well-limed soil. It can adapt to full sun or partial shade. Zones 3 to 9.

Planting and Care. Buy already-started plants, or sow seed indoors in late winter or directly in the garden in late spring. Space plants or thin seedlings to stand about 1 foot apart; mulch after planting.

Lady's Mantle

Monet used lady's mantle *(Alchemilla mollis)* as a border plant in his gardens, surely because of the way the plant's soft leaves and sprays of yellow-green flowers would cascade gracefully over the sides of a path. This hardy perennial herb grows to 1 foot tall.

Living on the Edge. Enjoy lady's mantle as an edging plant in your lasagna garden. It's best along a paved or chipped path, where it can sprawl over the edge without smothering the grass.

Site and Soil. Lady's mantle grows in practically any kind of soil, in sun or shade. I even find seedlings growing in my crushed-rock driveway. Zones 4 to 9.

Planting and Care. For quickest results, start with purchased plants and set them 12 to 18 inches apart. Mulch after planting.

Harvesting and Uses. Clip the flower stems as needed; they look wonderful as a filler in arrangements. The dried flowers are also used as a stuffing for sleep pillows.

Tips and Time-Savers

Lady's Mantle

Lady's mantle often self-sows. It's easy to transplant the seedlings to other parts of your garden or share them with friends. If you'd rather not have the seedlings, clip the flowering stems close to the base of the plant when the flowers fade. This will prevent seed formation and can encourage a flush of new leafy growth.

Lavender

Common lavender *(Lavandula angustifolia)* is a popular perennial herb beloved for its fragrant, gray-green leaves and pretty purple flowers. It grows in shrubby clumps to 2 feet tall. If you enjoy making crafts, lavender definitely belongs in your garden.

Site and Soil. Lavender needs full sun. It adapts well to average garden soil, as long as it is not soggy. The raised surface of a lasagna bed provides the good drainage lavender demands. Zones 4 to 8.

Planting and Care. Start with purchased plants, or sow seed indoors in late winter. Set plants out 12 to 18 inches apart. Trim plants lightly in fall to encourage a bushy shape.

Harvesting and Uses. Clip off the flowerstalks just as the blooms open; hang them in a warm, airy place to dry. Enjoy them in dried flower projects, such as wreaths or arrangements, or add them to potpourri.

Harvesting Lavender. Trim off lavender flowers just above the uppermost leaves on the stem if you only need the blooms, or cut back further into the plant if you want the leaves too.

Tips and Time-Savers

Lavender

I like to keep all of the lavender stems left from trimmings or craft projects and tie them into small bundles with raffia. Toss them into your fire or woodstove to enjoy the scent in winter. These decorative bundles make wonderful gifts, too!

Lemon Balm

A tasty tea herb, lemon balm *(Melissa officinalis)* grows in bushy perennial clumps of bright green, oval to heart-shaped leaves. The lightest touch releases their powerful lemon scent. The 1- to 2-foot stems bear clusters of small white flowers in summer.

Keep Clipping. Cutting lemon balm stems close to the ground before bloom encourages your plants to produce a flush of lush new growth—and give you another harvest later in the season.

Site and Soil. Lemon balm is not fussy but tastes best if grown in rich, well-drained soil. It can adapt to full sun or partial shade. Zones 4 to 9.

Planting and Care. Start with purchased plants for quickest results, or sow seed indoors or outdoors in spring. Space plants or thin seedlings to stand 18 inches apart. Mulch after planting.

Harvesting and Uses. Pick individual leaves as needed for fresh use; cut and dry whole leafy stems for winter use. The leaves make a soothing tea.

Tips and Time-Savers

Lemon Balm

Lemon balm self-sows freely and can become invasive if you allow the flowers to mature on the plant. Cutting all the stems close to the ground when the blooms open prevents seeding. (It also encourages plants to produce fresh leafy growth.) If you don't have a use for the lemon-scented trimmings, just scatter them around the base of the plant as a mulch.

Making the Transition. To help your lemon verbena recover from repotting, set it in a shady spot in the garden for a week or two before bringing it indoors for the winter.

Lemon Verbena

Lemon verbena *(Aloysia triphylla)* grows to 3 feet tall, with narrow, bright green leaves that smell strongly of lemon. This tender perennial herb is killed by frost, but you can keep it from year to year by growing it in a pot and bringing it indoors for the winter.

Site and Soil. This lemony herb thrives in full sun and rich soil. It's winter-hardy in frost-free areas; elsewhere, grow as an annual or bring indoors.

Planting and Care. Start with a purchased plant. Sink the plant, pot and all, into a lasagna bed. In late summer, lift the pot, remove the plant, wash off the roots, and repot the plant in a pot of commercial potting mix before bringing it indoors for the winter.

Harvesting and Uses. Pinch off leaves as needed for fresh use or drying. Add them to any recipe where you want a lemony flavor.

Tips and Time-Savers

Lemon Verbena

North of Zone 7, don't expect much of a harvest from this herb, as it needs warmth to really thrive. But it's still worth growing just for the pleasure of rubbing its leaves and releasing the pungent lemon scent. Give it a sunny windowsill indoors, and let the soil surface dry out a bit between waterings; soggy soil will lead to root rot.

Lovage

The giant of the celery family, lovage *(Levisticum officinale)* is a bushy perennial herb that needs lots of space. The clumps of long-stalked, green leaves can reach to 3 feet across, and the clusters of small, yellow, summer flowers bloom atop stems up to 6 feet tall.

Lots of Leaves. A single lovage plant will provide all the leaves you need! You can start harvesting shortly after transplanting, when the plant has at least five leaves.

Site and Soil. Give lovage a lasagna bed with rich, moist soil in sun or partial shade. Zones 3 to 8.

Planting and Care. You only need one lovage clump, so start with a purchased plant. Unless you want to harvest the seeds, cut off the flowerstalks before the blooms open to encourage leafy growth and prevent self-sowing. Other than mulching, lovage needs no special care.

Harvesting and Uses. Pick leaves as needed. Chop the fresh leaves into salads, or freeze them for later use as a celery substitute in winter soups or stews.

Tips and Time-Savers

Lovage

This herb is a treat for cooks, since it gives you the taste of celery without the hassle of growing real celery. Keep in mind that lovage has a much stronger flavor than celery, though, so use it sparingly until you get used to the difference.

Sweet Marjoram

Sweet marjoram *(Origanum majorana)* is a tender perennial herb usually grown as an annual. The bushy, 12- to 18-inch-tall plants bear aromatic green leaves and clusters of pink summer flowers.

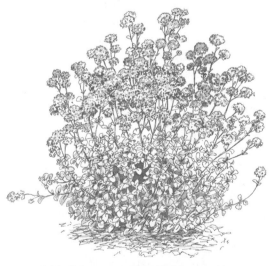

A Multipurpose Herb. Most recipes call for sweet marjoram leaves only, but the flowers are tasty too! It's worth growing just as an ornamental and to attract beneficial insects.

Site and Soil. Grow sweet marjoram in full sun. Good drainage is critical.

Planting and Care. Start with purchased plants, or sow seed indoors in early spring, 8 to 10 weeks before the last frost. Set plants out after the last frost date, spacing them 10 to 12 inches apart. Mulch after planting.

Harvesting and Uses. Snip leaves as needed for fresh use. Cut stems close to the ground just as the flowers open and hang in a warm, airy, dark place to dry. Use the tender leaves fresh in salads for a unique taste. Sweet marjoram is also excellent in soups and stews.

Tips and Time-Savers

Sweet Marjoram

For a special taste treat, rub salt, pepper, and chopped sweet marjoram on chicken before roasting; then sprinkle marjoram flowers over the chicken before serving.

Plan Before You Plant. Mint roots can spread quickly in the loose, rich soil of a lasagna bed. Give them a spot where they can romp without crowding out companions, or restrain them by planting in a pot sunk into the soil.

 *Mint*

Marvelous mints have a place in every herb garden. Two of the most popular mints are peppermint *(Mentha × piperita)* and spearmint *(M. spicata)*. Both produce bushy, 2-foot-tall plants topped with spikes of tiny flowers; spearmint has a milder scent and flavor. Once you get started growing mints, it's fun to look out for some of the other kinds; these perennial herbs come in dozens of different shapes, sizes, colors, and flavors.

Site and Soil. Mints thrive in the rich, evenly moist soil of a lasagna bed in partial shade. Most are hardy in Zones 4 to 9.

Planting and Care. Most mints spread rapidly by creeping roots if unrestrained, so it's smart to plant them in a pot, then sink the pot, almost up to the rim, in your lasagna garden. Mulch after planting.

Harvesting and Uses. Pinch off leaves or shoots as needed for fresh use. For drying, cut whole stems close to the ground just before bloom and hang in a dark, warm, airy place. Use the fresh or dried leaves in cooking or teas; add the dried foliage to potpourri.

Tips and Time-Savers

Mint

Mint seedlings can vary in scent and flavor, so buy already-started plants to get the aromas you want. To make more of your favorite mints, simply dig and divide the clumps in spring or fall.

Nasturtium

Nasturtiums *(Tropaeolum majus)* are equally at home in the herb garden and the flower garden. The bushy clumps of these easy annuals bear circular green leaves, each supported on a center stem, like an umbrella. From midsummer to frost, the 1- to 2-foot-tall plants produce showy blooms in a range of colors, including red, orange, yellow, pink, and white. You can also find "climbing" nasturtiums, with long, vining stems that weave along the ground among other plants or scramble up supports.

Site and Soil. Nasturtiums need full sun. They aren't fussy about soil; a well-drained lasagna bed suits them just fine.

Planting and Care. Start seed indoors or directly in the garden in spring; space or thin plants to stand 6 to 9 inches apart. That's it!

Harvesting and Uses. Gather the leaves and flowers as you need them; wash and shake the flowers vigorously to remove any hidden insects. Both the leaves and flowers are edible and add lots of radishlike flavor to anything prepared or garnished with them.

Pretty and Prolific. Nasturtiums do double duty, with beautiful blooms that add color to your garden as well as to your salads. The leaves also have a pleasing peppery flavor.

Tips and Time-Savers

Nasturtium

When you prepare a lasagna bed for nasturtiums, or mulch existing plants, hold off on high-nitrogen materials, such as manures and grass clippings. Otherwise, the extra nutrients can encourage your plants to produce more leaves than flowers. Of course, this isn't necessarily a problem if you grow cultivars with interesting foliage, such as the cream-splashed leaves of 'Alaska'!

Oregano

To get that great oregano flavor associated with pizza and pasta sauces, look for Greek oregano *(Origanum heracleoticum)*. This bushy perennial herb grows to about 2 feet tall, with clusters of whitish flowers in summer. Common oregano *(O. vulgare)* has showier pink flowers, but its flavor is rather bland.

Give Them a Pinch. Pinching the tips off your oregano plants will give you a harvest of tender, flavorful leaves—plus, your plants will end up being bushier, with even more leaves to pick.

Site and Soil. Oregano demands full sun and well-drained soil; a lasagna bed provides good growing conditions. Zones 5 to 9.

Planting and Care. Start with purchased plants. Rub a leaf before you buy to make sure you're getting the pungent Greek oregano. Set plants about 1 foot apart. For propagation, divide plants in spring.

Harvesting and Uses. Pinch off leaves or shoot tips as needed for fresh use. For drying, cut whole stems just above the ground and hang in a dark, warm, airy place. The fresh or dried leaves are a perfect addition to tomato-based dishes.

Tips and Time-Savers

Oregano

To promote bushy growth, pinch off the stem tips several times during the growing season; use the trimmings as part of your harvest. If you want a larger harvest all at once, cut all the stems close to ground level just as the flowers begin to open. The plants will produce a new flush of leafy growth.

Parsley

Parsley *(Petroselinum crispum)* grows in pretty 1-foot rosettes of leaves that are either flat and celerylike (Italian parsley) or tightly crimped (curly parsley). I find that the flat-leaved Italian parsley has the best flavor. The first year, this biennial herb produces only leaves; its clusters of tiny yellow flowers don't appear until the second spring.

Site and Soil. Although parsley grows best in full sun, it can take light shade. The rich, evenly moist soil of a compost-enriched lasagna bed is ideal.

Italian parsley

Curly parsley

Try Them Both. I like to grow both kinds of parsley in my lasagna beds. Italian parsley is more flavorful, but curly parsley is particularly pretty in the garden or as a garnish.

Planting and Care. Start seed indoors in early spring. Set transplants 8 to 10 inches apart in the garden. Mulch after planting; otherwise, parsley is practically work-free. The first-year leaves taste best, so set out new plants each year.

Harvesting and Uses. Snip off the leaves as needed for fresh use; they also freeze well for storage. I like to chop parsley in my food processor and add olive oil to make a loose paste, then freeze the results in ice cube trays. Pop out the frozen cubes and store in a bag for later use in just about any recipe. I particularly like using them for parsley pesto—a combination of chopped parsley, olive oil, walnuts, garlic, and Romano cheese. Add a dollop to a bowl of pasta for a quick and easy meal.

Tips and Time-Savers

Parsley

Parsley is wonderful for cooking, but it's also gorgeous in the garden! Curly parsley is especially pretty as a filler in flower arrangements, and the bushy, dark green plants make a beautiful border for flower gardens and foundation plantings.

Rosemary

The needlelike leaves of rosemary *(Rosmarinus officinalis)* have a pinelike scent that's a delight to the senses. In its native habitat, rosemary grows as large perennial shrubs, but in much of the United States, it is killed by winter cold. Plants brought indoors for the winter usually reach only 1 to 3 feet tall.

Site and Soil. Rosemary appreciates full sun and well-drained soil. If you plan to grow it in a pot, a commercial potting mix will work fine.

Planting and Care. It's easiest to begin growing rosemary with already-started plants. Move the plants out to the garden when all danger of frost is past. In Zones 8 to 10, set rosemary plants about 3 feet apart; elsewhere, space them 12 to 18 inches apart or grow them in pots. Mulch after planting to keep the soil evenly moist.

Harvesting and Uses. Trim off leaves or shoot tips as needed for fresh use or drying. Add crushed fresh rosemary to olive oil to make a great dip for crusty bread. Sprinkle

Enjoy Rosemary Year-Round. It's hard to imagine having an herb garden without rosemary! Grow it in the ground during the summer, then dig and pot it up to grow indoors in the winter.

chopped fresh or crushed dried rosemary on top of bread before baking for an incredible taste and aroma. Rosemary is wonderful with lamb, of course, but it also tastes great with chicken. I prepare one of my favorite meals by dredging boned, skinned chicken breasts in flour and dipping them in egg wash (egg and water) and then seasoned bread crumbs. I cook them in a sauté pan with olive oil and a sprig of rosemary. In another pan, I sauté sliced, peeled sweet potatoes in more olive oil and rosemary. Serve the chicken and sweet potatoes with a crisp green vegetable, such as broccoli or braised celery—fabulous! I also enjoy using fresh rosemary sprigs to brush marinades, sauces, or oil on grilled meats and vegetables. Crushing the sprigs first with a wooden mallet releases more of the flavor.

Tips and Time-Savers

Rosemary

A dry rosemary plant is a dead rosemary plant. To keep the roots evenly moist and cool during the summer, I plant my rosemary directly in the soil of a well-mulched lasagna bed. In late summer, I dig them up and wash the soil off the roots, then trim both the roots and tops back by a third before planting them in pots of commercial potting mix. (Adding some water-absorbing polymers into the mix before planting can help later on, as the polymers will release moisture to thirsty roots if you occasionally forget to water during the winter.)

To help my rosemary plants recover from the stress of transplanting, I set them in the shade of a shrub or tree for a week, then move them closer to the house (still in the shade) for another week or so. I bring the potted plants indoors before I turn on the heat and set them in a spot that's bright but out of direct sun. Covering the exposed potting mix with sphagnum moss acts like a mulch, keeping the mix from drying out too quickly. When I need to water, I just lift a bit of the moss to expose the mix, then replace the moss when I'm done.

If you keep a saucer under the pot, make sure you check it an hour or so after watering, and dump out any water that's drained there.

Rue

Rue *(Ruta graveolens)* is a lovely perennial herb with a bad rap. True, touching the leaves can cause skin irritation to some, but the 3-foot-tall plants are wonderful in the perennial garden, with their distinctive blue-green foliage and yellow flowers that resemble clusters of stars.

Site and Soil. Rue adapts to full sun or partial shade; good drainage is the important thing. It even grows in dry, stony, alkaline soil. Zones 4 to 9.

Planting and Care. Start with purchased plants, or sow seed indoors in late winter. Set out transplants 18 to 24 inches apart. Mulch after planting. Trim plants in fall to shape them and promote bushy growth in spring.

Harvesting and Uses. Enjoy rue's good looks in the garden. Clip off the dried seedpods; they are excellent to use in decorative wreaths and swags.

Protect Yourself. For some people, touching rue can cause skin irritation. To prevent problems, wear gloves if you're harvesting the seedpods for crafts.

Tips and Time-Savers

Rue

I like to use an electric string trimmer to prune and shape my rue plants in fall. It's quick and easy, and I don't have to touch the clippings—I just leave them on the ground as mulch.

Sage

Common sage *(Salvia officinalis)* is a shrubby perennial herb with fragrant, gray-green leaves. In summer, the leafy, 2-foot stems are topped with spikes of purple-blue flowers. You can also find cultivars such as 'Purpurea', with purple-green leaves, and 'Icterina', with yellow-edged green leaves.

Site and Soil. Sage needs a sunny lasagna bed with well-limed, well-drained soil. Zones 3 to 9.

Planting and Care. Start common sage from seed sown indoors in late winter or directly in the garden in late spring. Buy already-started plants if you are looking for particular leaf colors. Set transplants or thin seedlings to stand 12 to 18 inches apart.

Harvesting and Uses. Pick leaves as needed for fresh use or freezing. For drying, harvest leafy shoots before the flowers open, or wait until bloom if you want the flowers too. Tender, small leaves add a taste sensation to salads. The dried leaves and flowers, stripped from the stems, are a welcome addition to potpourri. Bundle the remaining stems, tie them with raffia, and toss them into a fire or woodstove to enjoy the aroma.

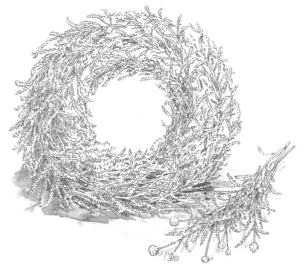

Santolina

Santolina *(Santolina chamaecyparissas)* produces bushy, 2-foot stems clad in aromatic, gray leaves. In summer, the stems of this perennial herb are tipped with buttonlike clusters of yellow flowers.

A Crafty Herb. Santolina's leafy shoots and buttonlike flower clusters dry well, making them great for crafts. Use the foliage as a base for a wreath; enjoy as is or spice it up with other dried herbs.

For the Birds. Sage is good for more than just stuffing! Its purple-blue flowers are rich in nectar, making them attractive to hummingbirds.

Tips and Time-Savers

Sage

I can't cook poultry without sage! Insert large sage leaves under the skin before roasting a chicken or turkey to give the meat a great flavor. Making a snack from the leftovers? Fresh-chopped sage mixed with cream cheese makes a wonderful spread for a turkey sandwich.

Site and Soil. If grown in rich soil with good drainage, santolina is dependable; a lasagna bed in full sun is ideal. Zones 5 to 8.

Planting and Care. Start with purchased plants, and set them 12 to 18 inches apart. Prune after the blooms fade to promote bushy growth. Replace old plants every few years with new plants made from cuttings.

Harvesting and Uses. Santolina is handsome enough to grow just for its good looks. For craft use, harvest the leafy stems just as the flowers open; hang in a warm, airy spot to dry.

Tips and Time-Savers

Santolina

Santolina's gray foliage mixes well with green foliage plants for low hedges in knot gardens or as an edging for other plantings.

Site and Soil. This easy-to-grow herb grows well in a sunny lasagna bed with well-drained soil.

Planting and Care. Sow seed directly in the garden around the last frost date. Thin seedlings to stand 6 to 8 inches apart, using the thinnings as part of your harvest.

Summer Savory

Summer savory *(Satureja hortensis)* is an annual herb with narrow, aromatic, green leaves on 18-inch stems. Small white flowers bloom along the tops of the stems from mid-summer to frost.

Tips and Time-Savers

Summer Savory

To extend your harvest of summer savory, trim plants lightly but often. This encourages the remaining stems to branch out, giving you more shoots to harvest through the season.

Harvesting and Uses. Snip off shoots as needed for fresh use, or harvest them just before flowering, place them in a paper bag, and hang the bag in a warm, airy place. Summer savory is a traditional favorite for flavoring bean dishes.

Easy Picking. For a quick and easy harvest, sow summer savory thickly in a wide band or a patch, then harvest it in bunches by trimming off the top-growth with scissors.

Winter Savory

Winter savory *(Satureja montana)* is one of my favorite herbs. I grow this rugged 6- to 12-inch-tall perennial in rock gardens and in rubble walls for its looks and hardiness; in the cook's garden for its flavor; and in the white flower garden for its tiny white blooms.

Flavorful Savory. Winter savory is worth growing just for its good looks and fragrant foliage, but it's also useful in the kitchen.

Site and Soil. Sun and good drainage—and not much else—are all winter savory asks. Zones 4 to 9.

Planting and Care. For quickest results, start from purchased plants; set them 10 to 12 inches apart. Mulch after planting—that's all they need.

Tips and Time-Savers

Winter Savory

To increase your stock of winter savory plants, mound a bit of soil over a few stems where they touch the ground (a technique known as layering). By the end of the season, these stems will have produced roots of their own; snip them off the parent plant and transplant them.

Harvesting and Uses. Clip off leaves or shoots as needed for fresh use. For drying, harvest the shoots just before the flowers open, place them in a paper bag, and hang the bag in a warm, airy place. Add the fresh or dried leaves to cooking meats and stews.

French Sorrel

French sorrel *(Rumex scutatus)* is a hardy perennial herb grown for its lemony leaves; they add a distinctive tang to soups and sauces. The leaves of true French sorrel are long and narrow in a shield shape, with a light green color; they grow in clumps to 2 feet tall.

Double Your Harvest. When you finish harvesting sorrel in the spring, cut the remaining leaves to the ground to get a new crop of tender foliage for a second harvest.

Site and Soil. French sorrel thrives in the rich, well-drained soil of a lasagna bed in sun or partial shade. Zones 4 to 9.

Planting and Care. Start with purchased plants, or sow seed indoors or directly in the garden in midspring. Space plants 12 to 18 inches apart. Mulch regularly.

Harvesting and Uses. This herb is one of the first greens up in the spring, so you can enjoy the tender new growth in salads, or cook it with other greens. Simply pinch or cut off the leaves as needed for fresh use.

Southernwood

Southernwood *(Artemisia abrotanum)* is one of my favorite herbs. Its shrubby, 3-foot mounds of gray-green leaves are beautiful in any garden, and the aromatic foliage makes a pleasant-smelling insect repellent. Best of all, this perennial herb is easy to grow.

Site and Soil. Southernwood grows in sun to partial shade. It thrives in the rich, well-drained soil of a lasagna bed. Zones 4 to 9.

Planting and Care. Start with purchased plants, setting them 2 to 3 feet apart, and mulch after planting. That's it!

A Natural Pest-Chaser. Grow a southernwood plant by your steps or door so it's within easy reach. For insect-repellent action, rub a sprig in your hands, then rub your hands on your exposed skin.

Harvesting and Uses. Although southernwood is mainly grown just for looks, you can harvest and dry the leafy shoots in midsummer for making wreaths and other crafts.

Sweet Woodruff

Sweet woodruff *(Galium odoratum)* is a delicate-looking perennial herb that grows wild as a woodland ground cover in the forests of Germany. It looks wonderful in a shady wild garden with its sweet white flowers that bloom in May. Plants grow no more than 10 inches tall.

Site and Soil. This beautiful herb grows well in partial to full shade and appreciates the evenly moist soil of a lasagna bed enriched with lots of compost. This sturdy little herb can also adapt to tough growing conditions, such as the deep, dry shade under trees and shrubs, although it will spread less quickly there. Zones 3 to 9.

Tips and Time-Savers

Sweet Woodruff

Within a year or two, sweet woodruff plants will spread and quickly fill their space. To control their spread, or to increase your plantings, dig and divide the clumps as needed in spring or fall. The plants may look a little ragged after transplanting, but they'll recover quickly.

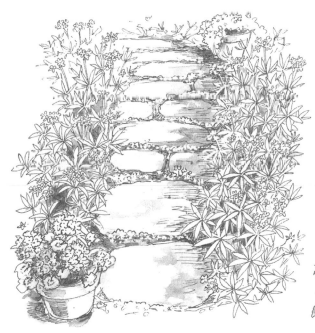

Made for the Shade. Sweet woodruff makes a wonderful ground cover in a shady spot. Grow it for its dainty flowers and interesting foliage; then dry the leaves and enjoy their vanilla-like scent in potpourri.

Planting and Care. Buy already-started plants, and set them 8 to 12 inches apart. Mulch well after planting to keep the soil cool and evenly moist.

Harvesting and Uses. To make May wine, a traditional German beverage used to celebrate the return of spring, add 12 sprigs of fresh sweet woodruff to a gallon of Rhine wine. Heat the sweet woodruff in the oven first to bring out its full flavor. For drying, harvest the foliage any time during the season, and hang it in a dark, warm, airy place to dry. Use the dried sprigs in wreaths or potpourri.

Tansy

Tansy *(Tanacetum vulgare)* is a perennial herb that grows to 4 feet tall and at least 3 feet wide. It needs plenty of room to spread, but if you have the space, it's worth growing. The ferny, bright green leaves have a strong scent that repels insects, and the flat-topped clusters of yellow flowers are great for crafts.

Harvesting Tansy. If you want the flowers for dried arrangements or other crafts, pick them when they are still yellow-green, and hang upside down in a warm, dark, airy place to dry.

Site and Soil. A tough plant that can grow in sun or shade, tansy thrives in just about any average soil. Zones 4 to 9.

Planting and Care. Start with purchased plants or—better yet—a division from a friend's tansy patch. (Once you get it established, you'll always have plenty of tansy to share!) Space plants 2 to 3 feet apart, then mulch.

Harvesting and Uses. Pick tansy when the flowers are fully open for fresh arrangements. The dried flowers and leaves keep their strong scent, which is said to repel ants and other insects.

Tips and Time-Savers

Tansy

If you are growing tansy in a flower border, give it a spot at the back of the bed, and stake it to keep the stems from flopping onto smaller companions.

French Tarragon

There's nothing like the taste of home-grown French tarragon *(Artemisia dracunculus)*. This perennial herb grows to 30 inches tall, producing bushy clumps of narrow, dark green leaves. French tarragon is often confused with Russian tarragon, a similar-looking but less flavorful relative.

Site and Soil. A lasagna bed in full sun suits French tarragon just fine. Zones 4 to 8.

Keep It for the Kitchen. French tarragon isn't especially showy, but it's a must-have if you like to cook. The fresh foliage is the most flavorful.

Planting and Care. Tarragon seeds produce the bitter-flavored Russian tarragon, so start with a plant labeled "French tarragon" to make sure you get the right herb. Set plants 2 feet apart. Mulch after planting.

Harvesting and Uses. Clip off leaves or shoots as needed for fresh use, or cut the leafy stems in summer, place them in a paper bag, and hang the bag in a warm, airy place to dry. I enjoy tarragon used fresh with chicken. It also adds a great taste to vinegars.

Tips and Time-Savers

French Tarragon

Try stuffing the inside of a chicken with tarragon and laying an extra sprig across the top before roasting. The distinctive licorice flavor of this herb will make the chicken extra tasty.

Bag It! For easy drying, toss thyme trimmings into a brown paper bag. Hang the bag in a warm, airy place for a few weeks.

Thyme

Every herb garden needs plenty of thyme! Start with the common culinary thyme *(Thymus vulgaris)*, which grows in bushy, 1-foot-tall mounds of small, gray-green, aromatic leaves and clusters of whitish blooms in early summer. Then branch out to try some of the other thymes, such as the purple- or pink-flowered mother-of-thyme *(T. serpyllum)*.

Site and Soil. Thymes need full sun and well-drained soil to thrive. Most are hardy in Zones 4 to 9.

Tips and Time-Savers

Thyme

Common thyme is fairly easy to start from seed, but the seedlings tend to grow slowly, and they may vary somewhat in flavor. When you start with purchased plants, you'll get a larger harvest sooner. Plus, you can make sure you get the scents, habits, and leaf and flower colors you want.

Planting and Care. Start with purchased plants, or sow seed indoors in early spring or directly in the garden in mid- to late spring. Set transplants or thin seedlings to stand 6 to 12 inches apart.

Harvesting and Uses. Pick leaves or sprigs as needed for fresh use. For drying, trim whole stems close to the ground just as the flowers open. Add fresh or dried leaves to soups, stews, and stuffings. They are also tasty in egg dishes.

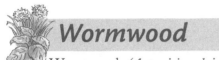

Wormwood

Wormwood *(Artemisia absinthium)* is a beautiful and useful perennial. Its shrubby stems clad in aromatic, deeply cut, gray-green leaves grow to at least 3 feet tall in the worst soil—taller in better conditions. Small, greenish yellow flowers bloom along the stems in summer, but they aren't especially showy.

Site and Soil. Wormwood grows equally well in sun or partial shade. A regular lasagna garden provides favorable soil conditions. Zones 4 to 9.

Planting and Care. For quickest results, start with purchased plants, and space them about 2 feet apart. Beyond that, wormwood needs little care, except for mulching after planting.

Harvesting and Uses. Cut the top 1 to 2 feet from each stem as the flowers open, and hang those trimmings in a warm, airy place to dry. Dried wormwood is great for wreaths and arrangements, and it also repels insects.

A Foil for Flowers. Wormwood is worth growing just for its lacy, gray-green leaves and shrubby habit. It makes a great "filler" for the middle or back of a flower garden.

Tips and Time-Savers

Wormwood

I plant a wormwood relative known as 'Silver King' in clumps here and there in my bulb garden to protect my tulip bulbs. The swaying stems and sharp fragrance of the gray plants discourage deer and other animal pests.

Yarrow

Few plants give so much for so little effort as yarrows (*Achillea* spp.). These dependable perennials come in a wide range of heights and colors. One of my favorites is a hybrid known as 'Coronation Gold', with yellow flower clusters and ferny, gray-green leaves on 3-foot stems.

Site and Soil. Yarrow grows practically anywhere, even in poor soil, so don't waste manure or compost on the site for this herb. Zones 3 to 9.

Planting and Care. Start with purchased plants to get the colors and heights you want. Space plants about 2 feet apart. Dividing clumps in spring or fall is an easy way to increase your yarrow plantings.

Harvesting and Uses. Gather the long-stemmed flower clusters when they show good color, but before they start to turn brown. For drying, hang them upside down in a warm, dark, airy spot. Enjoy the fresh flowers in bouquets; use the dried blooms in arrangements, wreaths, and other crafts.

Grow a Bunch. Yarrow's colorful flowers earn it a place in any garden. Plant extras so you will have enough to cut and bring indoors for bouquets.

Tips and Time-Savers

Yarrow

Don't think you'd be doing your yarrow plants a favor by giving them rich, moist soil. Sure, they'll produce lots of lush leaves, but they won't flower as well, and their stems will be floppy, so they'll need staking. That's too much work!

Chapter 4

Berries in the Lasagna Garden

My grandmother was a berry picker, and I was her shadow. My mouth still waters at the thought of one of her biscuit-topped, wild-blackberry cobblers. Each year, before the end of fall, her pantry would be filled with jars of preserved berries, jams, and jellies. When I had children of my own, we just naturally picked berries: blackberries and red raspberries in Tennessee, blackberries in Georgia, strawberries in Florida and New Jersey, and tiny, native huckleberries and blueberries in New York.

When we purchased our inn in upstate New York, I rarely had time to pick any fruit except blueberries. When I bought the property across the road, I found all the same wild fruits plus cultivated red raspberries down by the barn. In addition, there were cultivated red currants behind the garage and gooseberries near the chicken house. I picked the currants and gooseberries faithfully, but by the time I got down to the raspberry patch, most of the fruit would be gone already. I soon saw the need to plant more cultivated berries closer to the house, where they'd be within easy reach for regular picking. Lasagna gardening gave me a way to prepare new planting areas quickly, so I could easily grow all the fruit I wanted.

Growing Berries
the Lasagna Way

Starting a berry patch is no big deal when you use the lasagna method. You'll use the same basic technique for berries as for any other crop: cover the sod with wet newspaper, then cover that with alternating layers of peat moss and other organic materials to create a bed that's about 2 feet high. Sometimes I vary the ingredients I use, depending on the crop I'm planting. Blueberries, for instance, appreciate acid soil, so I use more peat moss, pine needles, and other acidic materials for building the layers. But the important thing is not so much exactly what you use, but rather that you use whatever is plentiful in your area and easy to get. The rich, moisture-retentive soil you'll create will provide ideal growing conditions for just about any berry.

Tips and Time-Savers

Garden Sharp

Ginsu knives are sold on TV as tools to cut through frozen foods and such. I find them invaluable in the garden, especially when I'm building lasagna beds for blueberries or other crops that like lots of peat moss. I like to cut peat moss bales open near the garden site, then leave them out for a few weeks so the peat can get evenly wet before spreading it. (Cutting the peat moss itself with a knife helps it get wet quicker.) Ginsu knives are also great for cutting sod, plastic containers, cardboard, or any other material that might ruin a sharper and more expensive tool.

Give Them a Good Start. Mound a ring of extra mulch about a foot from the base of your new plant. This will help direct water to the developing roots.

A newly built lasagna bed works fine for small plants, such as strawberries, but for other berries, I build the beds in fall and let them break down over winter for spring planting. An established lasagna bed has firmer soil, so it can support larger, bushier plants. To install berry bushes, canes, or small trees, pull back the loose soil to create a shallow depression, spread the roots out, and cover them with as much soil as you have. Make a "well" around each plant to catch water, then water thoroughly and mulch generously. Anchor the plants between two to four side supports, such as sticks or pieces of stout canes; if needed, tie garden twine around the plant and supports. You can remove the supports once the plant has sent out enough roots to hold itself in place. After that, just mulch regularly to keep the soil rich and moist, and enjoy your tasty harvest!

A Bounty of Berries for Lasagna Gardens

Berries are an excellent crop for home gardeners, providing generous harvests on relatively short, easy-to-maintain plants. Once you've experienced the incredible taste of homegrown berries, you'll want lots of lasagna beds to hold them. Below are some growing tips I've learned from my experiences with a variety of berry crops—some old favorites as well as some unusual berries that are worth trying.

Fabulous Fruit Confections with Rhubarb

As I began growing and cooking more berries, harvesting rhubarb became one of the best parts of gardening. I never cared for it alone, but it was wonderful cooked with any of the other fruits I grew. Rhubarb takes on the flavor of the fruit you combine it with, so you use half as much fruit and get rhubarb's wonderful texture as a bonus. I make fresh peach/rhubarb cobblers, blackberry/rhubarb and strawberry/rhubarb pies, and endless other combinations.

The absolute best is my blueberry/rhubarb jam. We served it at breakfast for inn guests, sold it by the jar in our gift shop, and gave it as thank-you gifts to those who helped us in some way. Try it for yourself!

Rhubarb adds a pleasant tartness and texture, but the flavor and color are all blueberry. Use this jam on biscuits, muffins, or toast as you would any special jam, but also try it on ice cream, on plain cake, or as a filling for crepes. Regardless of how you use it, blueberry/rhubarb jam is a treat!

For tips on growing rhubarb, see page 61.

Blueberry/Rhubarb Jam

2 1/4 cups blueberries
2 1/4 cups finely chopped rhubarb
2 tablespoons lemon juice

7 cups sugar
2 packages fruit pectin

Crush the blueberries, then add them to the rhubarb, lemon juice, and sugar in a large kettle. Bring the mixture to a rolling boil for 1 minute. Remove from heat, add pectin, and stir well. Ladle the jam into sterile jars, seal, and process in a hot-water bath for 15 minutes. Makes 4 1/2 pints.

Blackberries

Garden blackberries, a few generations away from their wild cousins, have upright or trailing, thorny canes and produce a main crop in late July or early August. By planting a backyard berry patch, you can get loads of plump, juicy blackberries for canning, freezing, preserves, and pies.

Site and Soil. Blackberries need average, well-drained, cool, moist soil. Lasagna garden beds provide perfect conditions. I find that beds in dappled sun or partial shade produce the best-tasting berries, which grow best in Zones 3 to 9.

Planting and Care. Prepare a lasagna bed in fall for spring planting. Set the roots of the canes in a slight depression, and pull soil up around them. If you have high winds in your area, anchor the roots with a stone or heavy clumps of overturned sod. Heavy mulching takes care of keeping the soil cool, moist, and weed-free.

Getting to Know Them. Upright blackberries bear their fruit on the tips of erect canes, while trailing types bear all along their stems. Trailing types tend to sprawl if you don't trellis them.

Controlling the Canes. A double-armed T-trellis will keep both kinds of blackberries contained, so you'll have an easier time gathering your harvest.

Tips and Time-Savers

Blackberries

Start new blackberry canes by layering and pinning. Before pruning, choose a new healthy cane, and scrape a wound in the stem at the point that will touch the ground. Pin the wounded spot to the soil with a U-shaped wire pin, pile soil over the pinned stem, and cover with mulch. After several months, clip the rooted layer from the parent plant and transplant it to a new spot.

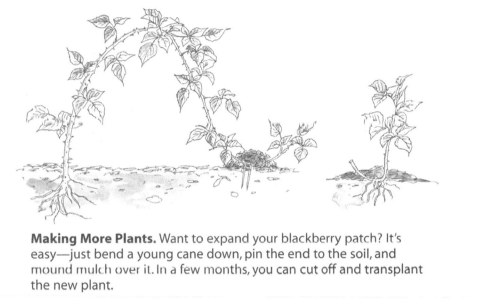

Making More Plants. Want to expand your blackberry patch? It's easy—just bend a young cane down, pin the end to the soil, and mound mulch over it. In a few months, you can cut off and transplant the new plant.

Whether you choose upright or trailing canes, they need to be contained between wires stretched between two posts. Trailing canes bear fruit up and down the stems, upright canes bear fruit at the stem tips. By keeping either kind contained between wires, you have an easier time harvesting the fruit. (It's also a good idea to wear long sleeves during harvest.)

Keep the soil around the plants weeded and well mulched. When new growth reaches 36 inches, prune off the tips to encourage branching. Fully ripe blackberry fruits are usually dull black and are easy to pull from the stems. After harvesting, prune out the canes that produced fruit.

Pat's Picks. 'Darrow' and 'Ebony King' are hardy and productive, with thorny stems. Thornless blackberry plants cost a few dollars more, but I think the easy picking makes up for the price. Look for 'Arapaho', 'Navaho', or 'Black Satin'; all three produce an early harvest on tall, upright canes.

An Experiment with Thornless Blackberries

Since thornless blackberries are not supposed to produce well north of Zone 6, I had not considered growing them until 1989. It was in the fall of that year I took one of my driving trips. The drive started in New York, through the Midwest, down South, then up the East Coast. During the trip I stopped for three days in my hometown, Crossville, Tennessee, to visit the aunts: Aunt Dorcus, Aunt Violet, and Aunt Judy. While taking a morning walk, I met an elderly woman raking and burning leaves. I stopped to ask, if I helped her rake, would she let me bag the leaves to take to Aunt Violet? After 20 years of reading about organic gardening methods, Aunt Violet at age 70 was ready to make her first mulched garden. She had no leaves to add to her compost and mulch materials, but I had just stumbled on the mother lode.

I spent the morning raking and bagging leaves. During one of our water breaks, the lady led me to the back of the house to show me her garden. It was a plot about 30 by 40 feet and gardened in the traditional tilled, bare-soil manner. She was in her eighties and, except for the tilling, cared for the garden alone. She led me past the garden to her thornless blackberry patch. The tall arching canes were growing between stout, 6-foot-high posts with two crossbars, one at the top and one

halfway down. Wire was strung and buckled tight to the crossbars, and the canes were neatly contained within the space between the strands of wire. Her harvest was amazing, and she had a nice little business selling berries during the season. I left there with a truckload of leaves and three blackberry canes.

I hauled those canes on to Georgia and up the East Coast to New York. Figuring they would not survive the harsh winters and Zone 3/4 growing conditions, I planted them in a protected area. When I say "planted," I mean I pulled back about 3 inches of soil in a lasagna garden and laid the roots in the depression. I weighted the roots down with a brick to keep the plants from blowing away, and gave them about 12 inches of mulch. The canes lived and multiplied. I moved them to a new location every year for five years—I was in the process of selling my property and wanted to take the canes with me—each time subjecting them to a bit more cold and winter winds. Every year they put out blooms and produced long, plump berries. In the fall of the sixth year, I moved them to a permanent location where they proved to be truly amazing in the amount of production. Which just goes to show that if you want to grow something bad enough, it's worth trying, even if the books tell you it won't work!

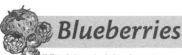

Blueberries

Highbush blueberries are one of the most rewarding investments you can make in your permanent planting scheme. Tuck single plants in foundation plantings, grow them in groups in a shrub border, or plant them out as a hedge. You'll enjoy their white flowers in spring, bountiful berries in summer, and beautiful color in fall.

Site and Soil. In a moist, well-drained, sunny spot with a pH between 4.2 and 5.0, highbush blueberries produce bumper crops, up to several quarts from each bush. When I build a lasagna bed for blueberries, I like to add lots of acidic organic materials, including peat moss, sawdust, pine needles, and wood chips. If a soil test indicates your soil is on the alkaline side, also add sulfur when you build your lasagna bed. Prepare the bed in fall for spring planting. Blueberries are usually hardy in Zones 4 to 8.

Planting and Care. Select plants that are best suited for your area; check with your extension agent for recommendations. If you buy from a mail-order nursery, you'll receive dormant shrubs that you'll need to plant right away (ideally within a few days). When buying locally, you'll have less of a selection to choose from, but the plants will be in a container or balled-and-burlapped, so you can wait a week or more to plant.

Set out your blueberries in the spring after the ground thaws or in the fall after leaves drop. To plant without digging, scrape away the soil to form a slight depression, and set the roots in the depression. (If the rootball was wrapped in burlap, make sure you untie

Tips and Time-Savers

Blueberries

My first experience with blueberries was with very old bushes. I wasn't sure they could be rejuvenated, but they were still trying to produce berries, so I decided to help them. I pruned them to the ground, covered the ground with several sheets of wet newspaper, and mulched with 6 inches of chopped oak leaves and a layer of pine needles. It took two years to get a crop, but they did come back. In six years, I was harvesting several quarts of blueberries from each bush.

My Favorite Mulch. I like to mulch my blueberries with pine needles. Besides looking nice, the needles help to keep soil pH on the acid side, so the plants thrive.

Blueberries for Beautiful Gardens

My first exposure to using blueberries as ornamentals came when I attended a meeting of my garden club at Judy Cook's house in the foothills of the Catskills. The house was at the end of a long driveway that wound through woods and old fields. As we turned in the gate for the last climb, the vista opened up and we were all spellbound. There was an unobstructed view of the stunning Shawangunk Mountains. Along one side of the driveway, Judy had planted 15 to 20 cultivated blueberry bushes. At the base of each bush was a small garden facing the drive.

After the meeting, Judy served plain cake with homemade blueberry sauce, and we heard how the Cooks had decided to plant their blueberry bushes along the drive to make picking easier. Each year they were able to fill a small freezer with their harvest. This let them enjoy their favorite fruit all year. They made pies, cobblers, jam, and sauce, and even had fruit for cereal every morning.

Back at our inn that fall, I watched the hill on the farm alongside the inn turn into a patchwork of glorious color. The most beautiful was the burgundy and magenta of frost-nipped blueberry bushes. When it was time for me to begin planting permanent foundation gardens around the inn, I knew there was a way to work blueberry bushes into the scheme as an ornamental.

I chose a plan similar to Judy's, using them as a windbreak around one side of the circular driveway. It was easy to get to the bushes to keep them pruned and to pick ripe berries. They also helped to break the force of the wind coming from the north. In the fall, they brought fabulous color to our landscape.

A Welcoming Sight.
Try growing blueberries along your driveway. You'll enjoy their beauty as well as their abundant harvests. Plus, they are withineasy reach for picking!

and loosen the burlap.) Fill in around the roots up to the crown (the point where the roots join the stem) and water thoroughly. Mulch generously; I like to use pine needles. Make a well of the mulch surrounding the base of the bush to catch and direct water to the roots.

To keep your blueberries producing well, prune off any dead, weak, or diseased wood each year in late fall, winter, or early spring. Feeding is simple: Scatter a mixture of bloodmeal, bonemeal, and rock phosphate around each plant in spring.

Blueberries can vary somewhat in "blueness" when ripe, so taste-test a few berries before harvesting. Gently twist the berries from the stems; they should come off with light finger pressure.

Red Currants

Red currants were growing on my property when I bought it, and I didn't know anything about them until I picked the first time. They produce beautiful fruit and need little care—that old planting had been there many years without anyone doing anything with it. I pruned deadwood and mulched to keep weeds out. That's it!

Site and Soil. Currants are a cool-climate crop, flourishing in Zones 3 to 7. They can grow in full sun or partial shade, and they thrive in the rich, moist soil of a lasagna bed.

Planting and Care. Red currants give you an almost carefree crop of berries, sometimes producing the same year you plant if you set out two-year-old canes in spring. Simply scoop out a hole with your hands or a trowel, remove the plant from its pot, set the roots into the hole, and pull the soil back around the roots. Water thoroughly, then add a generous layer of mulch. Prune out dead stems at ground level any time you see them. To har-

Tips and Time-Savers

Red Currants

One of the first fruits to ripen, red currants are ready at the same time you pick the first stalks of rhubarb. I include currants on the list of fruits I mix with rhubarb for jams, pies, and cobblers.

vest, pick off entire fruit clusters when the berries are fully red. Red currants are great for preserves and juices.

Pat's Picks. Jelly and jam makers love 'Red Lake' and 'Wilder'.

When to Pick? You'll know your red currants are ripe when the berries are tart and shiny red. They make beautiful jellies and jams.

Elderberries

Jelly and wine makers can never have enough of this undemanding fruit. Elderberries are rich in taste, as well as vitamin C, iron, and natural sugars. The plants themselves are also beautiful, with large, umbrella-shaped clusters of fragrant, white blossoms. Their sweet scent attracts hummingbirds and butterflies in droves. The berries hang down in loose clusters and are a favorite food for more than a hundred species of birds. The leafy growth also provides a desirable nesting area for many birds, including warblers, grosbeaks, and goldfinches.

Site and Soil. In the wild, elders are often found in the wet soil along streams and ponds. They adapt well in the acid soils found in mountain regions, as well as in the sandy soils of the South and West. In the garden, elders

Gathering Your Harvest. Elderberries are wonderful for making jams, jellies, pies, and wine. To harvest, simply cut the entire cluster from the main stem.

Easy Elderberries. If you're looking for a small tree that produces beautiful flowers, provides a good crop of fruit, and attracts a wide variety of birds, this is the plant for you!

Tips and Time-Savers

Elderberries

It's nice to have one or two elderberry plants nearby rather than hunting for them in the wild. My first experience with them was a seedling that came up by itself in my big perennial garden. Within a year it had grown to small-tree size, producing a visual feast when in full flower, followed by a large harvest of berries. Four years later, I pruned the plant vigorously, hoping to keep it small, and it responded by growing even larger. It grew to over 12 feet in height!

perform best when located in the moist, well-drained soil of a lasagna garden in full sun. American elder *(Sambucus canadensis)* is hardy in Zones 3 to 9.

Planting and Care. Elderberries are so easy to grow, they may even plant themselves in your garden if you live near an area where they are growing naturally! Of course, you don't have to wait for that—you can buy plants and set them out in an established lasagna bed. Pull back the loose soil, set the roots in the hole, and pull the soil back to cover the roots. Water thoroughly, then mulch to keep the soil cool and moist. Elderberries don't need much pruning; just trim out any dead stems at ground level whenever you see them. The berries are usually ripe in late August or early September. When they turn purple-black, taste-test for sweetness.

Pick for a Purpose. Harvest your gooseberries when they are green to yellow for a tart flavor, or let them ripen to pink or red for a sweeter flavor.

Gooseberries

Deciduous, thorny shrubs with arching canes, gooseberries begin to show bud early in the spring. Putting in a gooseberry patch is easy, and it doesn't require much time or effort to get years of tasty fruits for desserts, pies, and preserves.

Site and Soil. Gooseberries grow best in cool climates, in sun or light shade. They are not fussy about soil conditions or pH, but they grow best in sun in the rich, well-drained soil of an established lasagna bed. Gooseberries grow best in Zones 3 to 6.

When I bought my farm there were old gooseberry plants behind the chicken house. I took cuttings from them and made a new patch near other berry beds, preparing the soil as always by smothering the grass with wet newspaper. When I built the lasagna layers, I avoided using high-nitrogen ingredients,

such as grass clippings and barn litter, but I did give them extra dressings of wood ashes for potassium, and my plants seemed pleased with the results.

Planting and Care. Set out gooseberries in spring or fall. Pull back the soil to create a depression, set the roots in the hole, then replace the soil to cover the roots. Water thoroughly. Keep the ground covered with mulch so the soil stays cool and moist. Prune out any dead stems as soon as you spot them.

Tips and Time-Savers

Gooseberries

Gooseberries produce with little or no care for as long as 30 years, so make sure you choose the planting site carefully—they'll be there a while!

Gooseberries ripen in a range of colors. Those best for cooking or processing are usually ready in early summer; taste-test before picking sweeter "dessert" types in midsummer. Wear gloves to protect your hands from the thorny stems!

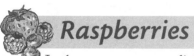

Raspberries

Is there a taste more divine than a just-picked, juicy, ripe raspberry? Is there a more fragile or expensive fruit? Wild raspberries have a short picking season, so they are easy to miss, and they tend to be small and seedy. Happily, it's easy to get a generous harvest of plump, sweet berries—just plant a patch of cultivated canes near your house for easy picking!

Site and Soil. Both red and black raspberries are hardy in Zones 3 to 9. They need rich soil, good drainage, and plenty of light, so plant them in an established lasagna bed with at least six hours of full sun. Both are susceptible to soilborne diseases that affect plants in the nightshade family, so pick a bed where eggplant, peppers, potatoes, or tomatoes have not been grown for three years.

Planting and Care. Prepare the bed in the fall by smothering grass and weeds with thick pads of wet newspaper. Cover with layers of organic soil amendments to 24 inches high. Use a good supply of compost for some of the layers.

Plant your raspberry canes in early spring, spacing them at least 4 feet apart. Pull back the soil to create a deep depression, so you can set the roots 2 inches deeper than they were growing in the nursery. Pull the soil back around the roots, set a few stones or bricks around the base of the plant to weigh down the roots, then prune the canes back to just above ground level. Water thoroughly, then cover the soil with at least 6 inches of mulch.

Through the summer, add more mulch as needed, and add a scattering of a general organic fertilizer. I like to pinch or cut off all blooms the first year. You'll have to wait until the second year for your first harvest, but in the meantime, the plants are putting their energy into good root growth.

Try a T-Trellis. A sturdy trellis will help contain your raspberry canes as they grow, making picking and pruning easier. It's best to install the trellis before planting, so you don't have to disturb the plants later.

Tips and Time-Savers

Raspberries

There are two distinct differences in red and black raspberries: the way they bear fruit and their growth habits. Red raspberries bear fruit at the tips of the canes; black raspberries bear on side branches. As for growth habit, red raspberries form suckers, which make clumps that you can divide. Black raspberries don't form suckers but spread by tip-layering; their arching branches produce roots (and then new plants) where they touch the ground.

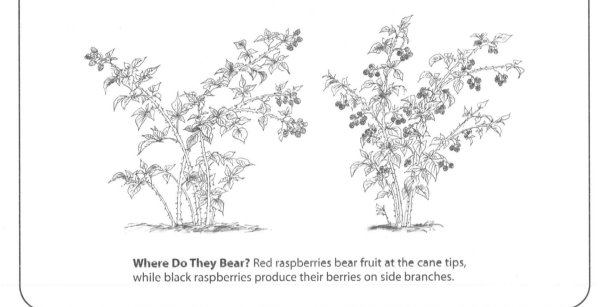

Where Do They Bear? Red raspberries bear fruit at the cane tips, while black raspberries produce their berries on side branches.

Ripe red raspberries range from light to dark red; black raspberries change from red to purple to almost black. Taste-test a few berries before picking more than a handful. After harvesting, prune out all of the canes that produced fruit.

Watch for aphids (small insects that cluster on shoot tips, causing curled leaves) and spider mites (tiny spiderlike creatures that feed on the underside of leaves, causing yellow stippling on the upper side). Spray with insecticidal soap if you see signs of infestation.

Pat's Picks. 'Heritage' sets red berries on first-year stems, so you can mow the entire patch in late fall or late winter and still get a crop each year. 'Mammoth Red' has thornless canes that make picking the large red fruit a pleasure. 'Black Hawk' is a dependable producer with firm black berries that are good for canning.

Strawberries

A home berry garden just isn't complete without a strawberry patch. With the lasagna method, it's easy to create a new bed and set out your plants all in the same day. For just a few hours' work, you can enjoy years of flavorful, juicy berries at the peak of ripeness.

Site and Soil. Strawberries grow best in full sun and rich soil with a pH of 6.5 to 7.0. Build your lasagna bed with generous amounts of compost, plus some scatterings of bonemeal over the layers, to get your plants off to a good start. Hardiness varies, so check catalog descriptions to find cultivars that are adapted to your climate.

Making Their Bed. I like to set out my strawberries in a wide bed, with the plants 4 inches apart. That leaves plenty of room for runners to fill in the bed.

Pretty and Productive. Strawberries are gratifyingly easy to grow, and they're beautiful too! By choosing your plants carefully, you can enjoy their fruits through most of the growing season.

Planting and Care. If you have a newly constructed lasagna bed, pull the layers apart just enough to stick in a plant, press the bed ingredients firmly around the roots, and water. In an established lasagna bed, just push the loose soil aside and put in a plant. Apply compost-rich mulch as you plant and continue to mulch as long as you have a strawberry patch. (Be careful not to cover the crown with mulch, or you will lose some plants to rot.) If a weed or patch of grass shows itself, get it out and apply more mulch. A strawberry bed prepared and planted this way will rejuvenate itself and continue bearing for years.

With this system, you don't have to worry about cutting back runners to keep rows open. There's no heavy weeding, and no watering except in times of drought. Mulch with rich compost, and broadcast bonemeal over the top of the bed each year, and there's no need to

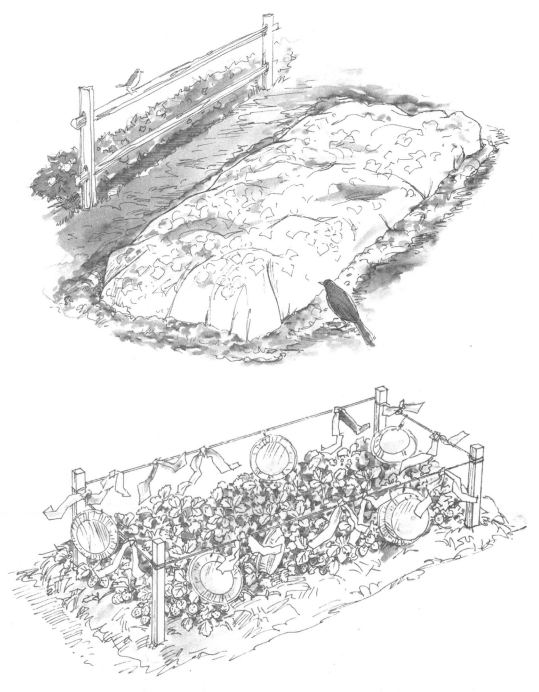

Guarding Your Harvest. Floating row cover keeps all kinds of critters out of your strawberry patch. If you just need to repel birds, try outlining the bed with stakes and string and hanging aluminum pie tins and/or cloth strips from the string.

Alpine Strawberries: A Taste Sensation

I once noticed a dozen fraise des bois *(alpine strawberry) plants listed at $36 in a mail-order catalog and wondered who would pay such a price for strawberry plants. Sure, they had a French name, but, really? I dismissed the thought as one would anything they can't imagine being true.*

Some years later, a friend gave me six tiny plants labeled fraise des bois, *and the memory of that catalog ad came back to me. I might have composted such puny plants if they had not had their label. That label set a dollar sign flashing in the back of my thrifty brain. Instead of tossing them, I planted them. Within a short time, I had six small, compact, bushy plants forming a short border in my herb garden outside the inn. They set dozens of white blossoms and bore tiny fruits that were so exquisite there is nothing to compare them with. They bloomed very early and continued until snow fell. I went out each morning and picked a handful to top my cereal or just stopped to browse.*

In the last 17 years, I have divided the descendants of those original six plants many times. They have outlined herb and vegetable gardens, marched down the edges of many stone paths, and been potted up and sold for profit. Alpine strawberries do not send out runners but propagate by seed or division.

They have few needs but like well-drained soil and mulch to keep the soil moist and cool. (I use a mulch of rich compost and cover that with a decorative mulch of buckwheat hulls.) Other than that, there's no work—just pure enjoyment!

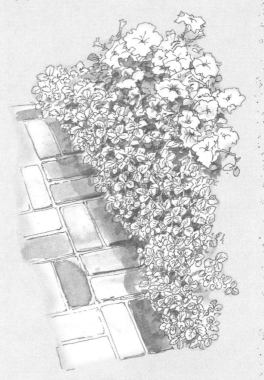

An Edible Edging. Alpine strawberry plants produce bushy little clumps that look great edging a path or border. They'll have fruits and flowers at the same time.

worry about extra fertilizer. If you install a large bed without paths, though, you need a way to access the middle. When you begin picking, pick from the outside of the bed first by reaching in as far as you can. When you are ready to do the middle, pull the leaves aside to allow you to step into the garden. Pick all around yourself, then stand up, turn, and pick around yourself again.

Strawberries benefit from having the foliage cut back after harvest. Strawberry

Tips and Time-Savers

Strawberries

Strawberries produce dense, leafy growth that provides a welcoming resting site for snakes. If you think you might have snakes in your patch, use a long-handled tool (an old broom handle is just right) to brush over the tops of your plants several times, in all directions. If you don't see any snakes leaving the bed, there probably aren't any. If you are still worried, don't pick from the middle of the bed.

farmers mow or burn off the foliage, but I like to use a gas-powered string trimmer to cut the old foliage back. By holding it just above the bed and moving it over the top of the bed, I trim just the upright leaves.

Pat's Picks. To get a longer harvest, buy two or three different disease-resistant cultivars that mature at different times. Some will ripen early in the season, some in midseason, and some late in the season. For a long harvest of Junebearers, which produce a large crop all at once, I like to plant a combination of 'Earliglow' (which sets and ripens fruit very early), 'Guardian' (a midseason ripener), and 'Sparkle' (a later-maturing cultivar). For a harvest spread out from spring to fall, plant three cultivars of everbearing strawberries that mature at different times; I like 'Ozark Beauty', 'Tribute', and 'Tristar'.

Weekend Gardeners. Using floating row cover is one of the ways weekend gardeners can have some of the fruit of their labors. By keeping your strawberry bed covered, you keep out wildlife, especially birds. Simply lay a floating row cover over the entire bed; it's easier to handle than netting. Water and sunlight can get in, but the critters can't. (Remove the cover after harvest.) If you don't have row cover, pound wood or metal stakes in the corners of the bed and connect them with string. Hang bright or shiny items, such as pieces of cloth, reflective tape, or aluminum pans, to scare the birds away.

Flower Gardening

At the opposite end of the spectrum from "what's-for-dinner?" vegetable gardening, flower gardening is food for the soul. The seed for a flower gardener was sown in the fertile field of my imagination at an early age. Even as my hardworking grandmother struggled to keep food on the table, she always took time to plant a 2-foot border of mixed flower seeds around her vegetable garden. She left me with indelible memories: posing for a photograph, standing in the front yard, admiring the enormous bloom on a hydrangea; picking fresh bouquets from her annual border and then putting them on the dinner table in a Mason jar; holding her apron up to form a container where she dropped seeds from the border for next year's garden; stooping to smell a bloom on the pink shrub rose next to the well.

During the busy years of work and raising a family, I thought I would never have time for a garden that was purely for pleasure. At age 55, I began a new journey, one that took me to a place where I had the time and energy to indulge myself. By the time I arrived at that point, I had mastered the art of lasagna gardening. Planning was still the same—picking the spot, designing the size and shape, and deciding what would go where. The difference was the amount of work involved and the time it took to make the garden. It was far easier and took less time than I had imagined because I didn't have to lift the sod, dig, or till. It was still a lot of work, but a breeze compared to traditional gardening!

Simple Steps to a Lasagna Flower Garden

Flower gardening the lasagna way isn't much different than creating any other kind of garden. The first step is to take a good look at what you have to work with—your climate, soil, and available space—then figure out where and how big you want your garden to be. (For a refresher on site selection, turn back to "Getting Started" on page 3.)

Next, make your step-by-step plan to get the job done: decide which beds you want to create right away, and which can wait for following years. It's easy to overdo it, as lasagna gardens are so easy to build, but remember—

you'll still need to take care of them! It can also be a challenge to find the plants you need to fill these new gardens all at once without going broke. It's smart to start with one or two beds the first year, then expand as you gather more materials and plants. Overall, the most important part of successful flower gardening is patience—to do the groundwork, put your plan into action, and wait for your plantings to do their stuff!

Laying Out Your New Garden

If you're creating square or rectangular flowerbeds, use stakes and string to mark the outlines. Adjust them as needed to make sure the beds are the size and shape you want before you start edging them and building the layers. If you're making a bed with a curved outline, a 100-foot, or longer, garden hose is the best tool: It's flexible and easy to move around until the design is pleasing. Once you have what looks right from the ground, go in the house and look at the outline from an upstairs window. After all, if you're going to

Shape It Up. To lay out your garden's shape, outline the area with stakes and string (for straight lines) or a garden hose (for curving lines). Use a funnel of sand to mark the outline, then remove the stakes and string or hose.

the effort of putting in a flower garden, you want to enjoy it from the house as well as close-up!

While string or a hose works great for shaping the outline, it can get in the way when you start building the bed, so I like to redraw the outline using a funnel of sand. Hold your finger under the opening of the funnel while you fill it with sand. Remove your finger and move along the outline to leave a line of sand to use as a cutting guide. (If you don't have any sand handy, you could use flour instead to mark the line. It's a little tricky to get the flour to flow evenly out of a funnel, though, so you might want to pour it from your hand along the string line or hose.) Once the line is marked, remove the string or hose.

I like my flower gardens to look neat, so my next step is to remove a 4- to 6-inch-wide strip of sod around the perimeter of each bed. I keep this strip mulched but unplanted, so it forms a clean, dark outline that keeps the beds looking tidy. It also makes mowing easier, as I can run the wheel of the mower inside the bed to trim the edge without running over the flowers. To make an edging strip, use a sharp-pointed shovel to cut along the sand line. (When the ground is too hard for the shovel, or I have to go over tree roots, I use the blade side of a mattock.) Make another cut 4 to 6 inches out from the line. Once both lines are cut, go back and cut out sections of sod. (I usually take them out in 1-foot-long sections.) These sod strips come out clean, leaving a trench around the perimeter. Set the strips aside on a tarpaulin, then add them to your compost pile or use them to build up the lasagna layers. Now you're ready to cover the planting area with pads of wet newspaper and start layering on the organic materials.

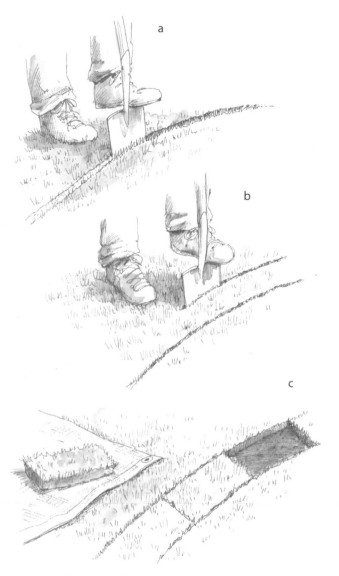

Cutting an Edge. There's nothing like a sharp edge to give a flower garden a finished look. I like to create my edging strips even before I start building the lasagna layers. *(a)* Start by cutting along the sand outline with your shovel. *(b)* Next, cut another outline 4 to 6 inches out from the first line. *(c)* Cut the strip into 1-foot sections and lift them out; set them on a tarp for later use.

Filling the Space

Once the layers are complete, you can plant right away, cover it with black plastic and let it "cook" for a few months, or allow it to break down over winter for spring planting. Whichever you choose, planting is easy—just pull back the mulch layers or soil with your hands, set the roots in the depression, and pull the mulch or soil back around the roots. Water thoroughly to encourage good root growth.

Unless you're lucky enough to have an unlimited budget, finding enough perennials to fill even a medium-size bed can be a challenge. Consider buying just a few larger plants, then add divisions from perennials already growing in other parts of your garden. Annuals—either from transplants or from seed sown directly in the garden—make great fillers while you're waiting for your perennials to expand.

Keeping the Garden Growing

Every year, I like to cut a clean edge around my gardens (and usually end up adding a couple of inches to the perimeter of the beds at the same time!). Lay the sod strips on the garden, grass-side down, to help build better soil. Other than that, lasagna beds don't need a lot of maintenance—just regular additions of mulch to keep the soil covered. Each spring, I empty my compost bins and spread the

Tips and Time-Savers

Keep a Visual Garden Record

It's smart to regularly photograph your garden from all angles, starting at planting time. Besides giving you something to look at over winter, the pictures will help you remember what you've planted and what you might want to replace or move.

The Part-Time Flower Garden

Few of us have all the time we'd like for working in our gardens, but that doesn't mean we can't have beautiful flowers. The trick is to ignore those traditional "rules" for starting a garden. Forget about spending days stripping off the sod and double-digging the soil: When you garden the lasagna way, you can create and plant a whole bed or border in a single weekend!

While any of the five gardens in this chapter can get by without much fussing from you, the "Perennial Garden" (starting on page 156) and the "Self-Sowing Garden" (starting on page 158) are particularly good choices for minimal maintenance.

contents on the gardens. When I mow grass in summer, I add 1 to 2 inches of clippings to the bed. And each fall, I mow the fallen leaves and add 4 to 6 inches of chopped leaf mulch to the garden. Remember, the important thing isn't so much *what* you add, but that you regularly add *some* kind of organic mulch—whatever you have easily available.

A Gallery of Gardens

The following five "theme" plantings are some of the gardens I have created with my easy lasagna method. They are not lists of plants compiled from research, but actual, existing gardens and the real plants that still grow there. I hope my experiences will inspire you to create your own beautiful, easy lasagna gardens!

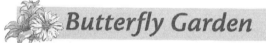

Butterfly Garden

People aren't the only creatures who enjoy gardens: Flowers provide a wealth of food and shelter for a wide range of wildlife as well. While there's no doubt that many insects play an important role in keeping a garden healthy, there's one particular group—namely, butterflies—that earns a special place of honor just for their beauty.

Plant any kind of flower garden, and chances are you'll see a few butterflies from time to time. But if you want to encourage a larger number and wider variety of them, it's fun to create a garden packed full of proven butterfly-attractant plants. Happily, many of the annuals and perennials that gardeners love are equally pleasing to butterflies, so you can all enjoy your beautiful butterfly garden.

Tips and Time-Savers

Planning Your Butterfly Garden

Flowers are certainly an important part of a butterfly garden, as they provide food for nectar-seeking adult butterflies. But to attract and keep the widest variety of butterflies, it's important to consider their other needs as well, such as sites for egg laying and suitable food for the developing larvae. Milkweeds (Asclepias spp.), for instance, are a vital food source for monarch caterpillars, while parsley is a favorite of black swallowtail larvae. Sure, your plants' leaves may end up looking rather chewed-up, but it's a natural part of butterfly gardening!

When I created my butterfly-attracting lasagna garden, I used plants I already had, and I was pleased with the butterflies that appeared. If your aim is to attract a particular type of butterfly, you'll need to do a bit of homework to find out its favorite plants. A field guide is a good place to start. Look for a book with information about the plants that caterpillars eat, the plants from which the adults take nectar, and the drinking, sunning, and other unique habits of the adults. Detailed, full-color illustrations of both the caterpillar and adult stages, and information about the geographical area in which the insects appear, are also valuable.

Spring and summer butterfly-watching expeditions in your neighborhood are a good way to establish your own checklist of local species. Use your list to develop a custom-tailored lasagna garden of favored food and host plants. A local natural history museum, college entomology department, or butterfly club can give you more pointers.

The Beginning

In the order of things, making a garden to attract butterflies seemed the right place to start when I began moving my gardens from our inn to my home across the road. I measured and staked out this first garden in the hay field next to my house. I covered the 8-by-12-foot space with thick layers of wet newspaper, then covered them with peat moss.

Back at the inn, I dismantled the formal garden that had been my first showcase for lasagna gardening and moved the plants across the road. As I wasn't yet ready to plant the butterfly garden, I "heeled-in" the clumps on an area of wet newspaper placed on top of the sod, then covered the roots with a mixture of peat moss and grass clippings. After wetting the area thoroughly, I piled wood chips on the rootballs to keep the moisture in.

Next, I removed the built-up soil from the old lasagna garden by scooping it up with a straight-edged spade to keep the area level with the surrounding grassy lot. Moving one wheelbarrow load of soil at a time, I traveled back and forth across the road until the original garden had disappeared. (The wood-chip paths were still there, so I raked them up and used them for mulch in other gardens.)

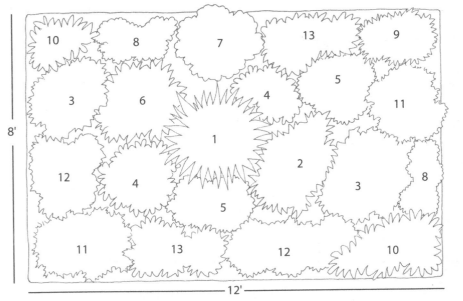

1. 'Red Magic' daylily
2. Spike gayfeather
3. Coneflower
4. 'Autumn Joy' sedum
5. Yarrows
6. Purple coneflower
7. Prairie mallow
8. Oregano thyme
9. Maiden pinks
10. Ajuga
11. Orange cosmos
12. Marigolds
13. Petunia

A Simple Butterfly Garden. This plot plan shows the layout of my butterfly garden. There are many other wonderful butterfly plants I could have included, but I used what I had on hand, and the results were terrific!

To build my new butterfly garden, I alternated the soil with layers of peat moss, grass clippings, chopped leaves, compost, and spoiled hay. When the beds were 24 inches high, I was ready to plant, so I sorted through my inventory to find herbs and flowers that would attract butterflies. After setting out the perennials, I sowed seed or set transplants of colorful annuals around them to give the garden a full look the first year. ("Plants for a Butterfly Garden" on page 134 lists the plants that I included; there are many others that work well too.) It certainly was a sight to see, with bright color from the masses of blooms as well as the many butterflies that came to feed!

Aftercare

This gorgeous garden didn't need any different care than my other lasagna gardens—just regular additions of mulch to keep the soil in top shape. I did have to replace one plant: a butterfly bush that didn't come back after the winter. But other than that, the perennials grew and thrived, getting better each season. After a few years, I stopped adding the annuals, just letting their self-sown seedlings fill the ever-decreasing gaps between the clumps of perennials. Beside attracting beautiful butterflies, this garden also hosted butterfly moths, hummingbirds, and a bevy of other interesting birds and insects.

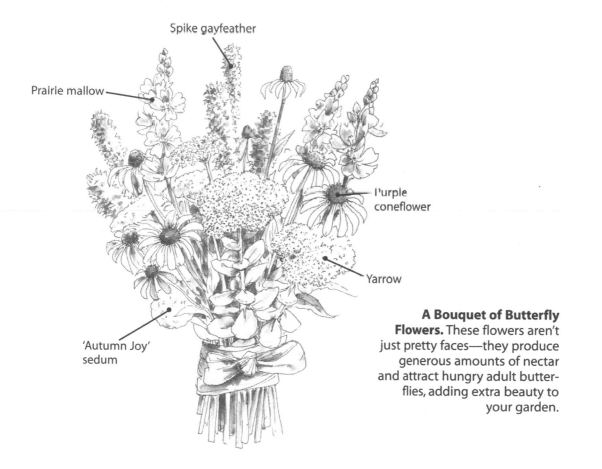

Spike gayfeather

Prairie mallow

Purple coneflower

Yarrow

'Autumn Joy' sedum

A Bouquet of Butterfly Flowers. These flowers aren't just pretty faces—they produce generous amounts of nectar and attract hungry adult butterflies, adding extra beauty to your garden.

Pat's Picks

PLANTS FOR A BUTTERFLY GARDEN

Here's a rundown of the annuals and perennials that I included in my butterfly garden with good results. There are many others to choose from, depending on where you live. To learn more about what the butterflies in your area like to feed on, check field guides or ask at your local nature center.

Name	Height	Notes
Yarrows (*Achillea* spp.)	3 to 4 ft.	Large, flat flower heads in a wide range of colors (including yellow, rust, red, pink, and white) in summer. Full sun. Zones 3 to 9.
Ajuga (*Ajuga reptans*)	6 in.	Short spikes of blue flowers in late spring or early summer. Full sun to shade. Zones 3 to 9.
Butterfly bush (*Buddleia davidii*)	6 to 8 ft.	Dense clusters of purple, pink, or white flowers in summer. It wasn't hardy in my Zone 4 garden, but it's a great addition to a butterfly garden in warmer areas. Full sun. Zones 6 to 8.
Orange cosmos (*Cosmos sulphureus*)	2 to 3 ft.	Broad-petaled, daisylike blooms through summer; usually bright orange but may instead be yellow or red. Full sun. Annual.
Maiden pinks (*Dianthus* spp.)	1 ft.	Red, pink, or white flowers in summer. Mine was a red-flowered one just labeled *"Dianthus."* Full sun. Zones 4 to 8.
Purple coneflower (*Echinacea purpurea*)	2 ft.	Daisylike summer flowers with a large center cone and swept-back, rose-pink petals. Full sun. Zones 3 to 8.

Name	Height	Notes
'Red Magic' daylily (*Hemerocallis* 'Red Magic')	3 ft.	Trumpet-shaped red flowers with yellow throats bloom in summer. Full sun to light shade. Zones 4 to 9.
Spike gayfeather (*Liatris spicata*)	2 to 4 ft.	Dense, fuzzy spikes of tiny red-violet or white flowers in summer. Full sun. Zones 3 to 9.
Petunia (*Petunia* × *hybrida*)	1 ft.	Trumpet-shaped flowers in a range of colors through summer. Full sun to partial shade. Annual.
Coneflowers (*Rudbeckia* spp.)	2 to 3 ft.	Golden-yellow summer daisies with prominent brown or green center cones. Full sun. Zones 3 to 9.
Sedums (*Sedum* spp.)	4 to 24 in.	Clusters of starry red, pink, white, or yellow flowers in spring or summer. I used 2-ft. 'Autumn Joy' sedum (*Sedum* 'Autumn Joy') plus an assortment of low-growing types. Full sun to light shade. Zones 3 to 9.
Prairie mallows (*Sidalcea* spp.)	2 to 4 ft.	Shell pink flowers like miniature hollyhocks in summer. Full sun to light shade. Zones 4 to 8.
Marigolds (*Tagetes* spp.)	6 to 36 in.	Flat or ruffled flowers from summer into fall in shades of yellow, orange, and red. Full sun. Annual.
Oregano thyme (*Thymus* 'Oregano')	10 in.	Clusters of tiny, light purple flowers in early summer over oregano-scented foliage. Full sun. Zones 4 to 9.

Edible Flower Garden

Whether you have a tiny lot or a large property, you have room for edible flowers. Even a single pot of nasturtiums or pansies can provide enough blooms for a special salad or pretty garnish. But if you enjoy preparing and serving food that is both tasty and beautiful, why not indulge yourself in a whole garden full of edible flowers? Once you find out how fun it is to use them, you'll be glad you did!

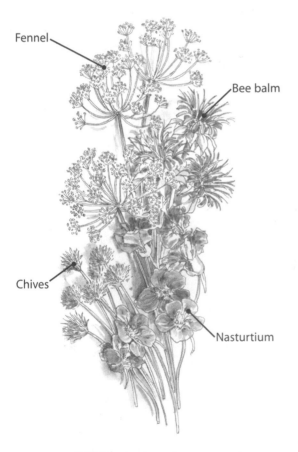

Fennel

Bee balm

Chives

Nasturtium

Pretty Edibles. You may be surprised to discover how many common flowers are edible as well as beautiful. For safety's sake, pick only from plants you know are safe, and never harvest from plants that have been sprayed with pesticides.

Planting My Edible Flower Garden

My inspiration for planting an edible flower garden was my close association with one of the first ladies of edible flowers, Cathy Barash. Cathy was in the thick of writing and photographing her book, *Edible Flowers—from Garden to Palate,* and needed lots of subjects. Plus, I needed lots of edible flowers to feed groups coming to see the gardens.

The site for this garden was the 8-by-12-foot area where I had "heeled-in" all the plants from our inn (as described in "The Beginning" on page 132). The newspaper and the first 4-inch layer of soil amendments were in place, so I could start building the bed as soon as I moved the plants. I didn't build up to the full 24 inches this time, but only about 12 inches, since I was in a hurry to plant.

I began in the center with a clump of the common tawny daylily *(Hemerocallis fulva).* Next to it, I placed a pale yellow hybrid that only grew to half the commoner's height but had flowers the size of salad plates. At opposite corners I planted large clumps of chives and bright yellow calendula *(Calendula officinalis).* Between the chives and calendula on one end of the bed, I left space for nasturtium; on the other end, I left room for lemon-scented signet marigold *(Tagetes tenuifolia).* I used pansies

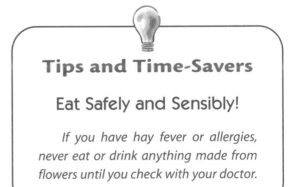

Tips and Time-Savers

Eat Safely and Sensibly!

If you have hay fever or allergies, never eat or drink anything made from flowers until you check with your doctor.

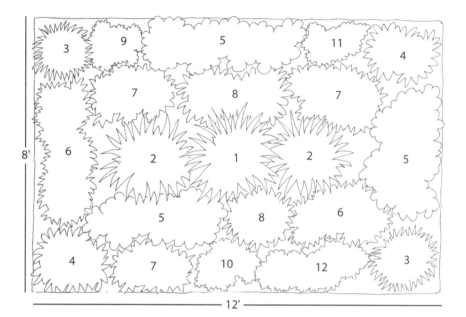

1. Tawny daylily
2. Yellow hybrid daylily
3. Chives
4. Calendula
5. Nasturtium
6. Signet marigold
7. Pansy
8. Sage
9. Common thyme
   (*Thymus vulgaris*)
10. Lemon thyme
    (*T. × citriodorus*)
11. Oregano thyme
    (*T. 'Oregano'*)
12. Caraway thyme
    (*T. herba-barona*)

An Easy Edible Flower Garden. If you like to cook and enjoy experimenting with new tastes and garnishes, I definitely recommend creating a garden, such as this one, just for edible flowers. While all of the flowers in this garden are safe to eat, not all are especially flavorful. I like to include some, such as daylilies, pansy, and signet marigold, just for their bright flowers—they make great garnishes!

(*Viola × wittrockiana*) wherever there was extra space for additional color. Plants of culinary sage filled out the middle "zone" of the bed, and an assortment of thymes hung over the edges.

Of course, these are just a sampling of the many wonderful edible flowers you can grow and enjoy. For more ideas, see "Plants for an Edible Flower Garden" on page 138. To expand on this theme, include vegetables with attractive leaves, blooms, and/or fruits for a beautiful blend of veggies, herbs, and flowers. Some ideas to get you started include red leaf lettuces, yellow- or purple-podded bush beans, red-stemmed Swiss chard, all kinds of peppers, red cabbage, tomatoes, and purple-leaved basil—just to name a few!

Using Edible Flowers Safely

Some commonsense rules apply when you're using edible flowers. First, eat only those you *know* are safe; don't be tempted to experiment! Eat the petals only, not the centers, and only in small quantities. Also, use only flowers you have grown yourself, without chemicals. (It's far better to have a few bugs—they are easy to shake or wash off—than to worry about pesticide residue.) Do not eat flowers that come from a florist, nursery, or garden center, since they may have been grown with chemicals. And if you are served edible flowers in a restaurant, don't eat them—they might not have followed these rules.

PLANTS FOR AN EDIBLE FLOWER GARDEN

Many flowers that are safe to eat have little or no flavor. I feel it's enough that they look so good. But for those who feel flowers in food must add something to the taste, I have a short list of "tasty flowers." Unless otherwise noted, all of these grow well in a sunny lasagna garden.

Name	Height	Notes
Anise hyssop (*Agastache foeniculum*)	3 ft.	Deep lilac flowers with a light taste of licorice in summer. Add them to your favorite butter cookie recipe. Zones 4 to 9.
Garlic (*Allium sativum* and *A. ophioscorodon*)	3 ft.	Each bulb produces a single curled flower stem in late spring. Once the flower bud is formed, cut the stem just above the leaves. The bud and stem have a milder taste of garlic than the cloves but can be used in the same way. Drop the entire bud and stem into soups, sauces, and stir-fry for a hint of garlic; remove before serving. Or cut the flower from the stem and julienne for adding to salads. The curled stem and flower also make an attractive garnish. Zones 3 to 9.
Chives (*Allium schoenoprasum*)	1 ft.	Lavender-pink pom-poms in early spring; harvest just when coming out of bud. The onion flavor is good in salads, stir-fry, vinegar, and salad dressings. Use the whole pom-pom for strong onion flavor or break it into florets for a delicate flavor. Zones 3 to 9.
Garlic chives (*Allium tuberosum*)	30 in.	Flat heads of white florets in late summer. Separate the florets and use for a mild garlic flavor that's especially good with lamb, veal, chicken, and seafood. Or sprinkle onto salads for flavor and garnish. Zones 3 to 9.
Dill (*Anethum graveolens*)	30 in.	Tiny yellow flowers in umbrella-like heads in summer. Pull the flowers off the head and toss into salads, especially potato salad, for a light licorice flavor. Annual.
Borage (*Borago officinalis*)	2 to 3 ft.	Starry blue flowers in summer. Their flavor is a bit like cucumber; sprinkle them onto salads as a garnish. My favorite use is to float them in punch. Annual.

Name	Height	Notes
Mustards (*Brassica* spp.)	2 to 4 ft.	Clusters of small yellow flowers in spring or summer. Add to salads for a spicy bite, or use as an edible garnish. Annual or biennial (Zones 2 to 9).
Summer squash (*Cucurbita pepo* var. *melopepo*)	to 3 ft.	Large, trumpet-shaped yellow flowers in summer. Best used as a receptacle for fillings or dipped in batter and fried. Zucchini is the preferred plant for blossoms. I like to use both male and female flowers: males for stuffing and females (with the small fruit at the base) for frying. Annual.
Arugula (*Eruca vesicaria*)	12 to 18 in.	Clusters of small white flowers in summer. The blooms add a spicy taste to salads. Annual.
Fennel (*Foeniculum vulgare*)	4 to 5 ft.	Small yellow flowers in umbrella-like heads in summer. Pull them off the heads before using. Their mild anise flavor is particularly good with cauliflower and chicken. Usually perennial in Zones 6 to 9; self-sows readily even in colder areas.
Sweet woodruff (*Galium odoratum*)	10 in.	Clusters of small white flowers in spring. They have a sweet smell and a nutty-vanilla flavor. Use in May wine and in custard. Prefers partial shade. Zones 3 to 9.
Sunflower (*Helianthus annuus*)	4 to 6 ft.	Dark-centered, daisylike flowers in summer. But instead of waiting until they open, harvest the buds when they are still small. Blanch, then bread and fry them; they taste like artichokes. Annual.
Bee balm (*Monarda didyma*)	3 ft.	Whorls of red flowers in summer. Pick the florets off the heads; their flavor is citrusy-minty. They look great in salads, but my favorite use is to chop them into softened butter. (Place the finished butter on wax paper, form it into tubes, then freeze for winter use as a spread on warm bread or melted over vegetables.) Zones 4 to 9.

(continued)

PLANTS FOR AN EDIBLE FLOWER GARDEN—CONTINUED

Name	Height	Notes
Basil (*Ocimum basilicum*)	18 to 24 in.	Spikes of small white flowers in summer. While it's usually a good idea to pinch out the tops of basil plants when they begin to set buds to encourage leafy growth, I allow a few flower spikes to form and enjoy their beauty and flavor. Their spicy flavor is good in soups, chowders, salads, pasta, and rice. Annual.
Greek oregano (*Origanum heracleoticum*)	1 to 2 ft.	Clusters of small white to pale pink flowers in summer. The blooms taste much like the leaves; use with veal, salads, and vegetables. Zones 4 to 9.
Sweet marjoram (*Origanum majorana*)	18 in.	Clusters of purplish red flowers in summer. A favorite herb vinegar, in which you can use the entire stem and flower head. In the kitchen, use just the florets in chicken, corn chowder, and salads for a mild, spicy flavor. Grow as an annual.
Scarlet runner bean (*Phaseolus coccineus*)	8 to 12 ft.	Scarlet bean flowers from midsummer into fall. The more you pick, the more you'll have, but you can never have enough once you've tasted their delicate beany flavor. Try them in salads and stir-fry. Annual vine.
Garden pea (*Pisum sativum*)	3 to 5 ft.	White or pinkish blooms in spring or summer. The flowers have a wonderful crunchy texture and pealike taste; great in salads or with seafood or pasta. Annual.
Radish (*Raphanus sativus*)	1 ft.	Small flowers, usually produced in spring or summer, have a "bite" similar to that of the root; great in salads. Annual.
Rosemary (*Rosmarinus officinalis*)	1 to 3 ft.	Blue summer or fall flowers have a milder rosemary taste than the leaves; sprinkle them on salads, rice, or sweet potatoes. Perennial in Zone 8 and south; grow as an annual or bring indoors for winter elsewhere.

Name	Height	Notes
Pineapple sage (*Salvia elegans*)	3 to 4 ft.	Beautiful red tubular flowers in late summer to fall. The blooms are sweet and fruity with a hint of spice and mint; enjoy them in salads, salsa, chicken, seafood, and cookies. Perennial in frost-free areas; elsewhere, grow as an annual or bring indoors for the winter.
Sage (*Salvia officinalis*)	2 ft.	Spikes of purple-blue blooms in summer. Sage flowers have a slightly milder flavor than the leaves. They are a zesty addition to salads, meats, and soups; also try mixing them into a dipping batter for fried vegetables for a knockout taste. Zones 4 to 8.
Elderberries (*Sambucus* spp.)	12 to 20 ft.	Large clusters of creamy white flowers in early to midsummer. Add them to muffins or corn fritters for a sweet taste. Zones 3 to 9.
Winter savory (*Satureja montana*)	6 to 12 in.	Small, white summer flowers have a hot peppery taste that's wonderful in seafood dishes and salads. Use as a garnish for root vegetables. Zones 4 to 9.
Thymes (*Thymus* spp.)	1 ft.	Clusters of tiny white, pink, or lavender summer flowers have a milder taste than thyme leaves. Use with fish and chowders. Zones 4 to 9.
Nasturtium (*Tropaeolum majus*)	1 ft.	Showy red, pink, orange, peach, yellow, or white flowers from midsummer to frost. The spicy-peppery flavor makes them a favorite in salads, vegetables, and pasta. Washing and vigorously shaking the flowers to remove hidden insects are the most important parts of preparation. Annual.
Sweet violet (*Viola odorata*)	6 to 8 in.	Purple or blue spring flowers have a sweet taste. Best used for beauty in salads or candied for cake decorations. Zones 4 to 8.

White Garden

While it's fun to plan a garden around any color scheme, there's something extra-special about a white garden. Of course, no garden is completely white—there are always the greens of leaves and stems, plus tinges of pink on petals, or yellow flower centers—but I think these light touches of color help to set off the white tones that much more. A white garden is a great choice if you want a garden you can enjoy in the evening, as white flowers are visible even after dusk has hidden darker colors. Some white flowers also have a wonderful fragrance that is especially noticeable in the still air of a warm summer evening.

stability of the two old trees, which had been planted too close together and too close to the house. The decision made, I hired a tree man, and in a brief moment the trees were down, with the stumps cut straight and close to the ground. The space opened up, and it was obvious to me I had found a place for my garden of flowers. It was not obvious to anyone else, though, because the compacted soil was full of rocks and tree roots. But I knew I was going to build this garden up, not down!

Once the trees were down, I got out my garden hose and began to mark my design. I had decided to make a free-form "island" bed that curved around the tree stumps. I cut the

The Site

My wonderful white garden grew from the most unpromising beginning: an oil spill and two overgrown hemlocks. When our insurance agent came to check out the oil spill, he voiced his concern for the

Obedient plant

Sneezeweed

Flowering tobacco

Cosmos

Shasta daisy

Zonal geranium

A Collection of Bridal Blooms. Once you start looking for white flowers, you'll be amazed at the wide range of plants you have to choose from. For the longest show, make sure you include both annuals and perennials.

edging strip and removed the sod, then placed two wooden half-barrels in the garden, one over each stump. The next step was to cover the remaining area completely with thick sections of wet newspaper, held in place by some of the rocks that had surfaced during the edging. Previously I had opened two bales of peat moss and allowed rain to soak into them. (I placed the bales close to the garden site before I opened them, because they are too heavy to move once wet.) I covered the paper with about 2 inches of the moist peat and removed the rocks, and the site began to look more like a garden. The next layer was about 4 inches of grass clippings, covered with another 2 inches of peat moss. I gave the whole thing a good sprinkle to make sure it was moist, and I was ready to start planting!

The First Year

When the time came for me to actually begin my flower garden, I chose to make a white garden. I love the subtleties and shades of white flowers with green, gray, and blue foliage. As I planned the design and began the layering process to make a good foundation for the new garden during the day, I researched white blooming plants at night. It's amazing how many varieties you have to choose from! ("Plants for a White Garden" on page 148 gives you an idea of some of the dozens of white flowers I ended up with.) Since I was working with a limited budget, I decided to invest in a few special plants to give the garden some height and structure, then put the catalogs aside for the time being and looked around for free plants.

For my birthday, I gave myself two large plants for the new garden. One was a spring-flowering spirea commonly called bridalveil, planted where the arching branches would

have room to grow. Nearby, I set another spring-flowering shrub, 'Palestrina' rhododendron, with a shading of pink in the center of large white blooms. It is a compact form that would not outgrow the garden.

Next, I moved in a plant of a favorite peony, 'Festiva Maxima'. This beautiful peony plant had tried to come up in one of my perennial beds at the inn for years. Not knowing what it was, I had chopped it down every year until one year I was too busy to notice and it grew and bloomed. I loved it so much I took it with me when I sold the inn and moved across the road. It had been growing in my foundation garden for a year before I started the white garden.

To get these three plants started, I placed them in position, then pulled back the layers and spread their roots as best I could. Using the strips of sod I had removed from the edges of the bed, I encircled the base of each plant (with the grass side of the strips facing down) to cover the roots and hold the plants upright. After watering each plant thoroughly, I added a 6-inch-thick cover of shredded bark from the old trees.

Tips and Time-Savers

Planning a White Garden

When planning a white garden, remember to look at the leaves as well as the flowers—plants with silvery, gray, blue, or white-variegated leaves definitely deserve a place for their season-long interest.

In the rest of the bed, I planted divisions of perennials that were growing in other parts of my garden. I was able to add three each of several plants that either bloomed white or had gray or blue foliage: feverfew, horehound, lamb's ears, silver thyme, silvermound artemisia, and 'Silver Queen' and 'Silver King' artemisia. I filled the half-barrels with a blend of compost and commercial potting mix, then planted them with annuals: 'White Orbit' zonal geranium, 'Snowdrift' petunia, sweet alyssum, and 'Rocket White' snapdragon.

Filling In

That first fall, I added a variety of bulbs, including 'Mount Hood' daffodil, 'Diana' tulip, 'Sterling Star' lily, snowdrop, and 'Joan of Arc' crocus, as well as lily-of-the-valley—planted in a pot sunken into the ground to keep its roots from spreading. This was the first time I tried planting bulbs in a new lasagna garden. I pushed the bulbs down through the layers until I felt them hit the paper, then mulched them with lots of bark mulch.

In the spring, all the bulbs bloomed—nothing had succumbed to shallow planting or the perils of winter. I could hardly wait for the weather to warm so I could continue planting. In anticipation, I scoured my other gardens and marked plants that could be lifted and divided to provide extras for the white garden. Sometimes I even moved plants in full bloom from other gardens. My established lasagna beds were all well drained and warmed up early, so I could lift a plant with lots of soil, place it on a tarp, and drag it to the new garden. This way, I was able to make sure a plant was going to be the right color before I moved it to the white garden!

Time passed quickly and my birthday was coming again. I picked the plants I would give myself as a gift: a dwarf form of potentilla called 'Abbotswood'; 'Souvenir de Alice Harding', a pure white, heavenly scented lilac

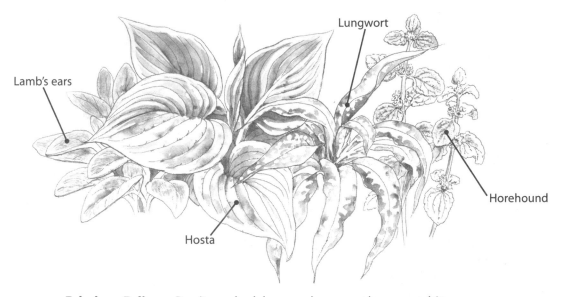

Fabulous Foliage. Don't overlook leaves when you plan your white garden. Plants with silver, gray, blue, or variegated leaves make a wonderful backdrop for white flowers and add extra interest.

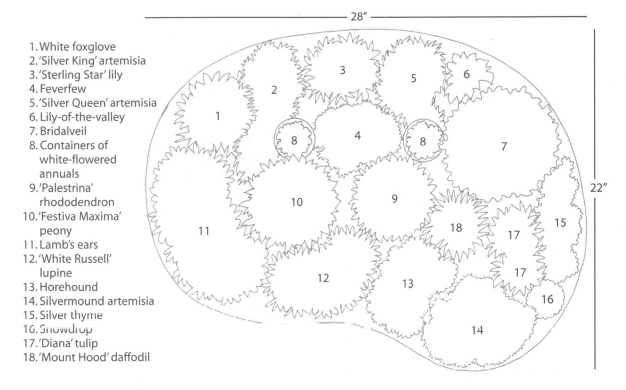

1. White foxglove
2. 'Silver King' artemisia
3. 'Sterling Star' lily
4. Feverfew
5. 'Silver Queen' artemisia
6. Lily-of-the-valley
7. Bridalveil
8. Containers of white-flowered annuals
9. 'Palestrina' rhododendron
10. 'Festiva Maxima' peony
11. Lamb's ears
12. 'White Russell' lupine
13. Horehound
14. Silvermound artemisia
15. Silver thyme
16. Snowdrop
17. 'Diana' tulip
18. 'Mount Hood' daffodil

A Wonderful White Garden. Here's a map of how my white garden looked at the end of its first year. By including a variety of annuals, perennials, bulbs, and shrubs, I created a garden that offered something to look at through most of the year.

with a lower growth habit than common lilacs; and a Siberian iris called 'White Swirl'.

As soon as the new birthday plants were installed, I began to move plants from other gardens: 'Alaska' shasta daisy, 'Floristan' white spike gayfeather, 'Snow Queen' bee balm, and 'The Pearl' yarrow. By the time I was finished moving perennials, it was time to plant annuals: 'Sonata White' cosmos, tall white snapdragons, pansies, and petunias.

Expanding the Garden

After a few years of adding more mulch layers regularly, the growing surface of the white garden was now 6 to 8 inches above the lawn. Each time I worked in the garden, planting and dividing, I saw lots of worm activity, a sure sign of good soil. I could easily dig down below where the paper had been and, except for large tree roots, find several inches of looser, worm-tilled soil.

Things were going so well that I started thinking about expanding the garden. About that time, our gift shop received a large order of jams and jellies packed in cardboard boxes. Telling myself I was saving time by taking the boxes directly to the garden instead of tying them in bales and taking them to the recycling station, I began the garden addition right

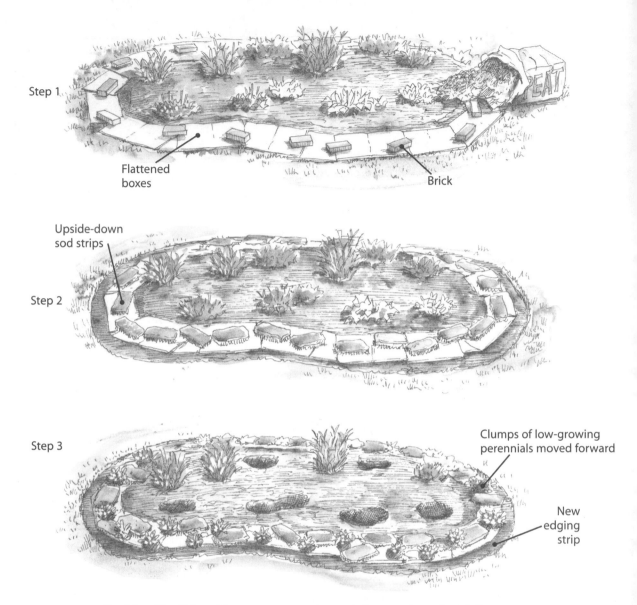

Step 1

Flattened boxes

Brick

Upside-down sod strips

Step 2

Step 3

Clumps of low-growing perennials moved forward

New edging strip

Pushing the Edge. It's easy to expand an existing garden—just follow these three simple steps. (1) Lay flattened cardboard boxes (or pads of wet newspaper) end to end around the perimeter of the garden and hold them down with bricks. (2) Cut a new 4- to 6-inch edging strip around the garden. Remove the sod strips and lay them upside down on the boxes; remove the bricks. (3) Dig up the low-growing plants that were growing along the original edge, leaving plenty of soil around the roots. Set them on the boxes, then fill in around the roots with lots of mulch. Add taller plants to the now-empty middle zone.

away. I collected some bricks, a bale of peat moss, my edging tools, and the garden hose. Instead of using newspaper to cover the sod, I used the flattened boxes, laid end to end. The boxes added about 10 inches to the outside of the garden, and there were just enough boxes to finish. It was meant to be!

Once the boxes were down and held in place with bricks, I covered them with a 2- to 3-inch layer of peat moss. Using a fine spray, I gave the bed a good wetting. A sharp-pointed spade and mattock helped me cut a narrow line in the sod around the outside edge of the boxes. I placed the sod-and-soil strips (grass side down) on the boxes to hold them in place so I could remove the bricks. In little more than an hour, I had added 10 inches to the garden perimeter.

Next, I moved some of the shorter-growing plants from the old perimeter closer to the new edge, lifting them with a good amount of soil around the roots. I set them down on the peat moss, then added more mulch around the roots. Behind these, I added taller-growing plants, including 'Whirling Butterflies' gaura, a white Siberian iris, 'Bridal Veil' astilbe, and two ornamental grasses: 'Morning Light' maiden grass and blue fescue. I also added more divisions from other parts of the garden to fill the extra space. The white garden was taking on a life of its own!

Finishing Touches

Part of the white garden was in dappled shade from a maple tree near one end. I had previously planted a circular garden of shade plants around the base of the tree. Now, with the expansion of the white garden, they cried out for an arbor to bring them together. I turned to my old friend Lou Temple to make one of his wonderful outdoor pieces. It came on a clear, sunny day in early fall, and I asked Lou to help me install it. When he saw where I wanted it to go, near the maple tree, he almost left. The ground around any tree is full of roots, and an arbor has to be installed where all four legs are level. We used shovels, mattocks, pickaxes, and steel bars to dig and chip through rocks, clay, and roots. I finished digging the holes with a tablespoon, removing bits of soil with my fingers until the arbor stood straight and tall.

The addition of an arbor to the garden gave me the opportunity to grow one of my favorite vines, a hybrid clematis known as 'Henryi'. I planted it in the white garden next to the side of the arbor that would be in the sun. After years of applying organic material in lasagna layers, the soil was rich and loamy. With my hands, I scooped the soil aside to make a depression 8 to 10 inches deep, added some compost and sand, and set the roots in the hole. At the base of the clematis, I planted a blue-leaved hosta, 'Big Daddy', to keep the clematis roots cool, then watered and mulched.

It took a year for 'Henryi' to bloom, but it was worth the wait: Big, saucer-size blooms in brilliant white covered the bottom rungs of the arbor that second summer. I had to get down to ground level to photograph them that first year. By the third year, I could stand to get a good shot. They were more than halfway up to the top of the 6-foot-high structure. I loved that plant! It was like having another child and watching it grow.

Each year, I'd add a bit more to my wonderful white garden—extending the edge here, adding a few plants there—and it was always a joy to see. Even if you have a small space, give a white garden a try: I know you'll enjoy it as much as I did!

PLANTS FOR A WHITE GARDEN

There's an amazing array of plants that are great for white gardens—not just white flowers, but silver, gray, blue, and variegated leaves as well. Here's an overview of the plants that performed well in my ever-expanding white garden. Unless otherwise noted, these plants all thrive in a sunny lasagna bed.

Name	Height	Notes
Annuals		
'Rocket White' snapdragon (*Antirrhinum majus* 'Rocket White')	3 ft.	Tall, dense spires of white blooms. Great for cut flowers.
'White Feather' flowering kale (*Brassica oleracea* 'White Feather')	1 ft.	Compact heads of frilly leaves with white centers and green tips. Wonderful for adding extra interest in fall.
Moonflower (*Ipomoea alba*)	20 ft.	Large, fragrant white flowers open in the evening on vigorous vining stems; needs a sturdy support.
'Sonata White' cosmos (*Cosmos bipinnatus* 'Sonata White')	2 ft.	Bright white flowers on bushy, lacy-leaved stems. Plants self-sow freely.
'Royal Wedding' sweet pea (*Lathyrus odoratus* 'Royal Wedding')	6 ft.	Fragrant, pure white blooms on long stems. Vining stems need support. Mulch generously to keep roots cool.
Sweet alyssum (*Lobularia maritima*)	4 in.	Clusters of small, sweetly scented white flowers. Great for the front of the border or in containers. 'Carpet of Snow' and 'Snow Cloth' are two of my favorites.
'Shade Star' flowering tobacco (*Nicotiana* 'Shade Star')	18 in.	Fragrant, creamy white trumpets on compact plants. Can take shade or sun.

Name	Height	Notes
'Orbit White' zonal geranium (*Pelargonium* × *hortorum* 'Orbit White')	18 in.	Clusters of white flowers over green leaves marked with a chocolate "zone." Compact, well-branched plants.
Petunia (*Petunia* × *hybrida*)	1 ft.	Several good white cultivars are available; my favorites include 'Snowdrift', 'Supercascade White', and 'Ultra White'.
Violas (*Viola* hybrids)	6 in.	Dainty flowers on compact plants. Two favorites are 'Sorbet Coconut' and 'Velour White'.
Pansy (*Viola* × *wittrockiana*)	6 in.	Larger flowers than violas. 'Majestic Giant White' has a dark center blotch; 'Delta' is pure white.
'Crystal White' zinnia (*Zinnia angustifolia* 'Crystal White')	5 in.	Yellow-centered white flowers on compact plants. Great for containers or the front of the border.

Perennials

Name	Height	Notes
'The Pearl' sneezeweed (*Achillea ptarmica* 'The Pearl')	18 in.	Creamy white, double flowers in early summer. Zones 3 to 9.
Woolly yarrow (*Achillea tomentosa*)	6 to 12 in.	Clusters of creamy yellow flowers through summer over mats of hairy, gray-green leaves. Zones 3 to 8.
Pearly everlasting (*Anaphalis margaritacea*)	1 to 2 ft.	Blooms midsummer to fall, with yellow-centered, snow-white flowers over gray leaves. Zones 3 to 6; hates hot, humid summers.

(continued)

PLANTS FOR A WHITE GARDEN—CONTINUED

Name	Height	Notes
Perennials—Continued		
'Silver King' artemisia (*Artemisia ludoviciana*)	24 to 30 in.	Both 'Silver King' and 'Silver Queen' have aromatic silvery foliage used to make wreaths and bouquets. Zones 4 to 9.
Silvermound artemisia (*Artemisia schmidtiana*)	12 to 15 in.	Dense mounds of finely cut, silver-gray leaves. Zones 3 to 7.
'Bridal Veil' astilbe (*Astilbe × arendsii* 'Bridal Veil')	3 ft.	White flower plumes in early summer. Also takes partial shade; mulch with compost to keep roots cool and supply extra nutrients. Zones 3 to 8.
Snow-in-summer (*Cerastium tomentosum*)	2 to 6 in.	White flowers over carpets of woolly, silvery leaves in late spring to early summer. Zones 2 to 8.
'Alaska' shasta daisy (*Chrysanthemum × superbum* 'Alaska')	20 to 48 in.	Yellow-centered white daisies in summer. Zones 4 to 9.
Lily-of-the-valley (*Convallaria majalis*)	8 in.	Fragrant, bell-shaped white flowers in spring. Plants prefer light shade. Zones 2 to 8.
'White Magic Fountains' delphinium (*Delphinium × elatum* 'White Magic Fountains')	5 to 7 ft.	Tall spires of white blooms from June to September. Zones 3 to 7.
Sweet William (*Dianthus barbatus*)	6 to 24 in.	Seeds usually produce mixed colors, so buy in bloom or sow elsewhere and transplant only those with white flowers. Zones 4 to 8.

Name	Height	Notes
White foxglove (*Digitalis purpurea* 'Alba')	3 to 4 ft.	Long spikes of tubular white flowers in summer. Zones 4 to 8.
'Whirling Butterflies' gaura (*Gaura lindheimeri* 'Whirling Butterflies')	2 ft.	Dainty, white summer flowers develop a light pink tinge as they age. Zones 4 to 9.
Baby's breath (*Gypsophila paniculata*)	3 ft.	Airy masses of tiny white blooms in summer. Zones 4 to 8.
'Big Daddy' hosta (*Hosta* 'Big Daddy')	12 to 30 in.	White summer flowers over clumps of large, blue-green leaves. There are also many other wonderful blue-leaved or white-variegated cultivars to choose from. Prefers shade. Zones 3 to 9.
'White Swirl' Siberian iris (*Iris sibirica* 'White Swirl')	3 ft.	Yellow-centered white blooms in late spring or early summer. Zones 3 to 9.
White spike gayfeather (*Liatris spicata* 'Floristan White')	24 to 36 in.	Spikes of fuzzy white flowers on stiff stems. Zones 3 to 9.
'White Russell' lupine (*Lupinus* 'White Russell')	3 to 5 ft.	Spikes of pea-shaped white flowers in late spring or early summer. Provide extra mulch to keep roots cool and moist. Zones 4 to 6.
Gooseneck loosestrife (*Lysimachia clethroides*)	2 to 4 ft.	Drooping clusters of white blooms in summer. Spreads quickly by creeping roots. Zones 3 to 9.

(continued)

PLANTS FOR A WHITE GARDEN—CONTINUED

Name	Height	Notes
Perennials—Continued		
Horehound (*Marrubium vulgare*)	20 in.	Clusters of tiny white summer flowers on branching stems clad in fuzzy gray leaves. Zones 5 to 9.
'Snow Queen' bee balm (*Monarda didyma* 'Snow Queen')	30 in.	Creamy white flowers in whorls in summer; aromatic leaves. Zones 4 to 9.
'Festiva Maxima' peony (*Paeonia lactiflora* 'Festiva Maxima')	30 to 36 in.	Double, scented, white blooms that have a hint of pink in late spring or early summer. Zones 3 to 8.
'Miss Lingard' phlox (*Phlox carolina* 'Miss Lingard')	3 ft.	Large, full heads of white flowers in summer. Zones 3 to 9.
'White Delight' moss pink (*Phlox subulata* 'White Delight')	6 to 8 in.	Pure white spring flowers over carpets of needle-like green leaves. Zones 4 to 8.
'Crown of Snow' obedient plant (*Physostegia virginiana* 'Crown of Snow')	2 ft.	Spikes of white flowers in late summer. Spreads quickly in good soil. Zones 4 to 8.
Primroses (*Primula* spp.)	6 to 24 in.	Bloom midspring to early summer. Seeds usually produce a mix of colors, so buy plants already in bloom, or grow seedlings elsewhere, then transplant only the white ones. Zones 4 to 8.
Lungworts (*Pulmonaria* spp.)	8 to 12 in.	*P. saccharata* and *P. angustifolia* have silver-spotted leaves and blue to pink flowers. Plants need some shade. Zones 3 to 9.

Name	Height	Notes
White sedum (*Sedum album*)	3 to 4 in.	Creeping carpets of narrow green leaves topped with clusters of white flowers. Zones 3 to 9.
Lamb's ears (*Stachys byzantina*)	10 to 24 in.	Small, purple-pink flowers on fuzzy spikes in late spring over silvery white, tongue-shaped, woolly foliage. Zones 3 to 9.
Feverfew (*Tanacetum parthenium*)	6 to 24 in.	Yellow-centered, small, white daisies on bushy plants. Self-sows readily. Zones 4 to 9.
Silver thyme (*Thymus x citriodorus* 'Argenteus')	1 ft.	Bushy clumps of small green leaves edged in white. Zones 4 to 9.
'Icicle' veronica (*Veronica spicata* 'Icicle')	15 to 20 in.	Tiny white blooms in dense, narrow spikes in summer. Zones 3 to 8.

Shrubs and Vines

Name	Height	Notes
'Henryi' clematis (*Clematis* 'Henryi')	8 to 20 ft.	Large, white summer flowers; vining stems need support. Provide shade for roots. Zones 4 to 9.
'Abbotswood' potentilla (*Potentilla fruticosa* 'Abbotswood')	2 ft.	White blooms on dense, bushy plants from early summer into fall. Zones 3 to 8.
'Palestrina' rhododendron (*Rhododendron* 'Palestrina')	24 to 30 in.	Large clusters of pink-tinged white flowers in late spring or early summer over compact stems with evergreen foliage. Zones 3 to 9.
Bridalveil spirea (*Spiraea prunifolia*)	8 to 10 ft.	Dense clusters of white flowers in spring on arching branches. Zones 4 to 9.

(continued)

PLANTS FOR A WHITE GARDEN—CONTINUED

Name	Height	Notes
Shrubs and Vines—Continued		
'Souvenir de Alice Harding' lilac (*Syringa* 'Souvenir de Alice Harding')	12 ft.	Upright trunk with a bushy crown bearing large clusters of delicately scented white blooms in late spring. Zones 3 to 9.
Grasses		
Variegated tuberous oat grass (*Arrhenatherum elatium* var. *bulbosum* 'Variegatum')	12 to 15 in.	Low clumps of narrow green leaves with ivory edges. Best in cool temperatures. Zones 4 to 9.
Blue fescue (*Festuca ovina* var. *glauca*)	10 to 12 in.	Dense mounds of narrow, powdery blue leaves. Great as an edging. Zones 4 to 8.
Maiden grass (*Miscanthus sinensis*)	4 to 5 ft.	Plumes of creamy white flowers in late summer over vase-shaped clumps of narrow green leaves. 'Morning Light' is more compact (to 3 ft.), with a narrow white edge on each leaf. Zones 4 to 9.

Name	Height	Notes
Bulbs		
'Joan of Arc' crocus (*Crocus* 'Joan of Arc')	2 to 4 in.	Goblet-shaped white flowers in early spring. Plant in a site protected from wind. Zones 3 to 8.
Snowdrop (*Galanthus nivalis*)	4 in.	Nodding white flowers in late winter to early spring. Leaves are narrow, flat, and green. Zones 3 to 9.
'Carnegie' hyacinth (*Hyacinthus orientalis* 'Carnegie')	9 in.	Dense spikes of fragrant, starry, white flowers in midspring. Protect from wind. Zones 4 to 8.
'Sterling Star' lily (*Lilium* 'Sterling Star')	20 in.	Showy white summer flowers atop compact stalks clad in narrow green leaves. Zones 4 to 8.
'Mount Hood' daffodil (*Narcissus* 'Mount Hood')	12 to 15 in.	Creamy white cup turns pure white shortly after opening to match the petals. Zones 3 to 7.
'Diana' tulip (*Tulipa* 'Diana')	10 to 12 in.	Single, luminous white blooms on short stems in spring. Looks best planted in large groups (at least nine bulbs). Zones 3 to 8.

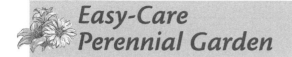

Easy-Care Perennial Garden

Contrary to what some people think, a perennial garden isn't a plant-it-once-and-enjoy-it-forever project. Sure, there are perennials that can live for decades without regular care, including daylilies, hostas, and peony. But there are other classic perennials that need lots of special attention to look their best. Hybrid delphiniums *(Delphinium × elatum)*, for example, demand staking, feeding, and cultivating to look their best. They take lots of maintenance time and have to be replaced every two or three years. If you have seen their tall, showy blue spires accenting the back of a border, you know why some gardeners feel these plants are worth the trouble. But you don't have to be a slave to your garden to enjoy beautiful flowers: Just choose a variety of easy-care perennials, such as those listed in "Plants for an Easy-Care Perennial Garden" on page 159. Combine these low-maintenance plants with a no-dig, no-weed lasagna garden, and you can enjoy a bounty of beautiful blooms all season long with a minimum of fuss.

From Disaster to Display Garden

In my case, the need for easy-care perennials became clear when I was faced with a big

(continued on page 160)

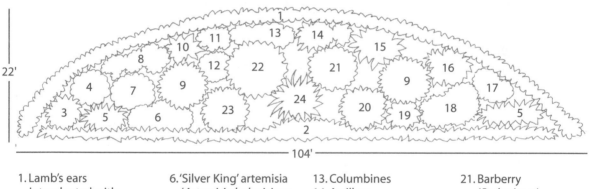

1. Lamb's ears interplanted with autumn crocus *(Colchicum autumnale)*
2. Daffodil *(Narcissus* 'King Alfred')
3. Peony
4. Yarrows
5. Siberian iris
6. 'Silver King' artemisia *(Artemisia ludoviciana* 'Silver King')
7. Asters
8. Lady's mantle
9. Elderberry *(Sambucus canadensis)*
10. Oriental poppy
11. Coral bells
12. Feverfew
13. Columbines
14. Astilbes
15. Foxgloves
16. Lupines
17. Coreopsis
18. Tansy
19. Bleeding heart
20. Yellow Japanese peony *(Paeonia suffruticosa,* yellow)
21. Barberry *(Berberis* sp.)
22. Purple-leaved plum *(Prunus cerasifera* 'Atropurpurea')
23. Pink Japanese peony *(Paeonia suffruticosa,* pink)
24. Daylilies

An Easy-Care Perennial Garden. I had a big space to fill, so I needed large, tough plants that would thrive without a lot of fussing from me. Along with a wide assortment of easy-care perennials, I added a few shrubs, including purple-leaved plum and barberry; the two elderberries planted themselves. For extra color, I scattered large annuals in the empty spaces, along with a hundred bulbs of purple-flowered giant alliums *(Allium giganteum)* for a dramatic display in early summer.

Pat's Picks

PLANTS FOR AN EASY-CARE PERENNIAL GARDEN

Here's a listing of some of the most dependable perennials around. All of these thrive in the nutrient-rich, well-drained soil of a lasagna bed. Those that like extra moisture, as noted in the entries below, appreciate some extra mulch.

Name	Height	Notes
Fern-leaved yarrow (*Achillea filipendulina*)	3 to 4 ft.	Large, flat, golden yellow flower heads in summer. Full sun. Zones 3 to 9.
Lady's mantle (*Alchemilla mollis*)	18 in.	Sprays of greenish yellow flowers in late spring to early summer. Good for light shade. Zones 4 to 9.
Columbines (*Aquilegia* spp.)	18 to 30 in.	Spurred spring or early-summer blooms in a rainbow of colors. Full sun to partial shade. Zones 3 to 9.
Asters (*Aster* spp.)	3 to 4 ft.	Daisylike flowers in a wide color range, including white, pink, red, purple, and lavender, in summer or fall. 'Harrington's Pink' and 'September Ruby' (both 3 to 4 ft.) are two of my favorites. Full sun. Zones 4 to 8.
Astilbes (*Astilbe* spp.)	3 ft.	Showy plumes of late-spring to early-summer flowers in white and shades of red, pink, and lavender. Full sun to partial shade; moist soil. Zones 3 to 8.
Coreopsis (*Coreopsis* spp.)	10 to 24 in.	Daisylike flowers bloom all summer—yellow in *C. verticillata* and pink in *C. rosea*. Plants may be short-lived but often self-sow. Full sun. Zones 3 to 9.
Bleeding heart (*Dicentra spectabilis*)	24 to 30 in.	Arching strings of pink hearts in spring. Full sun to partial shade; moist soil. Zones 4 to 9.
Foxgloves (*Digitalis* spp.)	2 to 4 ft.	Summer spikes of tubular white, pink, rose, or yellow flowers. Full sun to partial shade; moist soil. Zones 4 to 8.

(continued)

Plants for an Easy-Care Perennial Garden—Continued

Name	Height	Notes
Purple coneflower (*Echinacea purpurea*)	2 ft.	Daisylike summer flowers with a large center cone and swept-back , rose-pink petals. Full sun. Zones 3 to 8.
Hardy geraniums (*Geranium* spp.)	6 to 18 in.	Saucer-shaped white, pink, blue, or purple blooms in late spring to early summer. Full sun to partial shade. Zones 4 to 8.
Perennial sunflowers (*Helianthus* spp.)	4 to 5 ft.	Daisylike yellow flowers on sturdy stems in summer or fall. Full sun. Zones 3 to 9.
Daylilies (*Hemerocallis* spp.)	18 to 48 in.	Trumpet-shaped blooms in a wide range of colors; late spring, summer, or even fall flowers, depending on the cultivar. Full sun to partial shade. Zones 4 to 9.
Coral bells (*Heuchera sanguinea*)	24 in.	Spiky, branched clusters of tiny white, pink, or red flowers in summer over tidy clumps of rounded, evergreen leaves. Full sun. Zones 4 to 9.
Hostas (*Hosta* spp.)	12 to 30 in.	Lavender or white summer flowers over mounds of green, blue, yellow, or variegated leaves. Full sun to deep shade. Zones 3 to 9.
Siberian iris (*Iris sibirica*)	3 ft.	Showy summer blooms in white, yellow, blues, and purples over clumps of narrow, sword-shaped leaves. Full sun; moist soil. Zones 3 to 9.
Gayfeathers (*Liatris* spp.)	2 to 4 ft.	Dense, fuzzy spikes of tiny red-violet or white flowers in summer. Full sun. Zones 3 to 9.
Lupines (*Lupinus* hybrids)	2 to 3 ft.	Spikes of pealike, late-spring to early-summer blooms in a wide color range. Full sun to partial shade; cool, moist soil. Zones 4 to 7.

Name	Height	Notes
Bee balm (*Monarda didyma*)	3 ft.	Whorls of red, pink, purple, or white flowers in summer. Full sun to light shade. Zones 4 to 9.
Peony (*Paeonia lactiflora*)	30 to 36 in.	Large, fragrant white, pink, or red flowers in late spring or early summer. Full sun to light shade. Zones 3 to 8.
Oriental poppy (*Papaver orientale*)	3 ft.	Large, cupped blooms in white, pink, red, scarlet, or orange in early summer. Full sun. Zones 3 to 8.
Garden phlox (*Phlox* spp.)	2 to 4 ft.	The backbone of the summer garden, with large, full heads of white flowers. Full sun; moist, rich soil. Zones 3 to 9.
Coneflowers (*Rudbeckia* spp.)	2 to 3 ft.	Golden-yellow summer daisies with prominent brown or green center cones. Full sun. Zones 3 to 9.
Violet sage (*Salvia × superba*)	2 to 3 ft.	Narrow spikes of purple-blue flowers in early to mid-summer. Full sun. Zones 4 to 8.
Two-row sedum (*Sedum spurium*)	3 to 4 in.	Clusters of starry pink flowers over carpets of rounded green leaves often tinted with red. Full sun. Zones 3 to 9.
Lamb's ears (*Stachys byzantina*)	10 to 24 in.	Small, purple-pink flowers on fuzzy spikes in late spring over silvery white, tongue-shaped, woolly foliage. Full sun. Zones 3 to 9.
Feverfew (*Tanacetum parthenium*)	6 to 24 in.	Yellow-centered white daisies in summer. Self-sows readily. Full sun to partial shade. Zones 4 to 9.
Tansy (*Tanacetum vulgare*)	4 ft.	Flat-topped clusters of yellow flowers in summer. Spreads quickly. Full sun to light shade. Zones 4 to 9.

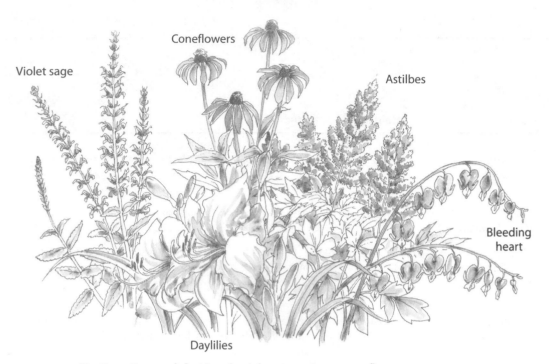

Violet sage · Coneflowers · Astilbes · Bleeding heart · Daylilies

No-Fuss Perennials. You don't have to give up on flower power to have an easy-care perennial garden! Many of the most dependable perennials also offer bright, beautiful blooms for weeks or even months.

space to fill with flowers. If I had planned the garden from the beginning, I would never have made it so large! But when a careless deliveryman let the oil tank overflow and spilled fuel oil on part of the hay field, we were faced with a big cleanup job. We hired a heavy-equipment operator with a backhoe to remove the contaminated soil, which left a scar on the field that looked like half of a circular driveway. I had to decide what to do next: have it filled in or make a driveway. Well, I hadn't planned on a circular driveway, but I decided to let him finish, since it would only cost me half of what I would have spent for a whole driveway. Made sense to me!

Once the drive was finished, the area inside the drive looked like a wonderful spot for a garden. I covered the entire space—104

by 22 feet—with wood chips from the two hemlocks that were removed to make the white garden. To plant, I pulled the chips back, added a few handfuls of peat moss as I dug and backfilled a planting hole, spread six to eight sheets of newspaper fanned out around the base of the plant, and covered the paper with the wood chips as mulch.

I would never have been able to buy all the perennials I needed to fill that huge space, but I got a good start with divisions of perennials growing in other parts of my garden. I planted big annuals to fill in bare spots between the new perennials, including cleome *(Cleome hassleriana)*, cosmos, marigolds, snapdragons, and giant sunflowers *(Helianthus annuus)*. With

Tips and Time-Savers

Extending Your Plant-Buying Budget

Garden-design books always tell you to set out clumps of at least three plants of each type. That's good advice, but what if you have a lot of space to fill and little money to buy plants? My solution is to buy one of each perennial I need and set them out in the garden the first year, with annuals around them for fillers. After one year of growth in good soil, most of the perennials are large enough to divide into three parts. Replant the sections close together so they make a big statement. Other ways to stretch your budget include starting perennials from seed instead of buying plants, and swapping plants with friends.

never watered or weeded, since the paper and mulch kept the soil moist and smothered weed seeds. I didn't fertilize—I just added peat moss to the soil during planting and sometimes spread more in the fall if I had open bags that needed to be used. If my neighbor didn't need all of his barn litter for his own garden, I spread the manure-rich straw around my plants. Occasionally, I added a scattering of lime as an afterthought.

Everything grew together, forming a mass of vegetation that bloomed in different stages from early spring to late fall. It was a roadside garden that slowed, and sometimes stopped, traffic. Many times I would look up from working in the garden and find a car parked across the road, its passengers taking it all in. I can't imagine how many people derived pleasure from that mistake garden. Give your own easy-care perennial garden a try, and see how much pleasure *you* can have without being a slave to garden chores!

the addition of a few shrubs and dozens of bulbs, that big old mistake of a garden became a sea of color!

Minimal Maintenance for Easy-Care Perennials

Every year, I laid months' worth of daily newspapers on the top of the garden and covered them with more bark mulch. As the plants grew, I divided them and planted the divisions. The garden kept getting bigger and better, with a minimum of time and effort. I

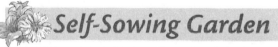

Self-Sowing Garden

The nature of lasagna gardening eventually leads you to wilder, rather than perfectly neat, gardens. Sure—neatness counts when you're *building* a lasagna garden. You may be recycling yard and kitchen wastes to build the layers, but the finished beds look tidy—not like piles of trash. Once the layered ingredients have broken down into a garden of rich, loamy soil, though, the conditions are ideal for self-seeding plants to produce lots of "volunteers." If you allow these seedlings to grow and mature, your lasagna garden will take on a style of its own: a casual, slightly wild, cottage-garden look.

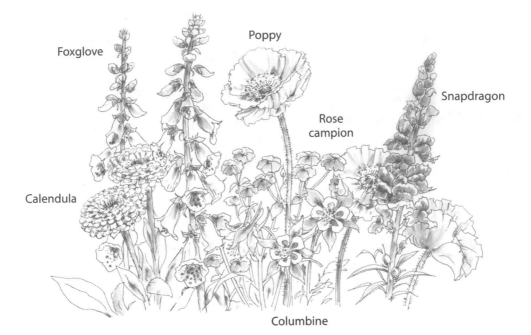

Foxglove   Poppy   Snapdragon   Rose campion   Calendula   Columbine

Sow Once, Enjoy for Years. You can't get much simpler than a garden that plants itself year after year! Since the colors of the seedlings may differ from their parents' colors, you'll enjoy a new display every season.

Choosing the Plants

So, which plants can self-sow? Well, just about all of them can, but we're interested in the ones that do it best. Annuals, which sprout, grow, flower, and set seed within one growing season, are a natural choice. They are genetically programmed to produce lots of flowers and seed so they can reproduce themselves; that's why pinching off spent flowers encourages plants to produce more blooms—they want to produce seeds! (To get the best of both options—long bloom season *and* seeds for next year's seedlings—simply stop pinching in mid- to late summer, so some flowers have a chance to go to seed.)

Biennials, such as purple foxglove *(Digitalis purpurea),* are also great at self-sowing. Their first year, they produce only a rosette of leaves, waiting until the second year to produce flowers and large amounts of seed.

Many annuals and biennials seed themselves so dependably that they actually seem like perennials. True perennials are generally less dependent on self-sowing, since they return each year from their roots, but there are exceptions. Columbines *(Aquilegia* spp.), for instance, are well known for their tendency to die out after a few years, but they produce so many seedlings that you may not even notice the original plant is gone. It seems that these and other short-lived perennials tend to self-sow more generously than longer-lived species.

For a list of annuals, biennials, and perennials that I've had good luck with, see "Plants for a Self-Sowing Garden" on page 165.

Starting a Self-Sowing Garden

Creating a self-sowing garden is easy—just scatter the seeds over the top of a new or established lasagna bed, or set out transplants for faster results. Once seedlings are a few inches tall, start adding mulch, and repeat a few times during the summer to keep the soil covered. When you clean up the garden in fall or early spring, scatter any remaining seedheads over the bed.

The first year, the results may look fairly formal, as the seedlings or transplants will be in organized patterns. By the second year, the look will be softer as the plants start mixing together. By the third spring, you can choose to let all the seedlings come up in a glorious jumble or else start "editing" the bed to thin out the seedlings and get the plants where you want them. If you choose the latter option, weed lightly at first, until you get to know what the seedlings of the different plants look like—otherwise, you may end up pulling out more than you planned to!

💡

Tips and Time-Savers

Self-Sown Surprises

Keep in mind that self-sown seedlings may look very different from the plant they came from. A beautiful yellow hybrid columbine (Aquilegia × hybrida), for instance, could produce seedlings in a rainbow of colors, from red and yellow to blue or purple. If you prefer particular color schemes, you might want to stick with a more carefully maintained garden, started with already-growing plants so you can be sure what the blooms will look like. But if you enjoy an ever-changing display of different colors, this is the garden for you!

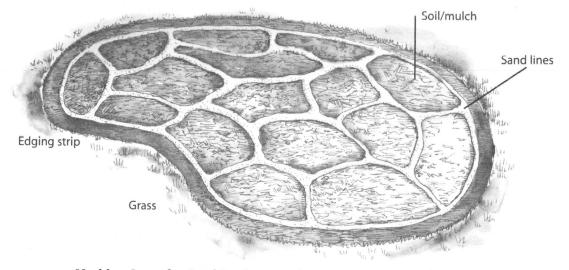

Soil/mulch

Sand lines

Edging strip

Grass

Marking Areas for Seed Sowing. You don't need a formal plan to create a self-sowing garden—just mark off sections of the bed with lines of sand or flour, then sow different seeds in the sections. That's it!

Keep Them Where You Want Them.
Plants growing close to or leaning over the edge of your garden may end up dropping their seeds in the grass, where you'll mow off the seedlings. To keep the seeds where they should be, bend the seed-bearing stems back into the garden or cut off the stems and shake the seeds where you want them to grow.

Walkabout Plants

Where have all the flowers gone? Are you sure this is where you planted your columbine? Didn't the coneflowers bloom here last year? What happened to the rose campion? Have your dependable self-seeders stopped seeding? Chances are, they seeded themselves in your lawn, where you mowed them down with the grass. When plants make seed, they tend to lean forward before they drop their seed. If you let them do this year after year, they will seed themselves out of the garden.

Fortunately, it's easy to keep your flowers where they belong. When a seedhead forms, bend the stalk back into the garden so the seed will drop where it is supposed to. (Or, if you want those seeds to grow somewhere else, pick off the seedhead and scatter or crumble the seed over the new garden.) It's also important to learn to recognize young seedlings so you don't weed them out or mow them down. If you notice one or more plants starting to take over, simply cut off their spent flowers or flowerstalks before they drop a new crop of seeds.

Pat's Picks

PLANTS FOR A SELF-SOWING GARDEN

Looking for some self-sowing plants to try? Here are some of the annuals, biennials, and perennials that have returned year after year in my garden. All of these grow and reproduce just fine in the rich, well-drained soil of a lasagna garden.

Name	Height	Notes
Annuals		
Snapdragon (*Antirrhinum majus*)	6 to 36 in.	Showy spikes of white, pink, red, orange, or yellow blooms from summer into fall. Full sun to light shade.
Calendula (*Calendula officinalis*)	1 to 2 ft.	Single or double, daisylike flowers in shades of yellow and orange. Full sun.
Bachelor's button (*Centaurea cyanus*)	2 to 3 ft.	Fluffy heads of blue, pink, red, or white blossoms through summer. Full sun.
Spider flower (*Cleome hassleriana*)	5 to 6 ft.	Clusters of white, rose, or pink flowers bloom all summer. Full sun to light shade.
Cosmos (*Cosmos* spp.)	2 to 4 ft.	Single or semidouble, daisylike flowers in white, rose, pink, red, or yellow in late summer and fall. Full sun.
Sunflower (*Helianthus annuus*)	3 to 5 ft.	Flat, daisylike, dark-centered blooms in shades of yellow, orange, rust, red, or cream from midsummer into fall. Full sun.
Sweet alyssum (*Lobularia maritima*)	4 in.	Clusters of small, sweetly scented white flowers from late spring to fall. Full sun to partial shade.
Forget-me-nots (*Myosotis* spp.)	12 to 18 in.	Sprays of dainty blue, pink, or white blooms in spring. Partial shade; moist soil.
Poppies (*Papaver* spp.)	1 to 2 ft.	Bowl-shaped, early-summer flowers in vibrant white, yellow, orange, red, or pink. Full sun.

(continued)

Plants for a Self-Sowing Garden—Continued

Name	Height	Notes
Annuals—Continued		
Gloriosa daisy (*Rudbeckia hirta*)	20 to 24 in.	Large, dark-centered, daisylike blooms in yellow, bronze, orange, or gold from summer into fall. Full sun.
Johnny-jump-up (*Viola tricolor*)	8 in.	Tricolored blossoms of purple, lavender, and yellow in spring to early summer. Full sun to partial shade; moist soil.
Pansy (*Viola × wittrockiana*)	6 to 8 in.	Large, flat flowers in a rainbow of colors—many with dark "faces." Full sun to partial shade; moist soil.
Perennials and Biennials		
Yarrows (*Achillea* spp.)	3 to 4 ft.	Large, flat flower heads in yellow, rust, red, pink, lavender, or white in summer. Full sun. Zones 3 to 9.
Hollyhock (*Alcea rosea*)	4 to 6 ft.	Showy, saucer-shaped, single or double flowers in red, pink, yellow, peach, or white in summer to early fall. Full sun to light shade. Zones 3 to 9.
Columbines (*Aquilegia* spp.)	18 to 30 in.	Spurred spring or early-summer blooms in a rainbow of colors. Full sun to partial shade. Zones 3 to 9.
'Silver King' artemisia (*Artemisia ludoviciana*)	24 to 30 in.	Bushy stems clad in silvery, aromatic leaves that look great all season. Full sun. Zones 4 to 9.
Sweet William (*Dianthus barbatus*)	12 to 18 in.	Dense, rounded clusters of white, pink, red, or maroon flowers (often with a contrasting "eye"), usually in spring or summer. Full sun. Zones 3 to 9.

Name	Height	Notes
Foxglove (*Digitalis purpurea*)	3 to 4 ft.	Summer spikes of tubular blooms in shades of rose, purple, pink, and cream. Full sun to partial shade. Zones 4 to 8.
Purple coneflower (*Echinacea purpurea*)	2 ft.	Daisylike summer flowers with a large center cone and swept-back, rose-pink petals. Full sun. Zones 3 to 8.
Dame's rocket (*Hesperis matronalis*)	2 to 3 ft.	Clusters of sweetly fragrant, white, pink, or lavender flowers in spring. Full sun to partial shade. Zones 3 to 8.
Blue flax (*Linum perenne*)	1 to 2 ft.	Cupped, sky blue flowers in early summer. Full sun to light shade; good drainage is important. Zones 4 to 9.
Lupines (*Lupinus* hybrids)	2 to 3 ft.	Spikes of pealike blooms in a rainbow of colors in late spring to early summer. Full sun to partial shade; cool, moist soil. Zones 4 to 7.
Rose campion (*Lychnis coronaria*)	2 to 3 ft.	Glowing magenta flowers in summer on branching stems over woolly, silvery leaves. Full sun to light shade; well-drained soil. Zones 4 to 9.
Oriental poppy (*Papaver orientale*)	3 ft.	Large, bowl-shaped, late-spring to early-summer blooms in white, salmon, orange, red, or pink. Plants die back to the ground soon after flowering; new leaves appear in late summer. Full sun. Zones 3 to 7.
Coneflowers (*Rudbeckia* spp.)	2 to 3 ft.	Golden-yellow summer daisies with prominent brown or green center cones. Full sun. Zones 3 to 9.

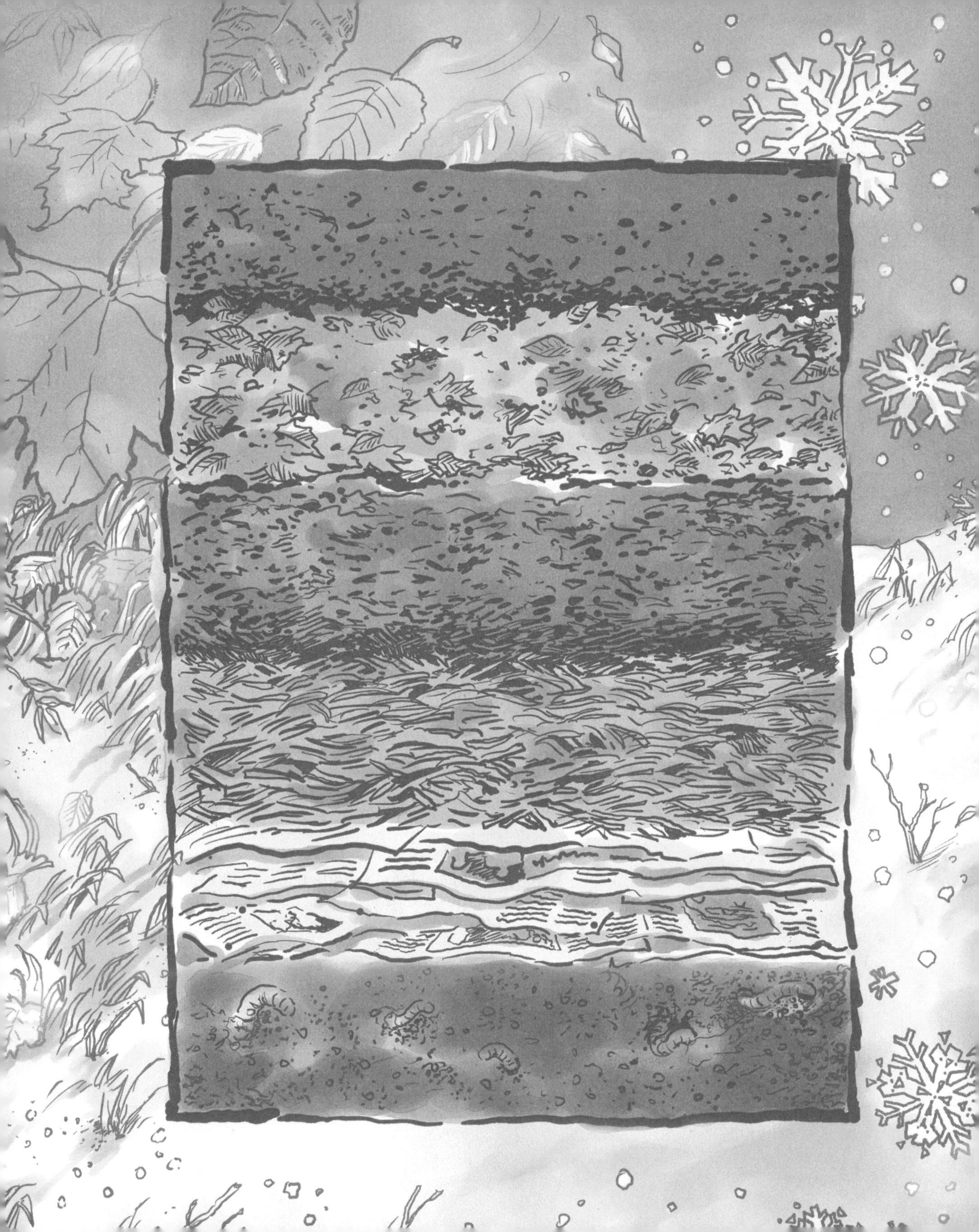

Chapter 6

Lasagna Gardening in Fall and Winter

For some gardeners, the growing season ends after the first frost—they put the garden to rest and are done with it until spring. For others, fall and winter offer new challenges for extending their harvest and their enjoyment as long as possible. I use both approaches. Some years, I just walk away, leaving green fruit on the vine and support poles to freeze in place, to be dealt with in spring. Other years, I get floating row cover out to help get my late crops through early frosts, and I sow other crops for early-spring harvest. There is no right or wrong way to handle your garden in the "off-season"; it just depends on how much time you have.

Of course, fall and winter gardening isn't just about the thrill of harvesting fresh vegetables and herbs for holiday dinners (though that's certainly a good reason to go to the effort!). It's also a great time to gather mulch materials for building new lasagna gardens or keeping the soil rich in established beds. You can enjoy the beauty of your outdoor gardens from indoors, if you've planned ahead and planted shrubs, perennials, and ornamental grasses that have interesting winter shapes or fruits. Including some berry- and seed-producing plants adds an extra benefit—attracting birds to your yard. And don't overlook the value of bringing some of your favorite flowers and herbs indoors for the winter, so you can enjoy them year-round. Any or all of these projects can help you make it through those dull winter days!

Extending Your Harvest

The first frost of the fall doesn't have to mean the end of your garden-fresh vegetable season. By planting cold-tolerant crops in late August or early September, selecting quick-maturing cultivars, and using row covers or other devices to ward off frost, even gardeners north of Zone 8 can harvest food into December.

Planting Crops for Cold-Weather Harvests

Fall is a great time for planting in all areas. With the cooler days and nights, those who live in warmer climates—the far South and desert Southwest—can begin gardens that would not have been possible during the hot summer. Gardeners in other areas can plant not only bulbs, perennials, and shrubs, but also food crops for a harvest later in the year or an early harvest the next spring.

Planting vegetables in late summer or early fall is just the same as planting at any other time. The secret is to choose crops and cultivars that tolerate or even thrive in cool weather. These include cabbage, chicory, kale, lettuce, spinach, and many other tasty leaf and root crops. For some specific suggestions, see "Late-Season Crops for Lasagna Gardens" on page 172.

Protecting Crops from Frost

Floating row cover is the late-season gardener's best friend. This spunbonded material is light enough to rest directly on top of plants, but it's dense enough to provide several degrees of frost protection. Of course, you can also use old sheets and blankets to cover your crops, but these heavier materials need some sort of support to keep them from breaking delicate stems. A-frames, bean towers, tepees, and tomato cages all make great supports for frost covers to protect late-bearing vegetables and edible flowers. Floating row cover lets sunlight through, so you can leave it on during the day as well as at night. Remove other types of covers as soon as the morning warms up.

Crop Covers Prolong Picking. Floating row cover makes it easy to extend your harvest season. I like to use metal support hoops, inserting them in spring and adding row cover to shield crops from late frosts. I remove the row cover in summer, but leave the hoops in place; then I replace the row cover in fall to protect against early frosts.

Growing Great Garlic

While you're taking advantage of cooler fall weather to plant flower bulbs and perennials, why not set aside a little time to plant a bed of garlic? When next summer comes, you'll be glad you did! A lasagna bed prepared in the fall will be ready for planting in the spring. A spring-prepared bed allowed to "cook" will be ready for planting a crop of garlic in the fall. For details on planting and harvesting this versatile crop, refer back to "Garlic" on page 45.

The plant we know as garlic comes in two subspecies: hardneck and softneck.

Hardneck Garlic

Hardneck garlic is acclimated to growing in cold regions. (My personal garlic-growing experience is in Zone 3/4, in upstate New York.) Up here, we plant hardneck garlic in the fall, about six weeks before the first hard frost, and harvest it in late summer or early fall of the next year. Hardneck garlic thrives in the loose, well-drained, organic-rich soil of an established lasagna bed. Mulching is necessary to prevent the alternate freezing and thawing of the soil, which can push the bulbs out of the ground; use 3 to 4 inches of compost, grass clippings, or chopped leaves.

As the name suggests, hardneck has a center stem that comes up in the middle of the narrow foliage and is almost woody when mature. This stem is formed when the bulb sends up a flowerstalk, which you need to remove to divert energy back down to the bulb. (The curled stem and unusual flower do have their uses, though. Add them to soups, stews, and sauces for flavoring; use them as a garnish; or include them in flower arrangements.) Of course, the bulbs are the main reason to grow hardneck garlic; they are easier to peel and have more complex flavors than softneck garlic.

Softneck Garlic

Softneck garlic is the kind most frequently grown for market. It fares better in warm zones and has a longer storage life, and its stems braid well. Gilroy, California, is the garlic capital of the United States, producing the most garlic for the produce market. Softneck garlic can be grown in colder regions, but it must be planted in the spring and harvested in the fall of the same year.

Growing conditions for softneck garlic are the same as for hardneck: loose, well-drained soil. Garlic isn't a heavy feeder, but compost-rich soil grows the best crops. It also needs a light mulch in warmer zones to keep the garden bed weed-free and to keep moisture in.

Late-Season Crops for Lasagna Gardens

Add a special touch to your Thanksgiving table with servings of just-picked vegetables right from your garden. Here's a listing of some great late-season crops for gardens in different parts of the United States.

Northern Gardens (Zone 5 and North)

Cabbage: *'Jingan' (55 days from planting to harvest) or 'Derby Day' (58 days).*

Chicory: *'President' (80 days); holds up best in winter weather.*

Collards: *'Champion' (60 to 80 days).*

Kale: *'Red Russian' (50 days).*

Leek: *'Durabel' (125 days).*

Lettuce: *'Red Montpelier', also known as 'Rougette du Midi' (65 days).*

Spinach: *'Bloomsdale' (50 days); the most dependable for overwintering.*

Temperate Gardens (Zones 6 and 7)

Beet: *'Kestrel' (53 days from planting to harvest for baby beets).*

Carrot: *'Minicor' (55 days for baby carrots).*

Collards: *'Champion' (60 to 80 days).*

Kale: *'Red Russian' (50 days).*

Lettuce: *'Sunshine' (50 to 60 days); performs best in cool weather.*

Spinach: *'Italian Summer' (40 days); bolt-resistant.*

Turnip: *'Purple Top White Globe' (57 days).*

Southern Gardens (Zones 8 and South)

Bush Bean: *'Nickel' (53 days); good heat- and cold-tolerance—pick beans for Christmas!*

Kohlrabi: *'Komet' (65 days from planting to harvest).*

Mustard: *'Giant Red' (45 days); plant in October and harvest until late March.*

Pea: *'Knight' (60 days); sow in mid- to late winter when garden beds begin to warm up and again in fall for winter crop.*

Radish: *'Gala' (26 days) or 'Redball' (24 days); radishes do not tolerate hot weather.*

(When you're not using your row covers, store them in clean garbage cans with lids. You'll know where they are when you need them, and the lids will keep mice from making nests in the material.)

For extra frost protection, hay or straw bales make a great cold frame. Stack them up around the bed to form a box, then cover the top with old windows or clear 6-mil plastic weighted down with stones.

Tips and Time-Savers

Fall Planting for Flowers and Herbs

Fall isn't just for planting vegetables—it's also a great time to sow seeds of cold-tolerant flowers and herbs, such as calendula (Calendula officinalis), pansy, chives, and parsley. In cold climates, they come up in the spring; warm-climate gardeners see plants and blooms in winter.

Gathering Mulch Materials

While building up your soil and rejuvenating old garden areas are ongoing processes, they're especially important in fall. By that time, most of your beds will be empty, or your perennials will have died back, so you can really pile on the organic matter. Fortunately, fall is a time of abundance. You may still be cutting grass when leaves begin to drop, but soon you will be mowing leaves. Fall is the time of year to take advantage of nature's bounty to cover growing beds with an insulating mulch, to fill composters, and to stockpile mulch for next year.

In addition to leaves and grass, which are free, the fall season usually brings discounts on bagged soil amendments, since garden centers are trying to get rid of their inventory before winter. Farmers who are cleaning out old hay to make room for new bales will, many times, let you haul the old bales away free. Livestock farmers are often looking for someone to take away their barn litter. Racetracks are another great source of manure-rich barn litter.

Keep a lookout for piles of wood chips where utility trucks have been clearing brush from roadsides, and cruise your neighborhood for bags of grass clippings and leaves from the unenlightened. If you live near the shore, collect free seaweed and kelp. Where pine trees are plentiful, their needles make great mulch for evergreens and other acid-loving plants. Once you develop a mulch mentality, you'll find a wealth of locally available materials for building and maintaining your lasagna gardens.

Tips and Time-Savers

Be a Considerate Mulch Gatherer

Over the years, I've learned two secrets for getting permission from farmers to haul away their spoiled hay, manure, and barn litter: Stay out of their way, and don't be a bother. If it is going to cost a farmer precious time and aggravation to deal with someone, he will just let the hay, manure, and barn litter lie and rot, rather than be bothered. Bring your own tools and containers, be prepared to do the work, and don't ask a lot of questions. Keep a low profile and say thank-you, then say it again with a card or gift so you will be welcomed back.

Stockpiling Your Mulch Materials

By the time you are a practiced lasagna gardener, you are also a constant worrier, wondering where your next layer of organic material is coming from. Just about the time the composter is empty and grass cutting is

Save Leaves for Spring. If you're lucky enough to have extra bags of leaves to save for spring mulching, consider piling them in an area where you plan to build a new garden. They'll make a good start on smothering the grass. Leaf bags also make great insulation around sheds and cold frames.

waning, fall arrives, bringing with it a host of free mulches and ingredients for composting. Each year, for instance, I use about 200 bags of leaves to mulch all my gardens and fill my composters. Fortunately, collecting that many bags is not difficult in the fall, and when I can, I gather twice as much as I need and save the extra leaves for spring and summer mulching. I use the plastic bags of leaves to kill the grass for a new garden and as insulation around my toolshed. Leaves are free!

When a local landscaper needs to get rid of a load of chipped bark, he knows he can dump it in a field near my gardens. We made arrangements years ago, and I still receive one or two truckfuls a year. The pile is out of the way, but I can still get my cart near to move it onto the gardens. Plus, wood chips are free!

You can see that you don't need to spend a fortune on organic mulches for your garden, especially if you have room to stockpile larger amounts of materials. Believe me, it's an incredibly satisfying feeling to have all your gardens covered in fall and still have piles of mulch ready and waiting for spring.

Gardening for the Birds

Besides feeding your own body and soul through the growing season, your lasagna garden can also be an important food source for wildlife in winter. By late fall, a garden is filled with a wealth of seeds, berries, and unpicked vegetables, which some tidy gardeners prefer to clean up before the snow falls. But if you groom your lasagna garden at this time of year, all that wonderful wildlife food is lost. If you leave everything in place (just mulching around the base of the plants), the birds that stay the winter will, to a great extent, sustain themselves on these seeds and berries. Once winter is over, clean up what's left of last season's growth, run it through the chipper, and put it back into the garden as mulch.

Northern bayberry

Winterberry

European mountain ash

Berries for Birds. Colorful berries are a welcome sight to hungry birds as well as winter-weary gardeners. Keep in mind that for some berries, such as winterberry, you need to grow both male and female plants to get pollination and fruits.

Leave the Seeds. Don't be in a hurry to cut down old flower stems in fall. These seedheads can provide a wealth of food for birds, and they add height and texture to the winter garden.

A combination of small trees, shrubs, and vines provides additional food, nesting sites, and protection for many birds. And by adding ornamental grasses to your garden, you not only create interesting height and movement in the winter garden but also provide even more valuable seeds. A garden with untrimmed perennials, berry-producing shrubs, tangled vines, and seed-bearing grasses makes an irresistible bird site. Add a highly visible feeder and a heated water source, and you'll have beautiful birds flocking to your backyard!

When you have a chance to choose new plants for your property, keep their bird-attracting potential in mind as well as their beauty. Grow as many food-bearing species as possible, with enough variety to assure birds a steady diet of fruit, buds, and seeds throughout the year. For some ideas of plants to try, see "Best Berries for Birds" on page 176.

BEST BERRIES FOR BIRDS

If you're thinking of adding a new shrub or tree to your yard, why not make it one that offers attractive berries? You'll enjoy the extra season of beauty, and the birds will enjoy the cold-weather bounty! Here's an overview of some of my, and my birds', favorites.

Name	Height	Notes
Japanese barberry (*Berberis thunbergii*)	4 to 6 ft.	Deciduous shrub with thorny stems bearing bright green leaves with variable fall color. Small, yellow spring flowers are followed by long-lasting, bright red berries. Full sun to light shade; average soil. Zones 4 to 8.
Red-twig dogwood (*Cornus alba* 'Sibirica')	8 to 10 ft.	Shrubby clumps of red stems bearing deciduous green leaves with variable fall color. Clusters of creamy white flowers in early summer are followed by gray-white fruits. Full sun; average to moist soil. Zones 3 to 8.
Flowering dogwood (*Cornus florida*)	15 to 30 ft.	Small tree with horizontal branches bearing oval, green, deciduous leaves that turn red in fall. Tiny spring flowers surrounded by showy white bracts are followed by clusters of shiny red fruit. Full sun to partial shade; evenly moist but not wet soil. Zones 5 to 8.
Washington hawthorn (*Crataegus phaenopyrum*)	25 to 30 ft.	Small to medium-size deciduous tree with thorny stems and dark green, leaves with variable fall color. Clusters of white flowers in early summer are followed by long-lasting, glossy red fruit. Full sun to light shade; average soil. Zones 4 to 8.

Name	Height	Notes
Winterberry (*Ilex verticillata*)	12 to 15 ft.	Deciduous shrub with dark green leaves that turn yellow in fall. Inconspicuous early-summer flowers are followed by long-lasting, bright red berries on female plants. For fruit production, you need at least two plants—one male and one female. Full sun to partial shade; average to moist, acid soil. Zones 4 to 9.
Eastern red cedar (*Juniperus virginiana*)	50 ft.	Pyramidal or columnar evergreen tree with blue, berrylike cones that ripen in fall. Full sun; average soil. Zones 3 to 9.
Japanese flowering crabapple (*Malus floribunda*)	15 to 25 ft.	Small deciduous tree with green leaves and pink to white spring flowers, followed by red fruit. Full sun; average to evenly moist soil. Zones 3 to 9.
Northern bayberry (*Myrica pensylvanica*)	6 to 8 ft.	Deciduous to semievergreen shrub with aromatic green leaves and long-lasting, waxy, bluish white fruits on female plants. A single plant might produce fruit, but setting out at least two (one male and one female) helps ensure fruiting. Sun to partial shade; tolerates poor, sandy soil. Zones 3 to 7.
European mountain ash (*Sorbus aucuparia*)	20 to 40 ft.	Small to medium-size deciduous tree with green leaves that have variable fall color. Clusters of white flowers in late spring are followed by orange-red berries in fall. Full sun; average soil. Zones 3 to 7.
American cranberrybush viburnum (*Viburnum trilobum*)	10 to 12 ft.	Deciduous shrub with glossy green leaves that turn red in fall. Clusters of white flowers in late spring are followed by long-lasting, brilliant scarlet berries. Full sun to light shade; evenly moist soil. Zones 2 to 8.

Planting a Garden for Winter Interest

The elements that attract wildlife to your garden in winter are the same things that make the garden pleasing to people. Bright berries add welcome touches of color, while standing seedheads offer interesting forms. Go a few steps further by adding a few plants with evergreen leaves or colorful or curiously shaped stems, and you've created a garden that's a joy to look at even during the dull days of winter.

If you enjoy walking through your gardens year-round, consider scattering these winter-interest plants throughout your yard, so you'll have an added incentive to go for a stroll. Otherwise, consider grouping several winter-interest plants in one highly visible spot—by your front door, perhaps. That way, you can frequently admire their beauty without bundling up for a winter walk.

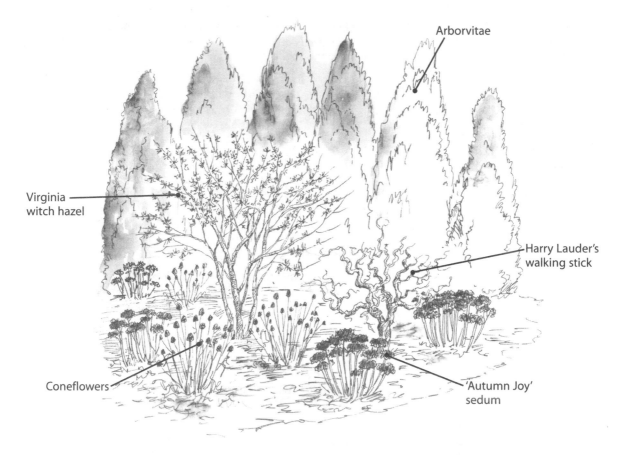

Extend the Show. Consider grouping a collection of plants that offer winter interest in a spot that's easy to see from inside your house. Include plants with late-fall or late-winter flowers, attractive stems, evergreen foliage, and interesting seedheads.

PRETTY PLANTS FOR WINTER GARDENS

Make the most of your lasagna gardening space by including plants that look as good in winter as they do the rest of the year. Here's a rundown of some of my favorite plants for winter interest.

Name	Height	Notes
Warty barberry (*Berberis verruculosa*)	6 ft.	Upright thorny stems with hollylike evergreen leaves that turn bronzy in winter. Yellow flowers in late spring or early summer are followed by blue-black berries in early fall. Full sun; average soil. Zones 5 to 8.
Harry Lauder's walking stick (*Corylus avellana* 'Contorta')	6 to 8 ft.	Contorted, shiny brown branches accented with long catkins in late winter. Prune out straight stems at the base. Full sun to light shade; average soil. Zones 4 to 8.
Rockspray cotoneaster (*Cotoneaster horizontalis*)	3 ft.	Horizontal branching habit with an interesting herringbone pattern. Pink buds open to white spring blooms, followed by red berries in fall and winter. Great for over a wall or bank. Full sun; average soil. Zones 5 to 8.
Virginia witch hazel (*Hamamelis virginiana*)	10 ft.	Sweetly scented yellow flowers bloom in fall, along with the yellowed leaves or just after the leaves drop. Other species tend to bloom in mid- to late winter. Full sun to light shade; average to moist soil. Zones 4 to 9.
Siberian iris (*Iris sibirica*)	3 ft.	Showy summer blooms in white, yellow, blues, and purples, followed by interesting brown seedpods. Full sun; moist soil. Zones 3 to 9.
Winter jasmine (*Jasminum nudiflorum*)	4 ft.	Trailing, vinelike shrub with green stems accented with yellow flowers in late winter. Full sun to partial shade; average to moist soil. Zones 4 to 9.

(continued)

Pat's Picks

PRETTY PLANTS FOR WINTER GARDENS—CONTINUED

Name	Height	Notes
Lavender (*Lavandula angustifolia*)	2 ft.	Bushy plants with fragrant gray stems and leaves offer interesting forms in winter. Full sun; well-drained soil. Zones 4 to 9.
Sumacs (*Rhus* spp.)	25 ft.	Curved, twisting stems offer interesting forms; upright, fuzzy clusters of dull red fruits stay all winter. Spreads quickly by suckers. Full sun; average to dry soil. Zones 3 to 8.
Rugosa rose (*Rosa rugosa*)	6 ft.	Pink, white, or red summer flowers are followed by large orange fruits, called hips. Full sun; average to dry soil. Zones 3 to 7.
Coneflowers (*Rudbeckia* spp.)	2 to 3 ft.	Golden-yellow summer daisies leave behind their prominent brown center cones; these seedheads last well into winter. Full sun. Zones 3 to 9.
Winter savory (*Satureja montana*)	6 to 12 in.	Small bushy herb with white flowers in summer and fragrant stems all winter. Good for rock gardens. Full sun; average to dry soil. Zones 4 to 9.
'Autumn Joy' sedum (*Sedum* 'Autumn Joy')	2 ft.	Flower heads mature over a period of months, from green to pink to bright red to rust red. Leave stems standing over winter; break them off when new growth appears in spring. Full sun; average soil. Zones 3 to 9.
Arborvitae (*Thuja* spp.)	Varies widely	Evergreen shrubs or trees with green or golden foliage; may take on a purplish cast in winter. Available in many forms, including rounded, bushy, pyramidal, and columnar. Full sun to light shade; average soil. Hardiness varies, depending on the cultivar.

Bring Herbs Indoors for Fragrance. Make the most of your garden by bringing a few plants indoors for wintertime enjoyment. I like to pot up creeping rosemary, so I can enjoy its good looks, fragrance, and flavor. Scented geraniums are fun to train into treelike "standards"; simply start with a fairly young plant and cut out all but one strong upright stem. Tie it to a stake so it will keep growing straight up, and pinch off sideshoots as they form on this trunk. When the shoot reaches the point where you want the head to be, pinch out the shoot tip to encourage branching. Pinch the tips of these branches regularly to create the bushy head.

Gardening Indoors in Winter

Bringing plants inside for the winter is more about saving yourself than saving plants. Herbs and flowers that have fragrance and beautiful forms brighten even the coldest day.

From the time I first spent a winter with a pot of prostrate rosemary sitting on a table in the living room, I have been unwilling to live without one. One year I just couldn't let go of a particular plant, so I lifted it from the garden in late summer and potted it for a gradual move inside. First I washed the garden soil from the roots and potted it in a clean soilless mix. After watering it thoroughly, I placed the potted plant in the shade of a shrub near the house. From there I moved it onto the porch under the eaves to protect it from the first frost, but kept it out of direct sunlight. Before I turned on heat inside the house, I brought the plant in and placed it near a window with little direct sun. The next move was to a permanent place on a table behind the sofa where the only light came from a pair of table lamps. For the next two years that rosemary brought me pleasure through several senses: the look of its shape, the texture of the foliage, the smell of its special fragrance, and the taste of it in numerous dishes.

The same steps I used to bring that rosemary plant indoors work well with many other plants, including scented geraniums. Just give them lots of light, but keep them out of direct sun. I find that covering the top of the pot with sphagnum moss helps keep the potting soil from drying out quickly, so I don't have to water as often.

Amaryllis bulbs are another fun indoor-gardening project, and they couldn't be easier.

Easy Amaryllis. For pure flower power, it's hard to beat the brightly colored blooms of amaryllis. They come in a wide range of heights and colors; some even have double flowers!

Everything the plant needs is enclosed in the bulb: roots, stems, leaves, bloom, and food to make it all happen. If the bulb you buy isn't already planted, simply choose a pot that's just an inch or so wider than the bulb itself. Add a few inches of potting mix to the pot, put in the bulb, and add a bit more mix around the sides. Leave the top third of the bulb uncovered. Set the pot in a sunny window and water thoroughly. All you do is place it in the light and give it water. With just occasional watering, a single bulb can reward you with one to four giant blooms. You can't beat that! In fact, amaryllis are so easy that they make great gifts, even for nongardeners.

Whether you use clay or plastic pots for your indoor plants is a matter of personal preference. But whatever containers you choose, make sure they have holes in the bottom, and place saucers underneath to catch the excess water. If you opt for unglazed clay saucers, be sure to use plastic liners to protect your furniture and floors. Or set pots and saucers on trivets or trays for protection.

Giving the Gift of Gardening

Sure, gardening is fun and rewarding—but it's even *more* fun and rewarding when you share the joy with someone else. With the holiday season coming up, fall and winter are great times to think of ways you can share the pleasures of gardening with your friends and family.

One of the ways I like to spread the fun is by what I call "remember-me plants"—gifts of beautiful, dependable bulbs or perennials. I either give something the recipients can plant or give something and plant it myself. Either way, I am planting myself in their gardens so they can remember me when that plant comes to life each year. I never give annuals or tender bulbs that need to be dug up and brought

indoors over winter to survive, and I hardly ever give biennials, because they are short-lived. My gifts are hardy perennials that need little care or bulbs that come back every year.

Sometimes I give the gift of a garden, one I create with my lasagna method, and leave it for them to work and play in. Of course, this is something that you'll want to discuss with the recipient before you go ahead and install it. Once you get the go-ahead, the lasagna method is a perfect route to go, since you can build the beds and plant them the

Plant a Memory. What could be more personal than a gift from your own garden? Sharing your favorite perennials and bulbs makes a very special present for friends and family alike. It's a good idea to include a card or note explaining the plant's needs, so the recipient can give it the right care.

The Gift That Keeps Giving

I've found that sharing plants is a wonderful way to build a friendship. For instance, when I first met a special friend of mine, I sent him 100 drumstick alliums (Allium sphaerocephalon) as a thank-you for lunch. Later he called and thanked me. Much later he called to tell me they were in bloom and were very beautiful. We had lunch again, and I sent him a box of my favorite old-fashioned white garden phlox (Phlox sp.). He planted the clumps in his silver garden and called to thank me. Later he called to tell me they were in bloom and how beautiful they were. In return, he gave me samples of his favorite grasses, a corkscrew willow (Salix matsudana 'Tortuosa') he started from a cutting and scotch thistle (Onopordum acanthium) plants that grew to 6 feet tall.

Over the years, my friend and I have exchanged plant gifts many times. When I visited his gardens, I would see all the plants I had given him: ground covers, poppies, divisions from my white garden, and many more. One day we stood at the edge of the border to his silver garden and he remarked that I had been planting myself in his garden. It was true!

same day—an instant garden! Prepare a little "fact sheet" explaining how to care for the garden through the year, or make your regular visits for garden maintenance part of the gift. Either way, you have the chance to share the beauty of a garden with someone who is too busy to start their own or who is intimidated by the idea of gardening. Once they see how easy lasagna gardening is, they'll be hooked for life!

Starting Seeds Indoors

Get a jump on spring this year by starting some of your garden plants from seed. You'll save money, since you can grow dozens of plants for the price of a single seed packet. You'll also have a greater variety of plants to choose from. Your local garden center may only stock one or two varieties of the most common plants, but seed catalogs offer a much wider variety of colors and sizes, as well as uncommon flowers and vegetables. Give seed starting a try at least once—it's easier than you think!

Deciding When to Sow

Late winter to midspring is a busy time for indoor seed-sowers. Cold-tolerant plants, such as broccoli and pansies, are among the first you can start, as are many perennials and slower-growing annuals, such as begonias. Wait until closer to midspring for starting faster-growing crops, such as squash. For best results, follow the sowing guidelines on the seed packet or in the catalog description. Don't be tempted to start your seeds too early, or the seedlings may get spindly and tangled by the time it's warm enough to plant them outside.

You'll often see seed-starting guidelines given in relation to the last frost date (as in "sow seeds around eight weeks before your last frost date"). This is the average date of the last spring frost in your area. In any given year, the last frost may occur several days before or after that date, but it's a helpful rule of thumb for planning seed starting. If you don't know your last frost date, ask other gardeners in your neighborhood, or ask at your local garden center.

Gathering Your Materials

First, you need something to sow your seeds in. You can buy plastic pots at your local garden center, or recycle deli food containers, plastic cups, and other items—pretty much anything that will hold 1 to 2 inches of seed-starting medium. Whichever container you choose, make sure it has at least one hole in the base so excess water can drain.

You also need some commercial seed-starting medium, available in bags at garden centers. (Don't use regular garden soil for indoor seed starting; it can carry disease problems and weed seeds, and it will pack down with regular watering, interfering with healthy root growth.) Before filling your pots, dump some of the seed-starting medium in a clean tub or bucket and add several cups of warm water. Knead the medium with your hands to help it absorb the water. Add more water as needed to get all the medium evenly moist, but not dripping wet. (If you add too much water, add some more dry medium until you get the right level of dampness.)

Scoop the moist medium into your containers, then smooth it out with your fingers. You want the surface of the medium to be 1/4 to 1/3 inch below the rim of the container. Lightly tap the bottom of the container on a firm surface to help settle the medium.

Let's Get Sowing!

Now you're ready to plant. Check the seed packet or catalog description for information on spacing and sowing depth. If it doesn't give any advice, sow large seeds about 1 inch apart, and cover them with ¼ to ½ inch of moist seed-starting medium. Plant medium-size seeds about ½ inch apart and cover with ⅛ to ¼ inch of medium. Scatter tiny seeds as evenly as possible over the surface of the medium; try to get them ¼ to ½ inch apart. Cover them with a light sprinkling of medium, or just press them lightly into the surface of the moist medium. Add some kind of label to each container immediately after sowing, so you won't forget what's planted in there!

Set the containers in a shallow pan of water and let them soak until the surface of the medium looks moist (usually in 30 to 60 minutes). Let the containers drain, then set them in a warm place with indirect light. Cover the containers with clear plastic, such as a large plastic bag, to help keep the air around the germinating seeds moist. Check the containers daily for signs of sprouting.

Raising Healthy Seedlings

When the seeds start to sprout, gradually remove the plastic cover. (Open it for 1 hour one day, then 2 hours the next, then a half day, then a whole day.) Seedlings need lots of light, so move them to a bright spot, such as a sunny windowsill. If windowsill space is limited, you can get great results with a simple fluorescent light fixture. Buy 2-foot or 4-foot "shop lights" at your local home center or hardware store, along with regular cool-white fluorescent bulbs. Hang the lights from a shelf or your ceiling. Suspend them from chains so it's easy to adjust their height as the seedlings grow; the lights should be about 4 inches above the tops of your seedlings. Keep the lights on at least 14 hours a day; 16 is better. Plugging the lights into an inexpensive timer helps ensure your seedlings get the light they need each day.

Water with room-temperature water when the seed-starting medium looks dry on the surface. For the first three weeks, fertilize once a week with a liquid fertilizer diluted to half its normal strength. After that, use a full-strength solution every two weeks. If your seedlings get crowded, snip off some of them at the base with scissors, or transplant them to individual containers. When they are ready for the garden, gradually introduce them to outdoor conditions, as explained in "Handling Hardening Off," below.

Handling Hardening Off

Indoor-grown seedlings are used to being pampered with warmth and water, so they need some help to adjust to the harsher conditions of the outdoor world. Two weeks before transplanting time, stop fertilizing and slow down on watering. About a week before planting, put the seedlings outdoors in a protected area, out of wind and direct sun. Leave them outdoors only an hour the first day, then two hours, then a morning, until they are used to being out a whole day. Water frequently, since they will dry out much more quickly than they did indoors!

Chapter 7

Ignoring Problems

 Flipping through the pest control section of most garden books is enough to frighten off even an experienced gardener. The army of nasty-looking bugs, dastardly diseases, and vicious weeds waiting to attack the minute your back is turned seems overwhelming. But what scares me more are some of the recommended solutions to these garden problems, including chemicals and toxins that are dangerous to man and beast.

Over the years, I've found that a hands-off approach to gardening generally works best: Ignore the problems, and they often take care of themselves. The key to this approach is starting with healthy plants, then creating a garden environment that encourages strong, vigorous growth, which is naturally less susceptible to pests and diseases.

Healthy-Garden Basics

Over the years, I've noticed that lasagna gardens aren't troubled by pests and diseases as much as traditional gardens are. Maybe it's because lasagna gardening creates and maintains healthy, fertile soil with the perfect environment for earth-worms. These natural tillers tunnel through the soil, allowing needed air and water to reach plant roots, plus they deposit nutrient-rich "castings" that build soil fertility. Continually renewing the top layer of mulch ensures a steady supply of food for earthworms, as well as conserving water and keeping plant roots cool. All these benefits come from laying down newspaper and soil amendments, some of which you used to dispose of by putting out for the garbage. Go figure!

Whatever the reasons, I know the soil in my lasagna beds is alive and healthy, since each garden has lots of earthworms and I run into few, if any, problems. To help keep it that way, I follow a few simple guidelines when I plan, plant, and care for my gardens.

Be a Smart Shopper

The most important part of keeping your garden healthy is knowing your enemies. You don't need a degree in entomology, but learning what the most common plant problems look like will protect you from bringing home problems with your new plants.

I learned the hard way not to blindly pick up plants from the nursery without a good inspection for pests. I once brought home annuals with whiteflies (tiny, white, winged insects that feed on the undersides of leaves) and put them in my greenhouse. I spent that summer removing all my plants and treating everything for whiteflies. Even if you've never had problems with plants from your local garden center before, it's still important to check every time you buy there. Garden centers buy their plants from many different growers, and any grower can have a problem that goes undetected and ends up in your garden. You can see why it's so important to recognize the

insects and the evidence of their presence. For pointers, see the "Checklist: Buying Healthy Plants" on the opposite page.

Every time you go shopping, take along a book on plant identification and growth habits, as well as a book with color photos of common insects and diseases, so you'll know what you're buying and what problems it might have. Also, find out where your garden center gets its perennials, shrubs, and trees. If they come from south of your growing area, they may not be suitable to your area. For instance, if you live in Zone 4 and your garden center gets its plants from a grower in Zone 8, those plants may not be able to withstand your cold winters. In other words, they will die. Get a guarantee from your landscaper or nursery-man that the plants you buy are hardy to your zone. (If you're not sure which zone you live in, refer to the "USDA Plant Hardiness Zone Map" on page 244.)

Look for Problem-Resistant Plants

It just makes sense to grow plants that are naturally less prone to the problems that are common in your area. If your bean plants come down with rust every year, for instance, look for a cultivar that is rust-resistant. Or, if you're tired of looking at gray patches on your garden phlox, replace it with a mildew-resistant selection, such as 'David'. "Resistant" doesn't mean that the plant will *never* get the problem, but that it will be much less likely to have a problem than a susceptible plant.

How do you know whether a certain cultivar is resistant? You'll usually find this information in the catalog description or on the seed packet. How do you know if you need a resistant cultivar? Mostly you learn by experience. If you're a new gardener, just go ahead and grow whatever plants you like best, regardless

Checklist: Buying Healthy Plants ✔

Before buying any plant, look closely at its stems and leaves (check the undersides too) for pests or signs of pest damage.

✔ Inspect shoot tips closely for aphids, small, pear-shaped insects that come in a variety of colors. They commonly feed on young, tender shoots, distorting growth and giving the lower leaves a sticky appearance.

✔ Look at both leaf surfaces for signs of spider mites. These tiny pests feed on the undersides of leaves, causing a stippled yellow or tan appearance on leaf surfaces; they may also produce fine webbing.

✔ Brush your hand over the plants to disturb the foliage; if whiteflies are present, they fly up in a small cloud.

✔ Check the leaves and stems for signs of scale (small dark lumps that scrape off easily with a fingernail) and galls (tumorlike growths that indicate the tree or shrub is infected with crown gall, a bacterial disease).

✔ Avoid any plants with stems or leaves that are wilted or discolored.

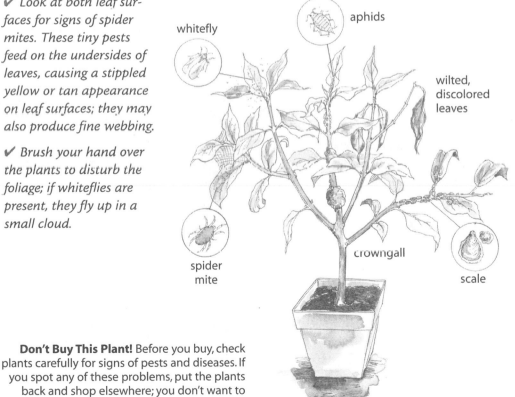

whitefly

aphids

wilted, discolored leaves

spider mite

crowngall

scale

Don't Buy This Plant! Before you buy, check plants carefully for signs of pests and diseases. If you spot any of these problems, put the plants back and shop elsewhere; you don't want to bring problems home to your healthy garden!

of their resistance to problems, and see how they do. If you notice a problem appearing, that's the time to look for plants that are resistant. Another way to find out about common problems in your area is to talk to local gardeners. You can learn from their experience and grow resistant cultivars from the start, so the problem may never appear in your garden.

Choose Companions Carefully

When you're building a healthy garden, *where* you plant can be just as important as *what* you plant. In some cases, for instance, combining certain crops can help minimize pest and disease problems—this is known as companion planting. Sometimes a companion is a strongly scented herb that seems to repel particular pests. In other cases, it's a "trap crop," a plant that the pests like better than your harvest crop. The pests congregate on the trap crop, where you can ignore them, spray them, or destroy them by pulling out the trap plants and disposing of them. There may not be a lot of scientific data to support the benefits of companion planting, but it works for me! Some of my favorite combinations include:

- Garlic and parsley next to roses (to protect the roses from black spot, a fungal disease)

- Chives and garlic next to peas and lettuce (to protect the latter crops from aphids)

- Radishes near cucumbers (to avoid cucumber beetles)

- Rosemary, sage, thyme, or tansy near cabbage (to deter cabbage moths, cabbageworms, and cutworms)

- Nasturtiums near broccoli (to lure aphids away from the broccoli)

My favorite trap crop is wild grapevines planted on a fence or arbor at the entrance to the garden. Japanese beetles love grape leaves so much that they go there first, saving your other crops from damage. Pick off the beetles regularly and drop them into a can of soapy water to control them.

When you're deciding where to plant your annual crops (mainly vegetables, but also flowers), you'll also want to consider what was growing in a certain site the year before. Growing a particular crop in the same spot year after year encourages the buildup of soilborne pests and diseases. While crop rotation—the practice of growing crops in different sites each year—can be complicated if you really get into the details, it can also be as simple as planting each crop in a different site each season. Keeping records of where you plant your crops each year will make planning future plantings easy.

I like to wait three or four years before I plant the same crop, or its close relative, in the same spot. For example, let's say you're growing cabbage in one lasagna bed this year. In the next two years, you might plant tomatoes, onions, or squash there—anything but cabbage and its relatives (including broccoli, cauliflower, collards, and kale). Other family relationships to keep in mind are eggplant, peppers, potatoes, and tomatoes (all in the botanical family Solanaceae) and cucumbers, melons, pumpkins, and squash (all in the family Cucurbitaceae).

Crop rotation has another benefit: It helps maintain your soil's nutrient balance. Leafy and fruiting crops are heavy feeders and rapidly use up nitrogen, while root vegetables and herbs tend to be light feeders. Peas, beans, and other legumes add nitrogen to your soil but need lots of phosphorus. Following a soil-building crop with a heavy-feeding crop and following a heavy feeder with a root crop or a soil builder will help balance your soil's nutrient supply.

Chives with lettuce

Thyme with cabbage

Nasturtiums with broccoli

Radishes with cucumbers

Compatible Companions. Some plants make good neighbors for other crops, either repelling pests or drawing pests toward themselves and away from your crops. Here are a few of the companion plantings I've had luck with in my garden.

Recruit Natural Allies

You're not alone in your battle against pests—beneficial insects, birds, and bats are on your side. While these helpful critters often just show up on their own, there are several things you can do to encourage them to call your garden their home.

Attracting and conserving the natural enemies of insect pests are important parts of managing your lasagna garden organically. The best way to protect beneficial insects is to avoid using toxic sprays or dusts in your garden. Even botanical insecticides kill beneficial species, so use them only when absolutely necessary to preserve a crop, and then only on the plants being attacked. Be careful when you handpick or spray pest insects, or you may end up killing beneficial insects by mistake.

You can make your yard and garden a haven for beneficial insects by taking simple steps to provide them with food, water, and shelter. Planting lots of herbs and flowers, for instance, will ensure a season-long supply of nectar and pollen for a wide variety of beneficial insects. Dry, dusty conditions can cause beneficials to dehydrate quickly; planting a hedge or building a windbreak fence around your garden will reduce dust problems. Also, fill a shallow birdbath or large bowl with stones and water so tiny beneficials can alight and drink without drowning. Lasagna gardens naturally have lots of mulch, which provides a great hiding place for beneficials; installing permanent pathways between the beds gives beneficials another protected area where they can hide between disruptions, such as planting and harvesting.

Unless your property is completely bare, at least some birds will visit with no special encouragement from you. Far more birds, however, will visit your lasagna garden if you take steps to provide their four basic require-ments: food, water, cover, and a safe place in which to raise a family. Food is the easiest of the four basic requirements to supply. A lasagna garden containing a mix of flowers, herbs, and vegetables will provide plenty of food during the growing season; perennials, shrubs, and trees with lots of seeds or berries provide food for birds in the off-season. Bird feeders help too. Some birds feed on the ground, while others eat their meals higher up. To attract as many birds as possible, set out a variety of feeders—seed tubes, broad platforms, and shelf and hanging types.

Provide a reliable source of water by setting a birdbath or shallow pan in the open and at least 3 feet off the ground. A spot near shrubs or overhanging branches will create handy escape routes from cats and other predators. Shrubs and trees also offer nest sites. You can add more nest sites and attract many types of birds to your yard with birdhouses. Different species have different housing requirements, but there are ready-made birdhouses, and build-your-own plans, for everything from bluebirds to barn owls. Whichever birdhouse you choose, make sure that it is weather-resistant, that its roof is pitched to shed rain, and that there are holes in the bottom for drainage and in the walls or back for ventilation. A hinged or removable top or front makes cleaning easier.

Feeders, birdbaths, and birdhouses play important roles in attracting birds. But trees, shrubs, and other vegetation can do the whole job naturally. Plants supply food, cover, and nest sites, and because they trap dew and rain and control runoff, they provide water too. When adding plants to your landscape, mix deciduous and evergreen species to provide cover all year long, and choose as many food-bearing species as possible. For suggestions, see "Best Berries for Birds" on page 176.

NATIVE BENEFICIAL INSECTS

It's easy to overlook beneficial insects, because most of them are inconspicuous in size and habit. They're so efficient, you may never have realized that pests were there. Here's a quick overview of some of the beneficials that are likely to visit a lasagna garden, along with tips on how to encourage them to stick around.

Name	Notes
Assassin bugs	Assassin bugs are robust, voracious insects with strong beaks to attack their prey. They squeak if you handle them, and they can inflict a painful bite. To preserve them, provide shelter with permanent plantings.
Braconid wasps	Rigidly mummified aphids or dying caterpillars with white cocoons stuck to their backs are signs that braconids have been at work. To attract them, grow nectar-producing plants with small flowers.
Ground beetles	Exceptionally long-lived (adults live up to two years), ground beetles are most active at night. Protect them by providing permanent pathways and ground-cover plantings.
Hoverflies	These insects hover over flowers and dart away like miniature hummingbirds. They often lay eggs in young aphid colonies to ensure their larvae will have enough prey. Flowers with plenty of pollen and nectar will attract the adults.
Lacewings	The delicate-looking adults flutter erratically in a zigzag flight through the garden at dusk. Plant pollen- and nectar-producing plants and provide a source of water during dry spells.
Lady beetles	Lady beetles abound in many sizes and colors, including solid black, ash gray, and yellow and orange with black spots or irregular blotches. Pollen- and nectar-rich plants will attract the adults.
Rove beetles	Often mistaken for earwigs, rove beetles are usually smaller and have no pincers. Provide cover by keeping plants mulched and maintaining permanent pathways.
Tachinid flies	One of the largest and most beneficial groups of flies, these are often mistaken for houseflies. To attract them, grow plants rich in pollen and nectar. Don't kill caterpillars with white eggs stuck to their backs; the eggs will become the next generation of flies.

Make Your Own Chemical-Free Sprays

If pests get past your natural defenses, don't run straight to your local garden center for a bottle of chemicals—make your own sprays from materials you have around the house. A simple high-force blast of water from a hose can knock pests off plants. Some will be killed, and others will get tangled in the mulch before they can climb back onto your plants. My favorite home remedy for aphids is a spray of 1 ounce of Murphy's Oil Soap mixed with 1 gallon of water. To make a good general pest spray, chop 1 garlic bulb and 1 small onion in a blender. Add 1 teaspoon of powdered cayenne pepper and 1 quart of water. Let stand overnight, then strain out the solids and spray the liquid on infested plants. (Keep this spray away from your eyes and nose, and wear rubber gloves to keep it off your skin, as it could cause painful burning.) To make a spray that controls aphids, whiteflies, and caterpillars, gather 1 to 2 cups of rhubarb or tomato leaves, chop them, and soak in 2 cups of water overnight. Strain out the leaves and add the remaining liquid to 2 cups of water. (Use care when handling the liquid, and avoid getting it on your skin.)

Foiling Animal Pests

Handling animal pests is a little different from dealing with pests and diseases. You can't just wait for natural predators to control the problem, or you'll be without a garden for the rest of the season. I've found that the best solution is a combination of approaches, including fencing some areas, changing my plant choices, and tolerating some damage when I can.

Deer

When I began lasagna gardening in the old hay field next to my house, I was aware of the deer that lived there and their habits. I had lived across the road at the inn for 14 years and watched them. In the predawn, they came up from the woods near the pond, traveled through the field by the inn, crossed the road, and disappeared behind the house into the woods on the other side. After dusk, they came back up through my big hay fields, through the cut in the windbreak, across my small hay field (where the new gardens would be), and crossed the road, heading back to the woods past the pond.

When I started gardening there, I had no illusions about controlling the age-old path of the large deer population. What I decided to try were some simple control methods that were possible and inexpensive. The first year, I erected a simple little fence near the road, across the front of the big perennial garden. I used 4-foot-high steel posts (they were easy to pound in), hooked plastic netting onto the posts, and tied fluttering white plastic tape to the top of the netting. The deer would see the flashing tape, then feel the netting with their nose. They began to cross further down the property. That year I only lost a few lily buds planted too close to the new crossing.

After two years I took the fence down and relied on my plantings of ghostly 'Silver King' artemisia (*Artemisia ludoviciana* 'Silver King') and applications of Milorganite (processed sewage sludge sold for garden use) around vulnerable plants. The swaying and fragrance of the gray plants and the smell of the Milorganite kept the deer away for several years. Eventually, though, they began crossing through the perennial garden again, so I had to start over again with the fence.

Simple Deer Fencing. I've had luck keeping deer out of my garden with a simple fence made of plastic netting attached to metal fence posts. I tie white plastic tape along the top and let the ends flutter in the breeze, as the flashing seems to help deter the deer.

In another area, I put in a new vegetable garden where the former owners had had a garden. I surrounded it with 3-foot-high wire fencing and steel posts. It would have been easy for the deer to step over it, but for some reason they didn't. Maybe it was all the things I hung from the fence posts: shoes, socks, gloves, hats, and bandannas, all worn that day and fragrant with my scent. In addition, when I had empty soil-amendment bags (from peat moss, manure, and the like), I would hang them over the fence posts to flutter in the wind. It all seemed to keep the wildlife at bay.

Overall, my best advice for keeping deer out of your garden is to try fencing, at least for a few years, then experiment with repellents for a while. Be prepared to switch back and forth as needed, as no one solution seems to work permanently.

Woodchucks

Woodchucks (also known as groundhogs, depending on where you live) are the bane of my existence. I am truly paranoid about them. They are there during the night, when my heritage beans are perfect and a group of gardeners is coming for a tour the next day. They pay a visit to my mesclun patch when it is just ready for harvesting and I have invited dinner guests who like to help pick the salad. These pesky critters are so bold they come out in full daylight to let me know they are going to eat whatever they want.

(continued on page 198)

Pest-Control Pointers

Controlling pests in the garden without chemicals isn't difficult, but it does take awareness and dedication. While I'm willing to ignore a reasonable amount of damage, there are a few pests that seem to be problems every year, so I make sure I'm ready with my control strategies.

Aphids, Spider Mites, and Whiteflies. Spray plants with a heavy force of water, followed with a spray of insecticidal soap. Spray with water again. To help repel aphids, cover the soil under aphid-susceptible plants with aluminum foil; it confuses the pests, so they're less likely to land on your crops.

Yellow sticky traps (sold in most garden centers, or through garden-supply catalogs) help control both aphids and whiteflies. One trap will help protect several plants. Wait several days, then add more traps if pests continue to cause damage. Place the traps near your plants, but not so close that the foliage gets stuck to the boards. You can form a guard of chicken wire around each trap to keep it from touching you and your plants. Set traps with the sticky sides facing your plants, but out of direct sunlight. Try to avoid placing the traps where the wind will blow dust and debris on them. Occasionally brushing the foliage of your plants with your hand will help drive the feeding pests into flight—and hopefully onto the boards!

Caterpillars. A wide array of caterpillars can damage your lasagna-garden plants, chewing large holes in leaves or devouring whole leaves. Cover transplants with floating row cover to keep these pests from reaching young plants. Pick caterpillars off uncovered plants by hand, and drop them into a container of soapy water. (If you see any green caterpillars with white-spotted black stripes, consider just moving them to another plant instead of destroying them—these are the larvae of the beautiful black swallowtail butterfly.)

Japanese Beetles. Pick Japanese beetles by hand and drop them into a can of soapy water. If you can't do this, use a battery-powered, handheld vacuum to suck them up. Be sure to empty the bag of beetles into soapy water to kill them.

Potato Beetles. If you see more potato beetles than you can pick and drop in a can of soapy water, try sweeping them off the vines with a broom. Do this when the beetles are young and haven't fed enough to be able to fly. Keep a mulch of straw or hay around the base of your potato plants. When you sweep the young bugs into the mulch, they can't find their way back.

Slugs. *Lay pieces of roof shingles (or other heavy material) near each of your gardens. Every morning, arm yourself with a spray bottle of ammonia and water, mixed half and half; lift each shingle and spray the slugs that have gathered underneath. Sweep the dead slugs under your garden mulch. Repeating this every day for two weeks will dramatically reduce your slug population. To protect individual beds or plants, circle them with a ring of wood ash or diatomaceous earth (a nontoxic mineral product available at most garden centers); slugs will not cross either line as it irritates their bodies. Yes, a pan of beer will attract slugs and they will die, but I hate to empty the pan of dead slugs. They are nasty when alive but dead they are truly repulsive.*

Safe and Simple Controls. *Before reaching for a spray, try some of the simple pest-control options illustrated below and at right.*

Trapping. To control slugs, lay pieces of shingles or boards on the soil; every morning spray the slugs that have gathered underneath with an ammonia-water mixture.

Excluding. Placing aluminum foil around plants can discourage aphids from landing on the leaves.

Hand picking. For larger pests, such as beetles, pick them off by hand and drop them into soapy water; removing them with a handheld vacuum or knocking them off with a broom or a strong spray of water are other options.

Controlling the Controllers

Cats are a big help in the garden, as they catch or repel a variety of animal pests. On the downside, though, they love to dig in the loose soil of lasagna gardens, especially in newly planted seedbeds. To discourage them from digging, I lay sections of short wire fencing across the top of a bed as soon as I finish sowing. Cats don't like the feel of the wire on their paws, so they will not walk or dig in the garden. When the seeds come up, I move the wire to the outside edge, in the grass, and the cats won't cross over it to dig out the seedlings. Once the seedlings are several inches tall, it's usually safe to remove the wire altogether.

Until this year, I thought I had found the perfect woodchuck deterrent: used cat litter! I mean *really used* cat litter. Not the kind with deodorants, not the kind that doesn't offend, even when overly used, but cheap, nasty, stinky cat litter.

It's easy to find where the woodchuck lives. It's usually under a building close to the garden. You can see the outside opening to its tunnel along the foundation of an outbuilding, such as a garage, barn, or toolshed. Once you find the opening, pour the used cat litter down the hole. Usually the woodchuck will move on to the neighbor's yard.

Of course, no method is foolproof. Last year I had a woodchuck that just wouldn't leave. I poured dirty litter down every opening under the toolshed and it didn't faze him. He stayed under the shed all summer, making frequent forays into the garden, and taunting me during the day by coming out, closer and closer to the garden, standing up between each encroachment and looking at me. I think that woodchuck liked living in a dirty, smelly place. And I think he was enjoying toying with me. Oh, well. I still recommend trying the cat-litter technique, as it seems to discourage *most* woodchucks!

Rabbits

Rabbits were not much of a problem at my farm, because there were a lot of cats, owls, and hawks. If natural predators are lacking in your area, or if they're not controlling the problem, try circling the plants the rabbits like with a sprinkling of bloodmeal (available at garden centers). If that doesn't work, enclosing your garden with fencing is the way to go.

Weeds Are Relative

What I think are some of the prettiest flowers in my garden, others think of as weeds. I once overheard a couple talking about a corner foundation garden at the front of my farmhouse. She said: "How soft Pat's gardens look!" He said: "Those are weeds and should have been cleaned out." They were both right, to a point. I had let Queen-Anne's-lace come and stay in a garden of trees, shrubs, and perennials. The lacy-looking flowers were beautiful and filled in empty spaces between

Rabbit Repellent. If you can't fence-in your garden, try repelling rabbits by surrounding their favorite plants with rings of bloodmeal.

Weed Control for Busy Gardeners

Some years, you just may not have the time you need to keep up with regular mulching. You can get away with it for one year, but by the end of the second year, your beautiful lasagna garden will revert to a weed patch. Fortunately, it's easy to reclaim the area—simply stomp the weeds down, cover with thick pads of wet newspaper, and begin the mulching process all over. For quick composting, cover the entire bed with black plastic, and let the sun bake it for two to six weeks. By "cooking" the garden, you hasten the composting process and bake the weeds and their seeds. Replant and keep mulching, and you're back on track!

other plants. I don't consider Queen-Anne's-lace a weed in a flower garden, but I do pull it out in the vegetable garden.

Overall, I like my gardens to have that soft, casual look, and it's easy to achieve by the second or third year of a garden. By this time, self-seeding biennials and perennials, plus a few "weeds," have filled in and hidden the mulch. It's almost a given result of a lasagna garden. The soil is receptive to seeds because it is naturally healthy and the mulch is soft. Seeds fall and sprout. You aren't poking about in a lasagna garden with a lot of unnecessary digging and tilling, so you don't dig out young, self-seeded plants. To my mind, if a young plant is tough enough to come up through several layers of mulch, it deserves to stay.

Back to the couple looking at my garden. She said: "I want a garden with lots of flowers that I can cut for bouquets." He said: "I only have time to keep the grass cut on weekends, not to maintain flowerbeds." My response is, why can't you have both? Planting swaths of wildflowers on the outside edges of your property is a super way to reduce the amount of lawn you have to maintain, and you'll have plenty of easy-care flowers to enjoy. It's simple to do the lasagna way: Just build new lasagna gardens each fall and sow wildflower seeds

WEEDS YOU CAN LIVE WITH

Gardening is a personal thing. It's creative, and you make choices about your creation. What is a problem or weed to one person is a thing of beauty to another. Here's a rundown of some of my favorite weeds, and why I like them.

Name	Notes
Wild white yarrow (*Achillea millefolium*)	When dried, the white flower heads turn a beautiful celadon green.
Pearly everlastings (*Anaphalis* spp.)	When cut just before fully opened, the flowers dry white with a tiny yellow dot at the center.
New England aster (*Aster novae-angliae*)	Masses of blooms in colors ranging from near-white to pink to deep purple.
Oxeye daisy (*Chrysanthemum leucanthemum*)	Brilliant white flowers with bright yellow centers.
Wild chicory (*Cichorium intybus*)	Beautiful blue flowers.
Queen-Anne's-lace (*Daucus carota* var. *carota*)	Lovely lacy, white, umbrella-shaped flower heads provide soft fillers in the garden and are good in fresh arrangements.
Joe-Pye weed (*Eupatorium purpureum*)	Tall stems topped with clusters of rosy pink flowers; remarkably adaptable.
Tawny daylily (*Hemerocallis fulva*)	An escapee from cultivated gardens, this daylily produces large, showy orange flowers. The buds are great in stir-fry.
Hawkweeds (*Hieracium* spp.)	Bright daisylike blooms in sunny yellow or eye-catching orange on fuzzy stems.

right over them. Each fall thereafter, add new layers of compost mulch mixed with peat moss, and broadcast more seeds.

So, what do you do about those "real" weeds? One of the benefits of lasagna gardening is that the thick layers you start with are enough to smother even tough weeds that are already on the site. After that, you rarely, if ever, need to disturb the soil, so you don't bring up weed seeds that are buried in the soil. Adding mulch regularly and setting plants close enough that they fill in and cover the surface of the bed are enough to discourage most new weeds from getting started. The few that do pop up are easy to pull out, since the soil is loose. The most challenging part of weed control in lasagna gardens is learning the difference between weed seedlings and seedlings of plants you want to keep!

Wonderful Weeds. Not all weeds are bad—some are beautiful. Some years, I leave certain "weeds" in my garden, other years I pull them out: It just depends on my mood!

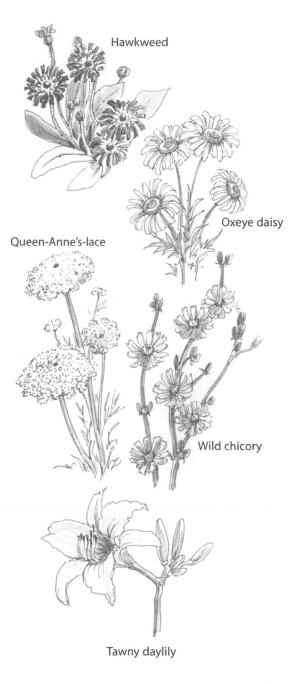

Hawkweed

Oxeye daisy

Queen-Anne's-lace

Wild chicory

Tawny daylily

Chapter 8

Finishing Touches

 Want to make your garden really fun and exciting? Add some special touches to express your personal style. These elements can be as practical as a picket fence or wood-chip path or as whimsical as some silly garden art. Arbors, trellises, walls, fences, edges, containers, paths, walkways, and accessories are all fair game for giving your garden some style. They provide a beautiful background for the seasonal progression of foliage, flowers, and fruits in your plantings.

Of course, finishing touches aren't limited to just flower gardens. Even if you only grow vegetables and don't have space for flowers or fanciful structures, you can use your imagination to create interesting supports for your vining crops. And there's no law that says you have to spend a lot of money on finishing touches. If you're a dedicated recycler, you can make use of items that others might throw away to decorate your garden.

Exclamation Points: Arbors, Arches, and Other Vertical Supports

Training vines and climbers to upright supports does more than add another dimension to your garden: It frees up valuable space for lower-growing plants. Most of us do not have enough gardening area, so my advice is to grow *up!*

Arbors, arches, A-frames, and other supports come in many guises. Some supports are sophisticated twisted iron, finished in verdigris. Others are made of wood from discarded pallets. Somewhere in between are kits that come ready to be screwed together and installed. Regardless of the material or style you choose, an arbor or trellis will make any garden more memorable.

Supports for the Vegetable Garden

Adding vertical supports to your vegetable garden is a wonderful way to increase your harvest without increasing the size of your garden. You can grow two crops—one upward and another at its feet—in the same amount of space you only grew one crop in before. Trellises also help to keep plants healthier, since they allow good air circulation around the stems and hold the leaves and fruits off the soil, discouraging the development of diseases. Trellised plants can provide welcome shade to lower-growing crops, such as lettuce, that dislike strong summer sun. Best of all, picking is a snap—no more bending over to gather your harvest!

In fact, a vegetable garden was the site of my conversion to vertical gardening. My first few gardens at the farm were flat and two-dimensional until I added 6-inch board siding to the beds. Just that 6 inches of board gave

Stepping Up Your Crops. Give your melons a lift by training them over an old stepladder! Anchor the ladder to protect it from being blown over in high winds, then train the vines up and over it. As melons form, place each one on a step; cover the fruit with old stocking or netting, and tie it to the ladder to hold it in place until it's ready for harvest.

the garden definition that had not been there before. Next, I added stone paths, then 6-foot bamboo tepees to support pole beans and other vining crops. My garden spaces, between the paths, were divided into squares, rectangles, triangles, and diamonds. I placed the tepees in the middle of the larger spaces for vining crops and grew low-growing crops at their base. In the smaller squares, I added one 2-by-2-inch stake. Each of these 8-foot stakes could support one tomato plant or four pole beans, leaving room at the base

Linguine Gardening

At my daughter Judy's house, a narrow, single-car driveway separates her property from her neighbor's. At the end of the house, the driveway curves a bit, leaving a long, narrow growing space in front of a picket fence sitting on the property line. I considered that strip under-used, and I began to visualize how Judy and other homeowners with similar sites could make the most of these small spaces.

My thoughts turned to vertical gardening. I could see low, vine-clad fences in the narrow spaces between the driveways in the front of the houses. The space on each side of the low fence would contain long narrow gardens facing each homeowner. The plantings at the base of the vines would reflect the individual gardeners' personal tastes.

The strip of land is long and narrow, so I adapted my lasagna-gardening method to linguine gardening. To create your linguine garden, first find your property line, then install your choice of vertical growing support—a fence, trellis, or other structure—within your property line. (Actually, it's a good idea to talk to the neighbor that shares that space before you install the support, so you avoid any misunderstandings!) Once the support is in place, prepare the soil as you would using the lasagna method: Lay pads of wet newspaper over the grass; cover the paper with 2 inches of peat moss. Add organic soil amendments (grass clippings, chopped leaves, compost, topsoil, and the like) in 4-inch layers, alternated with 2-inch layers of peat moss, until you have 12 to 24 inches of neat layers.

If you want to plant right away, pull the layers wide enough apart to get your plants in, pull the layers back up around the roots, water well, and you're finished. If you have planned ahead and your linguine garden has had 6 to 12 weeks to decompose, you will have 6 to 8 inches of loamy soil; scoop the soil aside to make the planting hole, insert plants, pull the soil back around the roots, then water and mulch.

A Simple Strip Garden. Make the most of a small space with a linguine garden. Even a narrow strip along a driveway has enough room for a climber-clad fence with some low-growing plants at the base.

for low crops like bush basil. In another section, I grew two rows of peas in a space 1 foot by 12 feet, with metal posts installed down the middle. Twine strung between the posts provided support for pea vines planted on both sides.

These structures gave my vegetable garden a whole new dimension, and this success encouraged me to seriously start "growing up." I turned my grandchildren's sandbox into a minigarden with a permanent wood-framed, wire support attached to one side. I may have gone too far when I made lasagna gardens under the children's old swing set, draped it with netting, and grew cucumbers and melons. It worked great, though! An old stepladder—one that's maybe not safe to stand on but not junky enough to throw away—is also a wonderful support for melons.

Ornamental Supports

When you're creating support structures for flower gardens, you can really let your imagination go wild. Sure, simple bamboo tepees can be fun here—in fact, they're great for fast-growing annual vines, which will cover the stakes quickly and be smothered in blooms by the end of the summer. (Bamboo tepees, by the way, are ideal for children's gardens, as they make wonderful hideouts! Runner beans are an excellent choice for covering the tepees, as they provide bright flowers as well as edible beans for a playtime snack.)

If you're looking for a bit more elegance, consider installing an arbor to create an enticing entrance or a shady spot for sitting. A wrought-iron arbor fits a formal garden best, while a rustic wood arbor fits well in an informal planting. Of course, you can also paint the arbor, using white or a bright color to make it stand out, or a dark color, such as green or brown, to help it blend in. One of my favorite vertical supports was a wooden arbor that bridged the space between my white garden and my shade garden. My favorite clematis, 'Henryi', grew up and over the arbor, drawing the eye to the back of the garden and up toward the maple tree. The structure was interesting in all seasons, not just during summer bloom, since it added height to the otherwise flat space.

Attractive supports come in a wide range of sizes and prices. Depending on your site

Recycled Rungs. Have some fun in your garden by using found objects as unusual vertical accents. Old ladders, for instance, make great supports for climbing vines.

Sweet pea

Love-in-a-puff

Scarlet
runner bean

Nasturtium

Quick-Climbing Color. Annual vines are great for quick color. These fast-growing vines can wind their way up a variety of supports, giving you a super show of bloom right at eye level.

and budget, you can build a trellis or arbor from scratch, buy a kit, or hire someone to install the structure for you. If your construction ability is limited, look for simple homemade structures, or buy them ready-made. On my barn, for instance, I trained grapes on twisted vine hearts, in place of a trellis that I found beyond my building capabilities. I placed ready-made fan trellises in planters on my deck to grow scarlet runner beans, and lattice trellises in half-barrels to grow hops.

Looking for something really quirky to liven up your garden? Old rakes and ladders make interesting supports. Lean them against the wall of a shed, or prop them up in the garden or in unexpected places. Decorate an arbor with old tools and broken pots wired onto it. Sections of freestanding fencing or old gates with minigardens growing on both sides are also fun for adding a touch of whimsy.

Keep in mind that while all vines climb, not all climb the same way. You need to know how a vine climbs so you can choose the best support for it. Some vines climb by twining around a support: Sweet peas and clematis wrap a tendril or leafstalk around a slender pole, while wisterias, morning glories, and beans wrap their entire stems around a post. Other vines attach themselves with adhesive holdfasts: English ivy *(Hedera helix)* has adhesive rootlets, while Boston ivy *(Parthenocissus tricuspidata)* and Virginia creeper *(P. quinquefolia)* have adhesive disks at the ends of tendrils.

MY FAVORITE CLIMBERS

Flowering vines are an obvious choice for vertical gardening, but don't stop there! Try vining vegetables, fruiting vines—even shrubs with long, arching stems can look great on an arbor, fence, or trellis. All of those mentioned below will thrive in full sun and the well-drained soil of a lasagna garden. I've given approximate heights, but the ultimate size of most vines is determined by the supports they're growing on. Vines that usually grow up to 10 feet are a good choice for lightweight supports, such as bamboo tepees or plastic trellises; larger vines need a sturdier support, such as a wooden trellis or arbor.

Name	Height	Notes
Love-in-a-puff (*Cardiospermum halicacabum*)	10 ft.	Delicate-looking vine with deeply cut green leaves and tiny white flowers from summer to fall. Blooms mature into balloonlike pods enclosing the round black seeds, each marked with a white heart. Annual.
Clematis (*Clematis* spp.)	8 to 24 ft.	Vines that climb by twining leafstalks, bearing deciduous leaves and showy, flat or bell-shaped blooms in a wide color range in spring, summer, or fall, depending on the species. Zones 4 to 9 (varies according to species).
Cotoneasters (*Cotoneaster* spp.)	12 ft.	Shrubs with arching branches bearing deciduous or evergreen leaves and small, pink or white spring flowers, followed by red berries. Zones 4 to 8 (varies according to species).
Melons (*Cucumis melo* and others)	8 ft.	Vining stems that climb by tendrils, producing sweet fruits in a range of flavors and sizes. Support the developing fruits with fabric slings tied to the trellis. Annual.
Cucumber (*Cucumis sativus*)	8 ft.	Tendril-climbing vine with yellow flowers followed by elongated or rounded fruits. Great on a fence or trellis. Annual.
Gourds (*Cucurbita* spp. and others)	10 ft.	Vining stems that climb by tendrils, with white or yellow flowers that mature into decorative fruits in a range of colors, sizes, and shapes. Annual.

Name	Height	Notes
Summer squash (*Cucurbita* spp.)	8 ft.	Vining stems that climb by tendrils, with tasty fruits in a range of shapes, sizes, and colors. Pick often to keep plants producing. Annual.
Hyacinth bean (*Dolichos lablab*)	15 ft.	Twining vine with three-part, green or purplish leaves and spiky clusters of pinkish purple blooms in summer, followed by glossy, deep purple seedpods. Annual.
Hops (*Humulus* spp.)	30 ft.	Vigorous twining vines grown for their large, three- to five-lobed leaves and green, conelike pods. They need a large, sturdy support. *H. japonicus* is annual. *H. lupulus* is a perennial, dying back to the ground each fall. Zones 3 to 8.
Morning glories (*Ipomoea* spp.)	15 ft.	Twining vines with heart-shaped leaves and large, trumpet-shaped, white, pink, red, blue, or purple flowers from midsummer to frost. Annual.
Sweet pea (*Lathyrus odoratus*)	6 ft.	Leafy vines that climb by tendrils, with dainty blooms on long stems from midspring into summer, usually in white or shades of pink, purple, or red. Grows best in cool climates. Annual.
Tomato (*Lycopersicon esculentum*)	15 ft.	"Indeterminate" tomatoes have long, trailing vines that grow and fruit well on stakes, strings, or trellises; they need tying to hang onto their support. Annual.
Scarlet runner bean (*Phaseolus coccineus*)	8 ft.	Twining vines with broad, green, three-part leaves and clusters of bright orange-red blooms from midsummer to frost. Flowers are followed by edible pods; you can pick them when young and cook like snap beans. Annual.

(continued)

MY FAVORITE CLIMBERS—CONTINUED

Name	Height	Notes
Pole beans (*Phaseolus* spp. and others)	8 ft.	Twining stems with white flowers followed by tasty pods for fresh eating or drying. Annual.
Pea (*Pisum sativum*)	6 ft.	Leafy vines that climb by tendrils, with white or pinkish flowers followed by long pods containing plump seeds. Annual.
Firethorns (*Pyracantha* spp.)	15 ft.	Upright to arching woody stems with evergreen to semievergreen leaves and clusters of white flowers in spring, followed by showy, orange-red berries. Zones 5 to 8.
Roses (*Rosa* spp.)	20 ft.	Long, flexible, thorny stems that bear showy single or double flowers in a range of colors in summer. Stems need some tying to help them hold onto a support. Zones 4 to 9 (varies according to species).
Nasturtium (*Tropaeolum majus*)	6 ft.	"Climbing" nasturtiums have long, trailing stems that grab onto a support with their leafstalks. The unusual, circular leaves are accented with large, showy blooms in a wide range of colors from early summer to fall. Annual.
Grapes (*Vitis* spp.)	50 ft. or more	Woody-stemmed vines with tendrils that cling to supports. Some species are grown primarily for their fruit, others for their handsome leaves, which turn red or purplish in fall. Zones 4 to 9 (varies according to species).

Fabulous Fences

There are as many kinds of fencing as there are reasons for having one. The style of fencing you choose depends on a number of factors, including your budget and the purpose you want the fence to serve—marking a property line, dividing areas within your yard, hiding unsightly views, providing privacy, keeping animals out, or keeping kids and pets contained. You also want a fence that fits in well with your neighborhood and garden style. A post-and-rail fence looks great in a suburban or rural setting, for instance, while a wrought-iron fence adds a touch of elegance to a city garden. Stone pillar-and-rail fencing

High-Style Fences. Make the most of your fences by accenting them with plants. A picket fence is a fun backdrop for a cottage-garden collection of flowers, while a row of daylilies can really dress up a plain post-and-rail fence. Make the most of a solid board fence by training a climbing vine over it.

is often used in the mountains because there are lots of stones for pillars and wood for rails. Stockade fencing is commonly used for privacy, while picket fences have a more inviting, decorative look.

A fence is one of the finishing touches to a garden, but I usually install it first. That way, I don't have to worry about disturbing established plants to dig fence posts. If you need to keep critters out or kids or pets in and you don't have the money to install a permanent fence, start with the relatively inexpensive wire fencing sold in rolls at garden and home centers. During the growing seasons, dress it up with some annual vines to hide the wire and add some color, until you can afford a more permanent fence.

Before you install a permanent fence along a property line, it's smart to check with local building codes, as some require a certain distance between the line and the fence; there may also be other regulations as to the style and height of the fence. It's also courteous to discuss your plans first with your next-door neighbor. You can avoid a lot of hard feelings and unpleasant surprises if you are both clear on where the fence is going!

Rubble Walls

What can you do with the stones and rubble you find in your garden? I make rubble walls—basically "boxes" made from the flattest stones, with the smaller, irregular stones filling the inside. My rubble walls were inspired by long-gone farmers and the fieldstone walls they built during the clearing of their fields to grow crops.

The idea to build these walls came to me as I walked the woods and fields to keep open the cross-country ski trails surrounding our inn. During my walks, I came across many

The $10 Picket Fence

If you're looking for a fence with some character—one that doesn't have that raw, new look—check around at auctions or antique shops. Sometimes, you can find some real bargains. Do keep in mind, though, that the price you buy the fence for may be very different than what you end up spending on it. Take a lesson from the story of my $10 picket fence. . . .

A friend called to tell me about fencing that was to be auctioned off that evening, and I made arrangements to attend. The old picket fence was stacked outside the auction house. As I inspected it, I thought of the work that had gone into making all those pickets, not to mention the work involved in taking it down and moving it there to be sold. I wondered if I could afford such a thing.

Toward the end of the auction, a handler brought out a section of the fence. I waited for the bidding to start as the auctioneer extolled the virtues of the fencing: all handmade, so big, such a wonderful gate, and on and on. From $200 asking, to $100, down to $75, down to $50 and finally, who will give $10. Knowing it would go on down to $1, I felt sorry for the fence and all the work involved, and lifted my number at $10. No one bid against me, so the gavel came down and the fence was mine for $10. My friend congratulated me on my buy and helped me load it on the truck. Once home we unloaded it onto pallets out in back of the shed.

Soon snow covered the stacks of fencing, so it stayed piled up until spring. I asked my neighbor Ed to do the repair work the fence needed, and he agreed. He fixed the broken pickets, dug holes, installed fence posts, put up the fence sections, and installed the gate.

When Ed was finished, I had a new garden space that measured 30 by 35 feet inside the fence. I liked the look of the old fencing with flaking white paint, but the repairs were done with new wood, so I promised myself I would get it painted at the first opportunity. After paying for the repair work and materials, I reckoned that the fence had cost me about $610. My resources were depleted, so painting had to wait.

Two years later, I asked Ed's wife, Doris, to help me paint the fence. Each day she would come for a couple of hours, sit on a little bench, and paint. From time to time, Ed would go to the hardware store and bring home yet another gallon of Wild Bayberry paint. I knew this paint was expensive but figured it was worth it; after all, how much paint could pickets take? It seemed this fence needed a lot, for the wood was dry and it absorbed the paint quickly. By the time the painting was finished, I totaled up the labor and paint and learned that the fence had now cost me $1,110!

stone walls crisscrossing the land. Some of the walls were just piled stones, running the length of a property line; others were more carefully laid up. The best-looking and most durable ones were actually two walls of flat stone with rubble inside and capped by interlocking flat stones. After hundreds of years, they stand as sturdy as the day they were built.

I built my first little rubble wall with stone that had surfaced during the removal of contaminated soil due to an oil spill and from construction of the circular driveway. I moved small piles of stone from the garden areas to a larger pile near the driveway, then finally to a spot on the edge of the gardens. Determined to move the stones only once more, I thought of building a short version of a farmer's stone wall. Once I made the decision, I built the wall in less than a day.

Beginning with the largest stones, I laid them end to end and tipped in slightly toward the center. In the next rows, I laid the stones so they crossed the cracks where each two lower stones met. As I went along, I tossed the rubble stones into the middle. By the time I had a 2-foot-high wall, the center was full of rubble. I dumped topsoil onto the rubble and washed it down with a strong spray of water. The soil settled in the spaces between the rubble, making places for roots to grow.

I planted the wall with several different thymes, as well as winter savory, sedums, and a number of ground covers. They took hold the first year, made it through the winter, and began to seed into the driveway. It was easy and very beautiful. During the next six years, I received more questions and comments about the rubble wall than any other aspect of the garden. If you spend a lot of time struggling with rocks, or if you're looking for a way to provide the excellent drainage that rock-garden plants demand, I definitely recommend giving rubble walls a try!

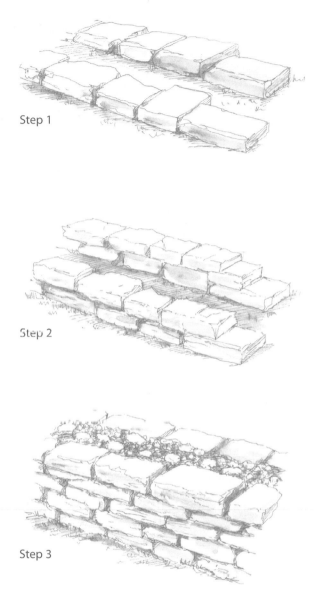

Step 1

Step 2

Step 3

Making a Wall. Make use of the rocks you dig up by building a rubble wall. (1) Start by laying the largest, flattest rocks in two rows to form the base of the wall. (2) Add the next layer of rocks, placing them so they overlap the cracks in the lower layer. (3) Continue building up, tossing smaller rubble in the middle as you work, until the center is even with the outer walls.

Easy Rock Gardening

A rubble wall is a great place to grow rock-garden plants, as the excellent drainage can help them survive damp conditions that might kill them in a ground-level garden. But what do you do if your whole garden is as rocky as a rubble wall? You use those same tough guys as the basis for all your plantings.

Our gardening season—as short as 6 weeks, and as long as 12 if we were lucky—seemed perfect for rock-garden plants. As an innkeeper, with little time for gardening in the early days, I had time to nurture only small areas. Instead of digging out rocks, I brought more in to protect my plants from harsh winds. I loosened the soil as best I could with sand, gravel, and grit, then used peat moss, more sand, and leaf mold to create pockets of planting material close to the heat-saving rocks.

I started out with early-blooming small bulbs—crocus, grape hyacinths (Muscari spp.), and snowdrops (Galanthus nivalis)—followed by miniature daffodils and lily leeks (Allium moly) for late-spring bloom, and they looked great. Then I bought alpine asters, woolly yarrow, and crested iris, all of which lasted only two or three years before they died out, due at least in part to the extreme cold, I think. I did have success with many others, though, including sweet woodruff and rock soapwort: enough success to keep me shopping for more rock-garden plants to try. Over the years, I've had my share of successes and failures, but overall, I found that the more care I put into choosing the plant, the more likely it was to survive.

If you are faced with a tough, rocky site, why not stop fighting the rocks and plant around them instead, like I did? For some suggestions of plants to try, see "Rock-Garden Plants for Rubble Walls" on page 216.

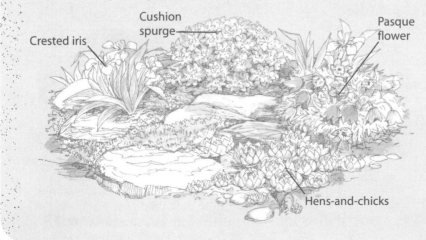

Crested iris

Cushion spurge

Pasque flower

Hens-and-chicks

Cheerful Color for a Tough Site. If your soil is too rocky to dig, try growing tough rock-garden plants between the stones. With careful planning, you can have color all through the season!

Down the Garden Path: Paths and Walkways

Sure, paths are practical, but they can be an attractive garden feature as well. Whether you need a straight walkway to get from point A to point B, or you'd like a meandering path to invite visitors to investigate hidden parts of your garden, the project deserves careful thought and preparation.

Picking the Right Path

The key to a successful path is to match the material to your needs, your budget, and your garden style. Grass paths are simple to make, inexpensive, attractive, and easy on the feet. If you want to change the width or shape of the path, it's a simple matter to cut away the sod or sow a bit of seed to fill in. I like to leave grass paths through new garden areas until I'm positive where I want a permanent path to go. On the downside, grass paths can quickly become worn and muddy. Setting flat stepping-stones into the center of the path can help provide a sturdier footing and prevent compaction.

Shredded-bark paths have a natural look that's wonderful winding through flower gardens. Bark is also a good choice for paths between beds in the vegetable garden. The footing on bark paths can be a little loose, but they tend to stay clean and drain well, so they're comfortable to walk on even in wet weather. They're a snap to make, too. I lay landscape fabric (available at garden and home centers) or pads of newspaper first to keep weeds and grass from sprouting up. Then, it's simply a matter of spreading 2 to 3 inches of shredded bark or wood chips over the fabric or paper, and your path is done! Just add more bark or chips every year or two to replace those that break down. This technique also works well with pine needles, and a pine-needle path looks wonderful through a shade garden.

Gravel lasts longer than wood-based paths, it drains well, and it scrunches nicely underfoot as you stroll through the garden. It

(continued on page 220)

An Easy-Care Path. Stepping-stones are a great way to prevent wear on heavily used grass paths. Set the stones into the soil a bit, so their tops are below the top of the grass; that way, you can easily mow over them without damaging your mower.

Rock-Garden Plants for Rubble Walls

Rock-garden plants have a reputation for being hard to grow, but there are many that can thrive in an average garden with minimal fussing. As with any plant, the key to success with rock-garden plants is giving them the growing conditions they need. For many of these, good drainage is critical; if you try to grow them in clayey garden soil, they'll rot in just a season or two.

Name	Height	Notes
Woolly yarrow (*Achillea tomentosa*)	6 to 12 in.	Clusters of creamy yellow flowers through summer over mats of hairy, gray-green leaves. Full sun to light shade. Zones 3 to 8.
Ajugas (*Ajuga* spp.)	4 to 6 in.	Short spikes of blue flowers in late spring or early summer. Full sun to full shade. Zones 3 to 9.
Alpine lady's mantle (*Alchemilla alpina*)	6 in.	Mounded clusters of yellow-green flowers in late spring over mounds of deeply lobed leaves edged with silver hairs. Full sun to partial shade. Zones 3 to 7.
Mount Atlas daisy (*Anacyclus depressus*)	2 in.	Daisylike white flowers in summer over mats of finely cut, gray-green leaves. Full sun. Zones 4 to 9.
Rock cress (*Arabis caucasica*)	6 in.	Clusters of sweetly scented white or pink flowers in spring over carpets of toothed, woolly, gray-green leaves. Full sun. Zones 3 to 7.
Sandworts (*Arenaria* spp.)	2 to 4 in.	Small, starry white flowers in late spring to early summer over dense carpets of narrow green leaves. Full sun to partial shade. Zones 5 to 9.
Thrift (*Armeria maritima*)	8 in.	Rounded heads of rose-pink flowers on leafless stems in late spring to early summer over mounds of grasslike evergreen leaves. Full sun. Zones 3 to 8.
Silvermound artemisia (*Artemisia schmidtiana*)	12 to 15 in.	Low, dense mounds of finely cut, silver-gray leaves. Full sun. Zones 3 to 7.

Name	Height	Notes
Alpine aster (*Aster alpinus*)	1 ft.	Yellow-centered, purple, daisylike flowers in early summer over low mounds of foliage. Full sun to light shade. Zones 4 to 8.
Basket-of-gold (*Aurinia saxatilis*)	8 in.	Masses of bright yellow blooms in spring over rosettes of gray-green leaves. Full sun. Zones 3 to 7.
English daisy (*Bellis perennis*)	6 in.	White, pink, or red, daisylike flowers in spring over clump-forming foliage. Full sun to partial shade. Zones 4 to 8.
Bellflowers (*Campanula* spp.)	6 in.	Cup-shaped purple-blue or white flowers in summer over mounding or trailing stems. Full sun to partial shade. Zones 3 to 8.
Snow-in-summer (*Cerastium tomentosum*)	2 to 6 in.	White flowers in late spring to early summer over carpets of woolly, silvery leaves. Full sun. Zones 2 to 8.
Hardy ice plant (*Delosperma cooperi*)	6 in.	Rosy purple, daisylike flowers through summer over mats of narrow, fleshy, gray-green leaves. Full sun. Zones 6 to 9.
Sweet William (*Dianthus barbatus*)	12 to 18 in.	Dense, rounded clusters of white, pink, red, or maroon flowers (often with a contrasting "eye"), usually in spring or summer. Full sun. Zones 3 to 9.
Fleabanes (*Erigeron* spp.)	10 to 18 in.	Yellow-centered, daisylike summer flowers in white, purple-blue, or pink over leafy rosettes. Full sun to light shade. Zones 4 to 8.
Cushion spurge (*Euphorbia epithymoides*)	16 in.	Bright yellow flowers in spring over compact mounds of blue-green leaves that turn reddish in fall. Full sun. Zones 4 to 8.

(continued)

ROCK-GARDEN PLANTS FOR RUBBLE WALLS—CONTINUED

Name	Height	Notes
Blanket flower (*Gaillardia* × *grandiflora*)	2 ft.	Daisylike, orange-and-yellow flowers all summer over clumps of lobed, hairy leaves. I like the compact cultivars, such as 1-foot 'Goblin' or 8-inch 'Baby Cole'. Full sun. Zones 4 to 9.
Sweet woodruff (*Galium odoratum*)	10 in.	Clusters of small white flowers in spring over creeping clumps of whorled leaves. Partial shade. Zones 3 to 9.
Hardy geraniums (*Geranium* spp.)	6 to 18 in.	Saucer-shaped, white, pink, blue, or purple blooms in late spring to early summer on mounded or bushy plants. Full sun to partial shade. Zones 4 to 8.
Creeping baby's breath (*Gypsophila repens*)	8 in.	Clouds of small white flowers in summer over carpets of narrow, gray-blue leaves. Full sun. Zones 4 to 8.
Rock rose (*Helianthemum nummularium*)	8 in.	Yellow, white, or pink single flowers in summer over spreading mounds of narrow, evergreen leaves. Full sun. Zones 5 to 8.
Perennial candytuft (*Iberis sempervirens*)	1 ft.	Rounded clusters of white flowers in late spring over mounded clumps of narrow, evergreen leaves. Full sun. Zones 3 to 9.
Crested iris (*Iris cristata*)	8 in.	Purple-blue flowers in spring over spreading carpets of short, broad leaves. Full sun to partial shade. Zones 4 to 9.
Lavender (*Lavandula angustifolia*)	2 ft.	Spikes of purple flowers in summer over shrubby clumps of narrow, aromatic, gray-green leaves. Full sun. Zones 5 to 9.
Edelweiss (*Leontopodium alpinum*)	8 in.	White flowers surrounded by star-shaped, woolly bracts in summer over clumps of gray, lance-shaped leaves. Full sun. Zones 4 to 7.

Name	Height	Notes
Moss phlox (*Phlox subulata*)	6 to 8 in.	Pink, blue, or white spring flowers over carpets of needlelike green leaves. Full sun to partial shade. Zones 4 to 8.
Pasque flower (*Pulsatilla vulgaris*)	8 in.	Cupped white, pink, reddish purple, or blue flowers in early spring, followed by fluffy white seedheads. Full sun to light shade. Zones 4 to 8.
Pearlwort (*Sagina subulata*)	2 in.	Tiny white flowers in spring over ground-hugging, mosslike carpets of narrow leaves. Full sun to partial shade. Zones 4 to 8.
Rock soapwort (*Saponaria ocymoides*)	6 in.	Small, bright pink flowers in early summer over creeping clumps of foliage. Full sun to light shade. Zones 3 to 7.
Winter savory (*Satureja montana*)	6 to 12 in.	Small, white, early-summer flowers on shrubby clumps of narrow, aromatic leaves. Full sun. Zones 4 to 8.
Sedums (*Sedum* spp.)	4 to 24 in.	Clusters of starry red, pink, white, or yellow flowers in spring or summer. Full sun to light shade. Zones 3 to 9.
Hens-and-chicks (*Sempervivum tectorum*)	4 in.	Pinkish red flowers on thick stalks in summer over tight rosettes of pointed, gray-green leaves. Full sun. Zones 4 to 9.
Lamb's ears (*Stachys byzantina*)	10 to 24 in.	Small, purple-pink flowers on fuzzy spikes in late spring to summer over silvery white, tongue-shaped, woolly foliage. Full sun to partial shade. Zones 3 to 9.
Thymes (*Thymus* spp.)	6 to 12 in.	Clusters of tiny white, pink, or lavender summer flowers over clumps or carpets of aromatic leaves. Full sun. Zones 4 to 9.

is a bit of an ordeal to install, though. You'll need to line the path with timbers, brick, boulders, or other edging to keep the gravel from spilling into adjacent grass and garden beds. If you have the room, it's best to get the gravel delivered and dumped, but you then have to haul it to the path site. Bagged stone is more convenient, but even small bags are *heavy,* and they don't hold much stone, so you can end up spending more than you expected. I had laid black plastic under my gravel path and was dismayed to see patches of it showing through after only one season. I'll warn you that children seem to find stones irresistible: I found stones in all the gardens, in the grass, and dangerously close to windows of our inn. There are certainly good spots for gravel paths, but consider the drawbacks carefully before you do all that work.

If you're ready to commit to a more permanent path, you have several options. Concrete pavers come in several shapes and colors, and they provide a durable, uniform surface that's good for high-traffic areas. Flagstones are elegant and formal, but they are also expensive. Brick is another classic choice. New bricks have a crisp, formal look, while older bricks have a more mellow, casual appearance. It's not difficult to lay flagstone or bricks on a base of sand and fill the gaps with more sand. If you prefer to have them set in mortar, it's worth paying a professional to get good results.

Pat's Path-Building Projects

For my first path project, I chose fieldstone because it was readily available, relatively easy to install, and beautiful. I had no experience installing fieldstone or any other kind of path, but I found a book with pictures and began.

Tips and Time-Savers

Planning a Pathway

An unmortared path is definitely within the scope of the average homeowner's skills. Before you install a path—especially a more permanent one—I highly recommend reading all you can find on the subject, looking at paths in magazines and gardening books, and talking to friends or neighbors who have installed their own paths. You'll get lots of ideas for patterns, as well as great suggestions. Keep in mind that main paths should be at least 4 feet wide, so two people can walk side by side. Paths through garden areas can be narrower, but don't make them much less than 2 feet wide.

I decided to build a 3-foot-wide, random-pattern, curving, fieldstone path, set on a sand base. I measured a piece of twine the width of the path and attached it to two large nails. I moved it along both sides of the path in a gentle curve. As I moved from one side of the path to the other, I drew the line with a third nail. I also removed a small trench of soil from both sides of the path with a small shovel.

Inside the two trenches, I excavated down 6 inches, then added a black plastic liner and 6 inches of sand. Fitting the stones into the path was a bit like working a jigsaw puzzle. I enjoyed fitting the pieces together into the sand bed, and when I had a small empty spot near the edge, I planted a patch of thyme. The final path drained well, was comfortable to walk on, and looked great. Seven years later, it still stands as one of the things I am most proud of.

Building paths inside the four gardens in my backyard was another kind of experience. This time I had help with the measuring and placement of stones. My friend Ron Tissot, a retired engineer, did all the measuring and stringing. We didn't excavate but placed the stones on top of the soil and filled in to level them. I still did all the stone collecting and had to hustle to stay ahead of Ron as he placed each stone in the right spot. As soon as he would see a pile of stone, he would begin to lay it in place until the pile was gone.

My neighbor Chancy Turk called one day to see if I would like to have some old bricks. I loaded my two grandsons, Anthony and Sean, in the truck and was at Chancy's in a flash. I was in heaven. The two little boys helped, and we loaded a small pickup bed full of all the bricks. Back home, we unloaded and I began to place bricks around the edges of the

beds in my picket-fenced garden. The paths here were made with newspaper on the sod and bark mulch on top of the paper. I only had to scoop up some mulch along the sides, and the bricks fit right on top of the paper!

Getting an Edge

A garden bed without an edge just isn't finished. A nice crisp edge gives a garden a clean, well-cared-for look, even if the plants within the beds get a little wild and woolly. It defines the line between the garden and the surrounding material, giving shape to both areas and discouraging people from walking on the soil. An edging also saves you weeding time, as it keeps grass from creeping into beds: You simply run the wheels on one side of the mower along the edge to get a neat trim.

The simplest kind of edge is just a strip where the grass was removed from the outer edge of the bed, then covered with mulch. (For complete details on making this kind of

Keeping Paths Tidy. Bricks make a wonderful edging for all kinds of paths, but they are especially good with loose materials, such as bark; they keep the path material on the path and out of the beds.

edging, refer back to "Laying Out Your New Garden" on page 128.) To keep the strip looking neat and weed-free, add more mulch as needed to keep the soil covered. Once a year, I recut the outer line of the strip to keep the grass from creeping in. (I tend to take off a strip of grass a few inches wide each time, so my gardens keep getting bigger!) Yes, it's a bit of work, but this kind of edge gives you the flexibility to easily change the size and shape of a garden bed.

If you're ready for a more permanent edge, you have many options, including metal strips, landscape timbers, cast-concrete edgers,

Filler Flowers. I like to keep a few pots of annuals on hand, so I can pop them into the bare spots in my borders. This simple trick gives me gardens that are full of flowers all season long.

stones, or bricks. If you're looking for something quirky to add a touch of fun, consider using recycled materials, such as tires or even bottles! If you choose an edging that sticks up from the ground, install a low strip in front of it. Set this low strip into the soil a bit, so the top of the strip is below the top of the grass. That will let you mow along the edge without bumping the taller decorative edging.

Lasagna Gardening in Containers

Container plantings make wonderful accents for all parts of your garden. Use them to dress up decks, patios, and porches, or to contain fast-spreading herbs such as mint. In the flower garden, pots full of colorful annuals make great fillers for bare spots left when early-blooming perennials or bulbs go dormant.

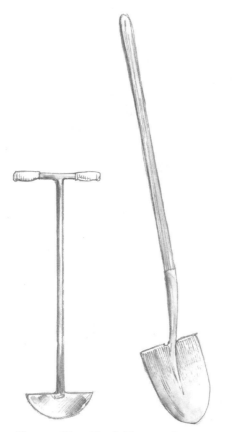

Choose Your Tool. You can buy a special tool with a curved blade to edge your beds, but I find a regular pointed shovel does the job just as well.

Preparing for Container Plantings

You can start a container garden anytime, though winter is a great time to begin gathering your materials. Start collecting containers: 5-gallon buckets and large pots for the biggest plants, and interesting, attractive containers for medium-size and smaller plants. Knock old soil out of previously used pots. If you choose a container that doesn't already have drainage holes, add a half-dozen or more holes in the bottom with a nail or drill. If containers need to be painted or decorated, do it during the winter when there's lots of time.

When prices are low, stock up on bags of planting material: peat moss, potting soil, and composted manure. Place the materials close to where you'll have your container garden so you don't have to move heavy bags several times. Leave them outside with holes cut in the bags so they will dampen during rains.

Another important step is selecting a site for your container garden. Pick a spot that's close to a water source and protected from the wind. A site with at least six hours of sun will let you grow the widest range of vegetables, herbs, and flowers. Keep in mind that filled containers can get pretty heavy, so make sure your deck or porch is up to the weight.

You'll also need to decide what you want to grow, so you'll know what seeds to start or which plants to buy. If you have room for large pots (ideally 16 inches or more across), you can grow large plants (such as potatoes or "determinate" tomatoes) or—if you provide a trellis or other support—vining crops (such as beans, cucumbers, and flowering vines). In front of the big pots, leave room for some medium-size potted plants, such as peppers, basil, or minisunflowers. Plan on placing small pots of herbs, patio tomatoes, or bush beans in front. Include baskets of trailing plants (such as strawberries, "indeterminate"

Fun Found Containers

Don't limit yourself to plain plastic or clay pots—use your imagination! You can plant in practically anything, as long as it can hold potting medium and it has some kind of drainage holes. Some of my found containers include coal shuttles filled with an assortment of brightly colored petunias; closely woven baskets planted with herbs and lettuce; and antique watering cans filled with Shasta daisies. If you don't want to put potting medium directly into the container, set the plant in a plastic pot, then slip that into the decorative container.

A Quirky Container. Don't discard that leaky old watering can! Plant some flowers in it and give it new life as a fun garden accent.

tomatoes, and prostrate rosemary [*Rosmarinus officinalis* 'Prostrata']) hung from the eaves, and you'll have a garden full of veggies, herbs, and flowers without setting foot off your deck!

Vegetable Crops for Containers

When choosing vegetables for your containers, look for compact or fast-maturing selections to get the best harvest from your limited space. Here are some good cultivars for container culture. Other crops to try include Swiss chard, greens, lettuce, peppers, and spinach.

- *Bush Bean: 'Rushmore' (49 days from planting to harvest)*
- *Carrot: 'Amini' (51 days), 'Round Baby' (60 days), 'Thumbelina' (60 days)*
- *Cucumber: 'Bush Pickle' (45 days), 'Bush Baby' (51 days)*
- *Lettuce: 'Black-Seeded Simpson' (41 days), 'Green Looseleaf' (41 days), 'Red Fire' (43 days), 'Red Looseleaf' (43 days)*
- *Onion (scallion): 'White Bunching' (60 days)*
- *Pumpkin: 'Sweetie Pie' (95 days); grow on deck railing or trellis*
- *Radish: 'Champion' (20 days), 'Red Boy' (22 days), 'Sparkler' (25 days)*
- *Snow Pea: 'Little Sweetie' (60 days); can be grown in a window box with a minifence for trellis*
- *Cherry Tomato: 'Patio Hybrid' (50 days), 'Lunch Box' (62 days)*

Filling Your Containers

Filling containers with the right growing medium used to be a big, messy job. When you use the lasagna method, though, you eliminate the messy mixing part—simply layer the ingredients right in your containers. When you move the material aside to plant, you will do just the right amount of mixing.

Start by covering the drainage holes with thin layers of wet newspaper (in large containers) or coffee filters (in smaller containers). In very large pots, fill the bottom with empty cans turned upside down. You'll need less material to fill the pot, and the container will be lighter and easier to move. (Actually, it's smart to place the containers where you want them *before* filling them, so you don't have to move them at all!)

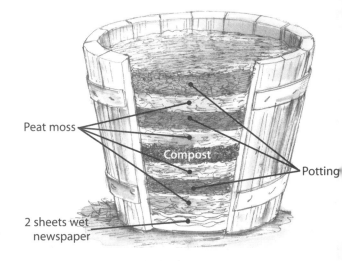

Lasagna Layers in Containers. Don't mess with mixing special soil for your container plants: Just lay a few sheets of wet newspaper on the bottom, and fill the pots with alternating 2-inch layers of peat moss and commercial potting mix. Add a layer or two of compost or other materials you have on hand; then you're ready to plant.

Next, add a 2-inch layer of peat moss, then a layer of potting soil, then peat moss, then more potting soil, and so on. Water after adding each layer to make sure all the layers are evenly moist. If you have compost, sand, or other ingredients available, add them in layers between the peat moss and potting soil. Don't use garden soil in any container: Besides possibly adding weed seeds and diseases, regular soil tends to pack down in containers and interfere with good root growth. Instead, I recommend a premixed potting medium, such as Sunshine or Pro-Mix, with vermiculite and perlite added to peat moss and other ingredients in the right proportions. You can also get potting mix with water-holding polymers added. These materials absorb water and release it slowly to your plants, so you won't need to water as often.

Caring for Container Gardens

Plant your lasagna-layered containers just as you would in a regular lasagna garden: Pull back the layers with your hands, pop in the plants, and pull the material back around the roots. After planting, water thoroughly, then cover the potting medium with a mulch to help it retain moisture and stay cool. I use one or two sheets of moist newspaper and cover it with a decorative mulch, such as chopped leaves or shredded bark. Just make sure you keep the mulch a few inches away from the stems, so it doesn't hold moisture against the stems and encourage rot.

Adequate mulch reduces the amount of watering your container plantings need, but still check them frequently. Large pots can usually go a day or two without watering, but smaller pots and hanging baskets may need daily watering, especially during hot or windy weather. Placing saucers under small pots and filling the saucers with water can help tide the plants over a weekend without additional watering, but don't let the pots sit in water constantly, or the potting mix will become waterlogged and roots will rot.

To keep plants looking their best, feed regularly with organic fertilizer. Scatter dry fertilizer over the top of the pot, or water with liquid fertilizer. You can make your own liquid fertilizer by putting a shovelful of compost in a burlap bag and suspending it in a bucket of water overnight to make "compost tea." (Use the liquid as fertilizer, and toss the soggy compost back onto your garden or compost pile, or use it to mulch a container.)

Container Care. Cut down on watering chores by covering the surface of the potting soil with mulch. Small pots tend to dry out especially fast, so add a saucer to hold a bit of extra water.

Container-Garden Smarts

Busy gardeners can enjoy containers too, but they need to be resourceful and plan ahead. If your watering time is limited, it's all the more important to place your containers near a water source, so you won't have to waste time hauling water from the tap to your pots. Make sure you add a layer of mulch on top of the potting medium, and place a saucer under smaller containers to hold an extra reserve of water.

One idea I really like for busy gardeners is wick watering. Simply place a bucket or dish of water in the middle of your container collection, then run a wick (such as a piece of clothesline rope or nylon stocking) from each pot to the water source. Tuck the plant end of the wick into the potting medium. As the potting medium dries, it will draw in more water through the wick. Check your wick-watering setup every few days to make sure the wicks are in place and to add more water to the bucket or dish.

A Simple Rope Trick. Wick watering is a great solution for busy gardeners who don't have time to water every day. Just run rope wicks from your pots to a container of water, and let the plants take up the water they need.

> ### Pat's Picks

PLANTS FOR CONTAINER GARDENS

An amazing array of plants can adapt to life in containers, but if you want the best yield or floral display from your potted garden, stick with those that are proven performers. Below are some that I've had success with in my own container gardens.

Plant Type	Specific Suggestions
Vegetables	Bush beans, "baby" carrots, bush-type cucumbers and squash, leaf lettuce, onions (scallions), chili peppers, early red potatoes, radishes, snow peas, and cherry tomatoes.
Herbs	Bush basil, chives, coriander (cilantro), lavender, lemon grass, mint, oregano, parsley, rosemary, sage, tarragon, and thyme.
Edible flowers	Calendulas (*Calendula officinalis*), 'Lemon Gem' marigolds, nasturtiums, and scarlet runner beans (*Phaseolus coccineus*) on a trellis.
Ornamental flowers	Dwarf cosmos (*Cosmos bipinnatus* 'Sonata'), trailing lobelia (*Lobelia erinus*), marigolds, petunias, and salvias (*Salvia* spp.).

Garden Accessories

Making a personal statement in your garden is easy. Every time you add an interesting container, a birdbath, or a piece of garden sculpture, you're expressing your individual taste. There are no rules here—it's your garden, so you can decorate it any way you want!

Where can you find great garden accessories? Mail-order catalogs that sell plants and garden supplies often sell ornaments as well, but don't limit yourself to these manufactured items. You can often find great accessories at auctions. That was the source of one of my favorites—a small bronze frog with a smaller frog perched on its back. Don't just think of statues, benches, and birdbaths; you can have fun with old pots, farm implements, birdhouses, and much more!

I think the best garden accessories are the personal ones: the ones with a history. When I move, I take my garden accessories with me. First are the two black iron kettles that were once my grandmother's cooking pots. They both have cracks, so they drain well, and one still has a lid I prop up next to the pot. Next are three pieces of "fence-post art" that were my mother's. One of her old friends was a mountain woman from Tennessee who could "see" people to carve into old fence pickets. My trio is of a man with a nail in his nose, a small girl with long hair, and a woman I think of as myself. These pieces were carved long before I was born, and abandoned to a firewood pile where my mother rescued them for her garden. I took them from her garden when she died, and they have been in mine ever since. It's these kinds of accessories that can give any garden that perfect finishing touch.

Epilogue

While working on this book, Pat sold her farm and moved to Wurtsboro, New York, a village 45 minutes east of the farm. Two zones warmer, her new garden site offers an added month on each end of the growing season. The property and the building, a 106-year-old former church, sit on a half acre in the middle of the village.

Pat opened a new business with her daughter Mickey. They call the business The Potager. The name just seemed right for the diverse products and services the Lanzas offer: café and catering; gift shop and garden center; gourmet gift baskets; and arts and crafts—a regular potage of garden-theme products.

The Potager has peeling paint, and the grounds are in the throes of constant change. The front of the property is lined with a picket fence painted bayberry green and accented with pergolas, arches, and arbors with vines climbing over them. The front garden is planted with antique roses surrounded by herbs.

In back of The Potager, the garden is made in tires and other recycled containers. Each container is a separate garden, growing vegetables, herbs, and flowers on vertical supports. Old ladders straddle tire gardens and support pumpkin vines with a pumpkin sitting on each step. Tomato cages sit in the middle of a tire garden with a clay saucer on top, making a birdbath, while tiny cucumbers crawl up the sides and leaf lettuce spills over the sides.

Wooden-rung ladders lie on the ground, with different herbs planted between the pairs of rungs. Assorted pieces of decorative iron that once held old sewing machines now stand in the middle of tire gardens with vines crawling over them, while bamboo poles tied into a tepee support pole beans. Best of all, the four tires from Mickey's Subaru hold the feet of an A-frame growing rack. Patio tomatoes are planted in each tire and grow over the frame.

A greenhouse installed on one side of the main building provides shelter for crops of baby lettuce and herbs for the kitchen. Outside the greenhouse is an array of plants for sale that reflects Pat's interests in rock gardening, white gardening, herbs, and antique roses. A small potager garden near the café door grows an unusual array of edible flowers for Mickey's beautiful salads. Window boxes march up the side of the entry ramp, spilling over with an abundance of nasturtiums and other annuals.

Along with her duties at The Potager, Pat continues to talk to groups across the country, including garden clubs, botanical gardens, and resorts. She writes for two local weekly papers and a travel guide. Pat also hosts a home-and-garden show on WDLC-AM radio out of Port Jervis, New York; the show airs each Friday at 8:00 A.M.

Pat is busy with her next book, *Grow Up! Small Space and Vertical Gardening*, using the lasagna method, of course.

229

Resources for Lasagna Gardeners

Seeds and Plants

Bountiful Gardens

18001 Shafer Ranch Road
Willits, CA 95490-9626
phone/fax: (707) 459-6410
e-mail: bountiful@zapcom.net
Website: http://countrylife.net/
ecoaction

W. Atlee Burpee & Co.

300 Park Avenue
Warminster, PA 18991-1447
phone: (800) 888-1447
fax: (800) 487-5530
Website: http://garden.burpee.com

The Cook's Garden

P.O. Box 535
Londonderry, VT 05148
phone: (800) 457-9703
fax: (800) 457-9705
Website:
http://www.cooksgarden.com

Gurney's Seed & Nursery Co.

110 Capital Street
Yankton, SD 57079
phone: (605) 665-1671
fax: (605) 665-9718

Johnny's Selected Seeds

Foss Hill Road
Albion, ME 04910-9731
phone: (207) 437-4301
fax: (800) 437-4290
e-mail:
homegarden@johnnyseeds.com
Website: http://www.johnnyseeds.
com

J. W. Jung Seed Co.

335 South High Street
Randolph, WI 53957-0001
phone: (800) 297-3123
fax: (800) 692-5864
Website: http://www.jungseed.com

Geo. W. Park Seed Co.

1 Parkton Avenue
Greenwood, SC 29647-0001
phone: (800) 845-3369
fax: (800) 275-9941
e-mail: catalog@parkseed.com

Pinetree Garden Seeds

Box 300
New Gloucester, ME 04260
phone: (888) 527-3337
fax: (207) 926-3886
e-mail: superseeds@worldnet.att.net

Ronniger's Seed & Potato Co.

P.O. Box 307
Ellensburg, WA 98926
phone: (800) 846-6178

Seeds of Change

P.O. Box 15700
Santa Fe, NM 87506-5700
phone: (888) 762-7333
fax: (888) 329-4762
e-mail: gardener@
    seedsofchange.com
Website: http://www.
    seedsofchange.com

Shepherd's Garden Seeds

30 Irene Street
Torrington, CT 06790
phone: (860) 482-3638
Website: http://www.shepherds.com

Stark Brothers

P.O. Box 10
Louisiana, MO 63353-0010
phone: (800) 325-4180
fax: (573) 754-5290
Website: http://www.starkbros.com

Stokes Seeds, Inc.

P.O. Box 548
Buffalo, NY 14240-0548
phone: (716) 695-6980
fax: (888) 834-3334

Territorial Seed Co.

P.O. Box 157
Cottage Grove, OR 97424
phone: (541) 942-9547
fax: (888) 657-3131
Website:http://www.territorialseed.
    com

Totally Tomatoes

P.O. Box 1626
Augusta, GA 30903-1626
phone: (803) 663-0016
fax: (888) 477-7333

Vermont Bean Seed Co.

Garden Lane
Fair Haven, VT 05743
phone: (802) 273-3400
fax: (888) 500-7333

Gardening Equipment and Supplies

Gardener's Supply Co.

128 Intervale Road
Burlington, VT 05401
phone: (800) 863-1700
fax: (800) 551-6712
e-mail: info@gardeners.com
Website: http://www.
    gardeners.com

Gardens Alive!

5100 Schenley Place
Lawrenceburg, IN 47025
phone: (812) 537-8650
fax: (812) 537-5108

The Greatest Gift

644 Enterprise Avenue
Galesburg, IL 61401
phone: (866) 259-0728
fax: (800) 362-4490

Harmony Farm Supply

P.O. Box 460
Grafton, CA 95444
phone: (707) 823-9125
fax: (707) 823-1734

A. M. Leonard

241 Fox Drive
Piqua, OH 45356
phone: (800) 543-8955
fax: (800) 433-0633
e-mail: info@amleo.com
Website: http://www.amleo.com

Peaceful Valley Farm Supply Co.

P.O. Box 2209
Grass Valley, CA 95945
phone: (916) 272-4769
fax: (916) 272-4794

Smith & Hawken

2 Arbor Lane
Box 6900
Florence, KY 41022-6900
phone: (800) 981-9888 catalog
requests only
fax: (606) 727-1166

Pat's Picks
(Recommended Reading)

Allen, Oliver E. *Gardening with the New Small Plants.* Boston: Houghton Mifflin Co., 1987.

Barash, Cathy Wilkinson. *Edible Flowers: From Garden to Palate.* Golden, CO: Fulcrum Publishing, 1993.

Bartholomew, Mel. *Square Foot Gardening.* Emmaus, PA: Rodale Press, 1981.

Benjamin, Joan, ed. *Great Garden Shortcuts.* Emmaus, PA: Rodale Press, 1996.

Better Homes and Gardens. *Step-by-Step Successful Gardening.* Des Moines, IA: Meredith Corporation, 1987.

Brookes, John. *The Country Garden.* New York: Crown Publishing Group, 1987.

Carr, Anna et al. *Rodale's Chemical-Free Yard and Garden.* Edited by Fern Marshall Bradley. Emmaus, PA: Rodale Press, 1991.

Chandoha, Walter. *The Literary Gardener.* Minocqua, WI: Willow Creek Press, 1997.

Clifton, Joan. *Making a White Garden.* New York: Grove Weidenfeld, 1990.

Cox, Jeff, and Marilyn Cox. *The Perennial Garden: Color Harmonies through the Seasons.* Emmaus, PA: Rodale Press, 1985.

Crockett, James Underwood. *Crockett's Victory Garden.* Boston: Little, Brown and Company, 1977.

De Verteuil, Anne, and Val Burton. *Planning Your Garden.* New York: Dutton, 1988.

Ellis, Barbara W., and Fern Marshall Bradley, eds. *The Organic Gardener's Handbook of Natural Insect and Disease Control.* Emmaus, PA: Rodale Press, 1992.

Faust, Joan Lee. *The New York Times Garden Book.* New York: The Lyons Press, 1991.

Gilkeson, Linda, Pam Peirce, and Miranda Smith. *Rodale's Pest and Disease Problem Solver.* Emmaus, PA: Rodale Press, 1996.

Halpin, Anne. *The Year-Round Vegetable Gardener.* New York: Summit Books, 1992.

Lawton, Barbara Perry. *Improving Your Garden Soil.* San Ramon, CA: Ortho Books, 1992.

McGrath, Mike, ed. *The Best of Organic Gardening.* Emmaus, PA: Rodale Press, 1996.

Miller, Crow. *Let's Get Growing*. Emmaus, PA: Rodale Press, 1995.

Organic Gardening and Farming Magazine staff. *Best Ideas for Organic Vegetable Growing*. Emmaus, PA: Rodale Books, 1969.

Pilcher, Rosamunde. *The World of Rosamunde Pilcher*. New York: St. Martin's Press, 1996.

The Reader's Digest Association. *1001 Hints and Tips for Your Garden*. Pleasantville, NY: The Reader's Digest Association, 1996.

———. *The Practical Gardener*. Pleasantville, NY: The Reader's Digest Association, 1993.

Simmons, Adelma G. *Herb Gardening in Five Seasons*. New York: Dutton, 1977.

Stewart, Martha. *Martha Stewart's Gardening: Month by Month*. New York: Clarkson Potter, 1991.

Stout, Ruth. *Gardening without Work*. New York: The Lyons Press, 1998.

———. *How to Have a Green Thumb without an Aching Back*. New York: Simon & Schuster, 1987.

Van Patten, George F. *Organic Garden Vegetables*. Portland, OR: Van Patten Publishing, 1991.

Index

USDA Plant Hardiness Zone Map

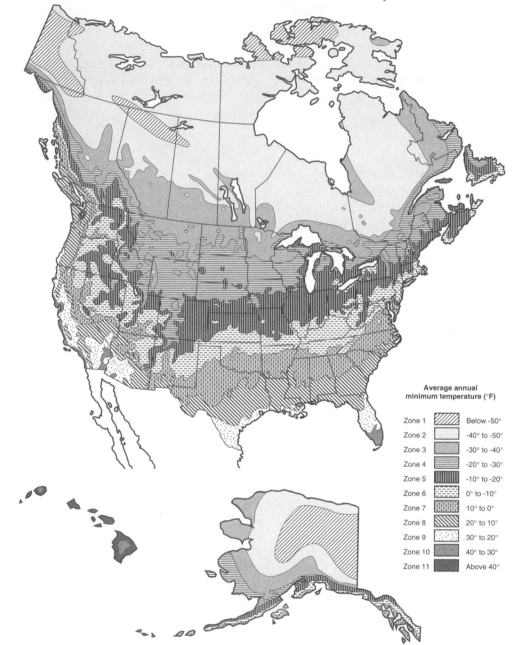

Average annual minimum temperature (°F)

Zone 1		Below -50°
Zone 2		-40° to -50°
Zone 3		-30° to -40°
Zone 4		-20° to -30°
Zone 5		-10° to -20°
Zone 6		0° to -10°
Zone 7		10° to 0°
Zone 8		20° to 10°
Zone 9		30° to 20°
Zone 10		40° to 30°
Zone 11		Above 40°

This map was revised in 1990 to reflect the original USDA map, done in 1965. It is now recognized as the best indicator of minimum temperatures available. Look at the map to find your area, then match its pattern to the key at the right. When you've found your pattern, the key will tell you what hardiness zone you live in. Remember that the map is a general guide; your particular conditions may vary.